PENGUIN BOOKS

VANILLA

Tim Ecott grew up in Ireland, the Far East and Africa. After studying anthropology he went into the film industry before joining the BBC World Service as a producer and correspondent in news and current affairs. A specialist on Southern Africa and the Indian Ocean states, he spent two years in the Seychelles, where he developed a parallel career as a dive leader. In 2003 he was scriptwriter for *Deep Blue*, the cinema version of the BBC's acclaimed *Blue Planet* series. Based in London, his journalism has appeared in numerous national and foreign publications. His first book was *Neutral Buoyancy: Adventures in a Liquid World*.

Vanilla

Travels in Search of the Luscious Substance

TIM ECOTT

PENGUIN BOOKS

PENGUIN BOOKS

Published by the Penguin Group
Penguin Books Ltd, 80 Strand, London WC2R 0RL, England
Penguin Group (USA) Inc., 375 Hudson Street, New York, New York 10014, USA
Penguin Group (Canada), 10 Alcorn Avenue, Toronto, Ontario, Canada M4V 3B2
(a division of Pearson Penguin Canada Inc.)
Penguin Ireland, 25 St Stephen's Green, Dublin 2, Ireland
(a division of Penguin Books Ltd)
Penguin Group (Australia), 250 Camberwell Road, Camberwell, Victoria 3124, Australia
(a division of Pearson Australia Group Pty Ltd)
Penguin Books India Pvt Ltd, 11 Community Centre, Panchsheel Park, New Delhi – 110 017, India
Penguin Group (NZ), cnr Airborne and Rosedale Roads, Albany, Auckland 1310, New Zealand
(a division of Pearson New Zealand Ltd)
Penguin Books (South Africa) (Pty) Ltd, 24 Sturdee Avenue, Rosebank 2196, South Africa

Penguin Books Ltd, Registered Offices: 80 Strand, London WC2R 0RL, England

www.penguin.com

First published by Michael Joseph 2004
Published in Penguin Books 2005

1

Copyright © Tim Ecott, 2004
All rights reserved

The moral right of the author has been asserted

Set by Rowland Phototypesetting Ltd, Bury St Edmunds, Suffolk
Printed in England by Clays Ltd, St Ives plc

Except in the United States of America, this book is sold subject
to the condition that it shall not, by way of trade or otherwise, be lent,
re-sold, hired out, or otherwise circulated without the publisher's
prior consent in any form of binding or cover other than that in
which it is published and without a similar condition including this
condition being imposed on the subsequent purchaser

For Jessica

What is it like — this plant, so beloved of nature that she has bestowed upon it a veritable magic wallet, in the shape of a little sheath, wherein reposes such wealth of usefulness and delight?

— Joseph Burnett, 1900

Contents

List of Illustrations   x
Prologue   xiii
Foreword   xv

1. Black Flower   1
2. An Indian Secret   20
3. The City that Perfumed the World   33
4. Mexican Money   54
5. From an English Garden   80
6. Ile Bourbon   94
7. Creole Hearts   108
8. The Slave's Crime   126
9. Homage to Albius   149
10. Empress of Tahiti   163
11. Murder in Madagascar   187
12. Ice Cream and Perfume   203
13. The Admiral's Legacy   218
14. Vanilla Prince   236

Epilogue   266
Acknowledgements   269
Select Bibliography   273

List of Illustrations

Photographs

1. The vanilla vine features in Diego Rivera's monumental mural in the Palacio Nacional in Mexico City
2. A crocodile woven from vanilla beans in Madagascar
3. Crucifix made from Mexican vanilla
4. In 1841, Edmond Albius first demonstrated how to pollinate *Vanilla planifolia* by hand
5. Mexican vanilla being dried in the sun in Papantla, 1910
6. In the 1930s almost all first-grade Mexican vanilla beans went to the USA
7. Young boys help the men to sort a mountain of green vanilla in Papantla in the 1950s
8. Mexican vanilla farmers in Zozozolco, in the hills of Veracruz
9. Some farmers sell just a kilogram of vanilla
10. Plump green vanilla will lose four-fifths of its weight during curing
11. Dipping the beans in scalding water by hand
12. Tahitian vanilla drying on the slopes of Taha'a
13. The vanilla orchid is a small flower
14. On the road to Antalaha, Malagasy farmers trade vanilla cuttings

15. The dried beans are lustrous, dark and moist
16. Graded by length and quality, the bundles of pods are sorted by workers at the Ramanandraibe warehouse
(All photographs by Tim Ecott, except no. 4 (courtesy of Archives départementales Réunion); nos. 5, 6 and 7 (courtesy of the Carreira Del Cueto family); no. 13 (P. Cribb).)

Text Illustrations

p. 21   The first known illustration of a vanilla plant appeared in 1552 in the Badianus manuscript (courtesy Royal Botanic Gardens, Kew)

p. 25   Francesco Redi, physician to the Medici court, made the first microscopic study of the vanilla pod in 1675 (courtesy Royal Botanic Gardens, Kew)

p. 124 By the middle of the nineteenth century vanilla vines were being grown in Europe's botanical gardens, but they did not produce fruits (author's private collection)

p. 146 Portrait of Edmond Albius (courtesy Archives départementales Réunion)

p. 183 The manual pollination of the vanilla orchid is a delicate process (drawing by Jessica Ecott)

p. 212 Early advertisements for pure vanilla extract (courtesy Jeff Lehman collection)

p. 235 The Malagasy have turned vanilla production into a lucrative art

Prologue

The best time for impregnation is from 8 o'clock in the morning to 1 or 2 in the afternoon and as far as possible the day after rain.
— Delteil, *La Vanille*, Paris, 1884

The Vanilla orchid opens in the pale light. Five celadon petals stand out around the centre of the blossom as it spreads beneath the earliest rays of the sun. Small and cream-smooth, they encircle a graceful yellow flute, the lip of the flower, which hangs outwards above the fleshy green stem of its climbing vine. Inside is the heart of the flower, filled with the makings of its own seed. There, pollen balls, sticky and heavy with desire, hang above the rostellum, a thick tongue-flap of tissue separating the mass from the moist female organs below. In the wild, a bee might creep across the interior of the flower, dragging its wings and legs between the tissues and melding the ingredients of its sex. Tiny pollen grains will cling to the bee and fly with it to another flute, mixing the plant's own character with that of another. But, left inviolate and unvisited, the gentle flower will bloom for five or six hours, and then wither in the tropical sun. By mid-afternoon it will be a shrivelled sack fallen to the ground.

A man's hand grasps the blossom firmly but gently, taking

care not to dislodge its rich seed load. One sunbrowned finger carefully pushes the lip down and away from the pollen mass while his other hand inserts a small stick no longer than a toothpick under the rostellum, gently lifting it out of the way. With his left thumb he presses the head of the flower downwards, smearing the pollen onto the waiting stigma which sits under the flap like an aspirin under a tongue. The stick withdraws smoothly and the pale flower is fertilized. Now it will brood.

Foreword

For more than a decade I have been in love with the islands. I have revelled in their heat and light, and been maddened by their remoteness. In Europe's dark winters and half-lit summers I have craved their equatorial brightness and wished myself on their silica-glint shores.

At times my love filled me with joy, occasionally anger, and even led to bouts of bitterness. Like any good love affair it made me obsessive. Years later, I cannot stop myself returning to the islands, though now we are more like old friends than lovers.

My first visit to the south-western Indian Ocean was hard work. The BBC had sent me on what they quaintly termed a 'duty trip' gathering interviews and material for radio programmes from the region. It was an eventful journey, a rapid immersion in the politics and culture of islands scattered from the Equator to the Tropic of Capricorn.

In Seychelles I caught Dengue fever, and in Mauritius I broke my ankle. In Madagascar I developed dysentery and by the time I reached the Comoros I also had a bout of pneumonia. It was an unusual concoction of maladies, and yet as I coughed feverishly, and limped agonizingly around the disparate capitals over a five-week period, I was deeply contented.

It was an interesting time to visit the region, an area that other English-speaking journalists didn't bother with, because they considered it too peripheral to world events. Whenever I made repeated visits to the islands, colleagues would sneer slightly at the idea that I was 'reporting from the beach again'. In fact, the Cold War had not yet ended and the political tensions within the region were as different as the topography of the island states were from one another. Here were slivers of Africa set afloat in the vastness of the Indian Ocean, and surrounded by deep waters in which the superpowers liked to hide their nuclear submarines.

Seychelles was then a one-party state, a closed and internally divided society where people lived by secrets and intrigue. In Mauritius the tourism industry was just gathering pace, and making money took precedence over the Byzantine complexities of a political system dominated by considerations of caste. Madagascar, the great island continent, was in the thrall of a dictator, and there were bandits and bubonic plague on the streets of Antananarivo.

My last stop was in the Comoros, then a Federal Islamic Republic and notorious for its tally of coups d'état and mercenary-led invasions. Nineteen coups in less than a quarter of a century is still something of a record, I believe. When I arrived, the president had just been assassinated and the country was in chaos. The civil service was on strike and my passport was soon locked up in the Ministry of the Interior, awaiting an exit visa. For some days it seemed as if I would spend much longer in Moroni than planned. When the strike eventually ended I was free to return to Europe, and late one night I waited at the tiny airport for the aircraft that would take me first to Nairobi, then Marseilles and Paris to catch a final connection to London.

The 747 came down out of the evening sky like a visiting swan and trundled to within yards of where I stood on the tarmac. The scented night air hung close, wrapping everything in a mix of sea-salt and tropical flowers. I have never forgotten the moon that night, a white pearl hanging above the island, casting its shadow over the crouching bulk of the volcano called Karthala.

Ahead of me in the crowd waiting to climb the steps to the plane, there was a tall elegant Comorean woman dressed in colourful cotton robes. Her hand luggage consisted of a rattan basket wrapped inside a large plastic bag. From the holes where the handles opened the long thick tendrils of a green climbing plant seemed to be struggling to escape.

'What is it?' I asked.

'Vanilla,' she whispered, looking around to make sure no one was watching. 'In my apartment in Paris I will keep it very warm, and it will remind me of home.'

Vanilla. A word that fills the mouth and exercises the tip of your tongue. The word meant little to me: a taste, a flavour – something that went into ice cream. I hadn't ever thought about the plant that might give fruit to the long dark sticks I had seen for sale in supermarkets. Vanilla 'pods', that's what we call them. Or are they 'beans'?

That night the vine in the rattan basket was leaving the tropics for a captive life in Paris. The plant was returning to the very city from where its ancestor had been brought to the Indian Ocean more than a century and a half before. That first cutting had not travelled in a plastic bag on an aeroplane, but on a wooden ship to nearby Réunion, from where it would eventually move to Madagascar, Mauritius, Comoros and Seychelles. But like me, that original vine had begun its journey not in France but in London.

The Comorean woman with her plant was one of a hundred

images from the islands that I would keep with me from that journey. As I stepped onto the plane that night I had a very strong premonition that I would return to the region, a conviction which frightened me in its certitude.

The next time I saw the vanilla vine was in Seychelles, where I made my home for a time, captivated by the islands' beauty and enticed by the intimacy of a country with just seventy thousand inhabitants. I originally wanted to live in Seychelles because I had developed an obsession with scuba diving, a passion that became a lifeline for my sanity when island fever set in. Underwater, I could always escape the claustrophobia of living in a society where everyone knew everyone else's business. Subsequently, I have made a career from writing about the underwater world, and it is a happy coincidence that vanilla grows in a band around the world which stretches roughly twenty-three degrees north and south of the Equator. These are the same latitudes where most of the world's coral reefs are found.

At the southern end of Mahé island, there is a twisting road named Les Cannelles. Following it inland away from the glimmering bays of the sinuous coast I climbed a rough track barely wide enough for one car at a time. The track rose steeply and the forest pressed in around me, blocking the view of the slopes of a hidden valley. Native hardwood species, *bois rouge* and *bois blanc,* grow here, mingling with exotic neighbours, thick-trunked breadfruit and broad-leaved jamalac trees hung with their light green water-apples. Eventually the road petered out and I came to a dead end, a small plateau in the shadow of a massive granite outcrop which the locals call Roche Gratte Fesse. It is a beautiful place, though in Kreol the name means 'Scratch Your Arse Rock'.

The valley slopes have been planted with cinnamon trees,

pineapples, patchouli and cloves, and the owners of the plantation call it the Jardin du Roi. They trace their descent from a mysterious character who arrived on the island shortly after the French Revolution. For more than fifty years he worked as a planter on Mahé, while intermittently writing letters to the Archduke of Austria whom he claimed as an uncle. The planter called himself Pierre-Louis Poiret and the letters asserted his claim to be the lost Dauphin, the child of Louis XVI and Marie-Antoinette. He was one of several claimants to the title, a dynastic mystery which to this day is still not satisfactorily resolved, in spite of DNA evidence that the Dauphin died in prison.

Poiret maintained his story even on his deathbed, swearing to the priest who gave him absolution that he had been robbed of his birthright by relatives who wanted the leadership of the Bourbon dynasty for themselves. In staunchly catholic Seychelles, such *in extremis* utterances acquired further credibility. Poiret sired seven children, calling all four boys Louis and the three girls 'Marie', the firstborn being Marie-Antoinette. After Poiret's death his children found pieces of silverware decorated with the royal crest among his private possessions and a letter stating that he had adopted the name 'Poiret' after the man who had smuggled him out of the Temple prison on the eve of his mother's execution.

The plantation house is an old wooden building, one of the few to survive in Seychelles. It is a simple, elegant structure raised up on stilts to protect the timber from the termites. The old wood is painted white and there is a pitched roof made of corrugated iron. Neat rows of small trees stand like a platoon of guards in front of the house and the ground slopes away sharply down the valley, draining the soil of the heavy monsoon rains. The trees have been kept closer to the house than any other plant, and they are in clear view of the balcony and the bedroom windows where they can always be seen. The trees themselves are simply props, for around their trunks and low branches precious vanilla vines curl and drape themselves for support.

On Mahé they grow only a little vanilla now, and there are a few small plantations on the nearby island of La Digue. The local tea is often flavoured with vanilla but no one exports the pods which once contributed a large part of the islands' wealth.

Walking in the forests of Mahé I found untended vines clinging to tall straight trees, green shoots heading for the heights, untethered from the supports they would have been tied to by men. These vanilla plants would never bear fruit, for they had escaped from abandoned plantations and would have no one to fertilize their flowers. Like the people of Seychelles, islands totally uninhabited until the eighteenth century, the vanilla vine is a visitor, transplanted and taking root where it can.

1. Black Flower

The vanilla plant is a tropical vine, which can reach a length of over one hundred feet. It belongs to one of the oldest and largest group of flowering plants – the orchids – currently known to contain over twenty-five thousand species, and counting. Of all the orchids, the vanilla family is the only one that produces an agriculturally valuable crop, as distinct from orchids which are cultivated and traded simply for their decorative value. These are not rare, bizarrely shaped hothouse exotics to inspire orchid collectors with their well-documented fanatical relish. The vanilla orchid has its own appeal, a fruit with a scent so unique, so distinctive to the human palate that it was once worth its weight in silver.

The vanilla orchid is not a showy flower; it has only a slight scent, with no element of vanilla flavour or aroma. When its pale yellow flowers are pollinated the ovaries swell and develop into the fruits, just like extra-long green beans, we call 'pods' or 'beans'. They contain thousands of tiny black seeds. The growing process lasts up to nine months, but only when the pods turn brown after being dried and cured do they develop the distinctive aroma we call vanilla. Drying, curing and conditioning the pods is an art, which if done properly takes another nine months. Vanilla is the most labour-intensive agricultural product in the world.

Like all agricultural commodities vanilla goes through periodic cycles of boom and bust prices. Even at its lowest level, there will always be farmers in Madagascar, Mexico or Indonesia who are so poor that they will cultivate vanilla vines. As I write, the price for gourmet-quality vanilla beans is at an all-time high – more than $500 a kilogram – inspiring growers to stand guard over their plants in the tropical jungle. Men carrying vanilla beans to market in Madagascar and Mexico have been murdered for a few kilos of their crop, and the handful of commercial buyers who control the world market are desperate to secure their lines of supply in the face of a world shortage of their commodity. In America and Europe the value of cured vanilla beans is so high that importers cannot afford to insure large stocks in their warehouses. One US importer has been forced to split his stock into three separate warehousing units several miles apart, because his insurance company was concerned that if an aeroplane were to crash onto one of the buildings it would wipe out the firm's entire profit.

In Mexico, Indonesia, Madagascar and Papua New Guinea the buyers charter private jets to visit the vanilla areas, avoiding commercial flights so as to keep their destinations secret from other members of their small select club. Buyers also prefer private planes because they are carrying suitcases stuffed with cash – at the top of the market, a tonne of vanilla will cost almost half a million dollars. When they do fly on commercial aircraft these brokers often disguise their movements by taking an indirect route to where they want to do business.

There is one buyer based in France who always flies to Madagascar via an African country, rather than travelling direct from Paris. He is wary of meeting any of his competitors on the regular Paris–Antananarivo route and thus giving away his presence on the island. He knows that if he can sneak into the country and make a contract, or collect pricing information, just a day ahead of his rivals, it can give him a significant advantage. Even in Europe and the USA, the vanilla dealers are wary of admitting which city they may be travelling to – because large commercial food companies are often linked to one particular city. If one dealer knows that a competitor is visiting Zurich or Chicago, for example, he may deduce that a meeting with company X is taking place. The industrial flavouring companies also make the vanilla dealers sign stringent confidentiality agreements, making them promise never to reveal that vanilla is an ingredient in their products.

Rumours and counter-rumours spread fast. A few years ago the vanilla farmers on their isolated islands and forested hillsides were unaware of what was happening in the outside world, but now they have access to cell phones and affordable satellite connections. From one side of the world to the other they can now pass on information about the price of their crop, giving them an advantage over the foreign buyers who fly in from the developed world to negotiate a contract. Meanwhile, rumours fly around the globe by mobile telephone faster than any aeroplane.

On a sunny morning in Mayfair, in one of London's smartest hotels I drank tea with a vanilla buyer. He had telephoned me the previous evening saying he had 'important news' that he wanted to share, something he didn't want to discuss on the telephone. 'Do you know about the container load of beans that's gone missing?' he asked as soon as I sat down. He had just arrived from America en route to Madagascar, and he wondered if I had already heard more details about the story.

'No, what container?'

The man's eyes swivelled, scanning the room to see if anyone was within earshot. 'Two tonnes,' he whispered, swearing me to secrecy about the name of the company involved. 'But guess what? The insurance company won't pay out – they've got satellite photos that prove the ship made an unscheduled stop and the containers were offloaded. Now the exporters are going to have to answer some tough questions.'

The story was a familiar one. Rumours about another exporter of vanilla trying to recoup a large amount of cash by illicit means. Such stories often have cash value. Speculators vie with one another to supply market intelligence to the industry, hoping either to drive up demand or discourage it, leaving them free to buy beans at a better price. A few weeks later a rival dealer telephoned with another story: a well-known middleman in Madagascar was buying cured beans at a very high price, equivalent to what they would fetch when they came to be exported.

'How will they make a profit?' I asked.

'Exactly!' he exclaimed. 'Financially, these prices don't make sense, but I have reason to believe that someone inside the exporting company is ripping the owners off. The insider is buying the beans at the export price, then he's soaking the beans in water so that they gain weight. The exporter still makes a profit because he gets to sell more kilograms than he originally bought. But it's high risk – if you add water you run the risk of the beans going mouldy.'

Like any cash commodity, the trade in vanilla sometimes attracts unscrupulous individuals who see an opportunity for quick profit. In recent years the high price of vanilla has made legitimate dealers especially wary of newcomers in case they might use this cash-rich business for money laundering. Drug smugglers have also tried using the heavily aromatic beans as a way of concealing their own merchandise to avoid detection by sniffer dogs. Sometimes, the business attracts simple old-fashioned fraudsters, and there was recently a case of a dealer in central America being swindled in Sri Lanka. The dealer had lodged several million dollars as a security deposit for beans only to find that his Sri Lankan contact had persuaded the bank to allow him to withdraw those funds for his own ends. It was all an elaborate confidence trick, and the 'supplier' never had access to commercial quantities of beans. The price of good quality beans from Madagascar has even led one dealer to ship vanilla from Indonesia to Madagascar, unload it and then repackage the beans as Malagasy – so as to secure a higher price. By creating bills of lading that proved the beans came from Madagascar the dealer could shift the blame onto his Malagasy suppliers if any of his customers ever discovered that the vanilla was not what they had been expecting.

Unlike other agricultural crops the amount of vanilla beans available each year is comparatively small – approximately two thousand metric tonnes. Demand is so high that nothing is left unsold, and vanilla brokers often sign a contract to supply their customers with a year's worth of beans in advance. As part of those contracts they may have to commit beans from next year's crop without knowing how many tonnes of beans they will actually get in their hands. The quality and size of the crop depends on weather conditions and how well it is cured. Meanwhile, the price of vanilla depends on who is buying, how much competition there is, and how quickly the money changes hands. The potential for panic among the buyers is always there.

One crucial factor in vanilla dealing is this: vanilla farmers will only trade for cash. They sell their crop to local agents, buyers who work for the bigger businessmen who dry and cure the beans to sell for export. Foreign buyers, the brokers who search for vanilla on behalf of their customers in the USA and Europe, have to guess how much stock they will need in a given season. They also need to calculate how much green vanilla will be available in the coming season, a process that can only be learnt by years of experience in the field. From this, they estimate how much dried vanilla will come onto the market half a year later — and they must also guess how honest their local agents will be when the time comes to exchange the money for beans. This trade is not for the faint-hearted.

On my desk there is a small bamboo tube decorated with carved pictures of vanilla pods. Whenever I remove the lid the room is filled with the smell of Bourbon vanilla — the name given to the best quality crop in the world. Inside there is a mixture of pods grown on the islands of Réunion and Madagascar. Next to it lie two small gold-plated vanilla pods, a gift from a vanilla dealer in Tahiti. The golden pods are rigid, immobilized and petrified in their shining gilt coat, but the ridges on the surface of their flesh have been preserved. In a small box I also have vanilla-scented tea from Seychelles. My favourite treasure is a crocodile, about fifteen inches long, complete with open mouth, clawed feet and a fine tapering tail. It is made entirely from woven vanilla beans — perhaps a hundred or more — by an old man on the north-east coast of Madagascar. Finally, there is a strong-smelling bottle of vanilla liqueur on my desk. The name on the bottle says it is '*Sangre negra*' (black blood), and it comes from the state of Veracruz on the Gulf Coast of Mexico.

In the country we now call Mexico, people were using vanilla long before any Europeans set foot on their land, and the dried pods were rare enough to be valued as a form of currency. Indeed, by 1519, when the Spanish conquistador Hernando Cortés reached Mexico, the ruling Aztecs were demanding vanilla as tax from the people of the central and eastern tropical plateau. The Aztecs, like the Maya before them, knew that the black pods could be dried and ground up as flavouring for *xocoatl*, the bitter liquid made from cacao, which we know today as chocolate. It was a drink reserved for the aristocracy, or for soldiers about to go into battle.

The vanilla story begins in the salt-thick air of Veracruz. Here, the first vanilla plants were cultivated and tended by the people who call themselves Totonac. These people found the wild orchids and called them *xa'nat*. The Totonac say that the flowers and their scented seed pods sprang from blood. Not just ordinary blood, but the blood of a princess who was so beautiful and so pure in spirit that her father decided she should never be possessed by any mortal man.

According to the Totonac legend the princess was the daughter of King Teniztli, and he named her Tzacopontziza, after the Morning Star. To keep her pure, the king had his daughter blessed by the priests and consecrated to Tonacayahua, the Goddess of Fertility. Inevitably, a young man of the tribe, named Zkata Oxga – Running Deer – fell in love with the girl and abducted her, making off with her into the mountains. The legend says that before the young couple could reach safety they were intercepted by a fire-breathing monster who blocked their escape, allowing Teniztli's high priests to capture them.

Princess Tzacopontziza and her lover had committed a mortal sin, and the priests decapitated them both and threw their bodies into a mountain ravine. As their blood seeped into the ground it dried the earth, and after some days a bush sprang from the ground where their blood had spilled. Very soon an orchid was seen growing among its branches. The plant grew rapidly and produced small pale flowers which in time sprouted several beans, delicate yet strong. When the beans matured they darkened, eventually emitting an exquisite perfume more beautiful than anything the subjects of King Teniztli had ever known before. People believed that the scent was the pure sweet soul of the dead princess and the orchid that grew in the mountains was declared sacred.

Today, the Totonac people still call it *xa'nat* and in the north of their domain they use the word to mean anything to do with vanilla, the flower, the pods and what they call the 'fat' or oil from the pods, which gives them the scent they value. Perhaps the earliest known use for vanilla pods was as a simple but effective deodorant for the Indians' houses, and it is still used in that way in central Mexico today, where a bunch of dried beans is tied together and suspended with string from a hook on a wall. Traditionally, the Totonac women, and women from other tribes in whose territory the plants grew, would place oiled vanilla beans in their hair, perfuming it with the subtle scent from the plant.

There is no record of the Totonac using vanilla as a foodstuff, or flavouring, but when they were subjugated by the Aztec Empire it was their duty to send vanilla pods to the great capital at Tenochtitlan. The empire relied on its trading alliances as much as if not more than its military power, and Tenochtitlan was at the centre of a trade network which covered 125,000 square miles. Aztec traders known as *pochteca* acted as informants, spies and intermediaries between the emperor and his allies, and they ensured the supply of riches to the capital, including treasured cocoa beans, vanilla pods, quetzal feathers, turquoise, gold and all manner of foodstuffs.

The pre-Columbian history of vanilla can be linked to the better known story of the cacao nut, another New World commodity which had a huge impact on the European diet. Archaeological remains tell us that the kernels of the cacao tree were in use in Central America for more than two thousand years before the Spanish Conquest. The cacao nuts were originally transported as trade items from the Amazon basin northwards to Mexico, and the Aztecs always regarded them as sacred, knowing their stimulant and restorative properties. It is probable that around the same period vanilla was also well known as a condiment, something to ameliorate the bitter taste of the cocoa powder which in the Aztec period (1200–1500 AD) was turned into the royal delicacy. In the Aztec language, *xocoatl* means 'bitter water', and the concoction they drank was sweetened with honey in the absence of cane-sugar, which was introduced by the Spanish invaders. The Aztecs also added peppers, maize and vanilla, whipping it all up into a kind of gruel.

Bernal Diaz, a soldier and historian who accompanied Cortés into the great city of Tenochtitlan, first described seeing Montezuma's servants bringing him 'a drink made from the cocoa plant, in cups of pure gold, which they said he took before visiting his wives'. According to Diaz the servants 'brought a good fifty large jugs, all frothed up and they always served it with great reverence'. The Spanish soldiery, who soon found themselves at war with the Aztecs, became interested in what they called 'the divine drink which builds up resistance and fights fatigue. A cup of this precious drink enables a man to walk for a whole day without food.'

Like chocolate, vanilla was not an everyday ingredient for ordinary people in Mexico, and even the Aztec aristocracy used it mostly as an after-dinner luxury. They never saw for themselves the plant that produced the dark pods they used to soften their 'bitter water'. Hidden deep in the tropical forests far from Tenochtitlan, it was known only to the people who lived within its range. Because they knew only the dark fruits of the vanilla, the Aztecs mistakenly called the plant *tlilxochitl* – the black flower.

On a featureless industrial estate in Illinois I could smell vanilla. It seemed to emanate from the very bricks of the modern office block in front of the Nielsen-Massey factory. Here, in the satellite town of Waukegan, an hour's drive north of Chicago, millions of vanilla beans reach the final stage of their journey which begins in a rucksack on a collector's back on the northeast coast of Madagascar. Picked by the farmer, bought by a collector and sold to a curer, they have been dipped, dried, sorted and bundled. Having been inspected and sold to an American exporter they are packed into gleaming white tin boxes. Loaded into forty-foot-long steel shipping containers they make a two-day voyage in a rusting cargo boat to the deepwater port at Toamasina where they are winched onto larger ships for a journey northwards through the Indian Ocean. Around the tip of Madagascar and past the Comoros they go, skirting the east coast of Africa and passing through the Suez Canal to reach the Mediterranean. After three weeks they reach the French port of Marseilles. Then on they go across the Atlantic in another ship for eight or nine more days, before docking at New York. They have travelled nine thousand nautical miles. Transported by truck to a warehouse in Pennsylvania they have been repacked, swapping their glittering and battered white tin boxes for cardboard cartons for the final eight-hundred-mile road journey to Waukegan. There, they are unpacked and processed by Nielsen-Massey Vanilla, the world's largest company specializing in the production of pure vanilla extract.

More than half of all the world's vanilla beans end up in the United States. Half of those are used in the dairy industry, mainly in the form of vanilla extract, or essence. Massey's, as they were originally known, began making pure and imitation vanilla flavours a century ago and they continue to produce top-quality extract using highly traditional methods. Outside the factory I spotted two cars, one bearing the registration 'VANILLA', and beside it another which read 'VANILA 2'. Inside, Craig Nielsen, a bear-like man with a deep voice and a bristling moustache, welcomed me to the plant.

'Those number plates are kinda' funny, aren't they? My uncle even had one that said "ESSENCE",' he said, giving a high tinkling laugh at odds with his large frame. 'I guess we were just lucky that in Illinois you need seven letters on your number plate!'

Craig made it clear that he could not reveal the names of any of the ice cream companies or other food firms to which he supplied vanilla extract. 'I'll show you the plant,' he said. 'But our client list and the formula for vanilla extract are trade secrets.'

The factory was a clean bright space with dozens of cardboard cartons of vanilla beans piled into one corner. Craig led me over to a metal machine nearby.

'This is where it all starts. Basically this is a big version of a kitchen blender,' he said. 'We feed the beans in here at this open funnel-top and they get torn up into shredded pieces.'

When he turned the machine on, it made a noise like a coffee grinder. I watched as he threw a handful of beans into the open maw and seconds later saw them drop down onto a metal tray. The glistening pods, so carefully packed and sorted by Malagasy women on the other side of the world, had been turned into dull brown shreds barely two inches long. 'We chop them up so as to expose as much of the surface area as possible before we extract the flavour.'

Apart from the sound of the grinder, the factory was quiet with only a gentle humming sound in the background. A few workers clad in white overalls and protective hair nets moved silently between a row of steel tanks lined up along the other side of the open space. The tanks, like upended baby bottles, were big enough to hold a thousand gallons of liquid and they had narrow metal pipes stretching from the funnel at the base up their flanks and back in a loop to the top. One of the pipes had a transparent section through which I could see a trickle of brown liquid, like strong cold tea. On a wall nearby there was a computerized control panel no bigger than a television screen. Digital displays revealed code numbers relating to individual extraction mixtures which varied according to the strength of extract being produced.

'Don't write any of those numbers down,' Craig admonished with another rattling giggle. 'That's where we enter the code numbers for the amount of alcohol that goes into the tanks.'

'Is that all there is to it?'

'Pretty much. You chop the beans, put them onto grilles that sit at the top of the tanks and percolate pure alcohol and water through them several times until you've got all the flavour out. We use a cold extraction method which means we take about three weeks to produce an extract; plenty of other companies do the same thing but they heat the alcohol to speed up the process.'

'Is that bad?' I asked.

'I can't say it's bad,' Craig replied cautiously. 'But it changes the chemical reaction slightly and we think our method gives a purer extract. Some of the chemicals in vanilla are present in tiny quantities and it's possible that they could change or lose some of their characteristics under heat – or pressure.'

'How much quicker could you extract the liquid if you used heat?'

'You could do it in three to five days, instead of three to five weeks. But we sell a premium-grade product, and our customers know they get reliable and consistent quality. We think that's due to doin' it slow.'

Nielsen-Massey produces a wide range of different strengths and flavours of vanilla extract, and they also create specific and individual flavour blends according to customer needs. 'Sometimes they'll send us ice cream or dry baked goods and ask us to match the flavour,' Craig explained as he led me to a partitioned area of the factory where colour-coded hoses were fed through the wall into the bottling area. Craig knew from the colour on the hose what strength or variety of extract was being pumped. The hoses looked exactly like those on a petrol pump, and there was a man using them to fill large plastic barrels which would feed the assembly line nearby. Stacked on massive racks around the walls were rows of barrels and larger square plastic 'totes' holding as much as 275 gallons apiece. On a little track, like a miniature baggage carousel, there were hundreds of glass bottles jiggling along in a line like toy soldiers. A nozzle descended from a machine and gave each bottle a blast of air to clean them of any dust particles. *Pfsst, Pfsst, Pfsst* it went, and then an automated piston-filler came down and squirted the rich brown extract into their necks. Little metal caps flipped down a track and plopped onto the bottles. They passed through a succession of rotating rubber wheels that tightened the caps by revolving in opposing directions. Inside each cap was a tamper-proof circle of silver paper that sealed onto the open neck as the cap tightened. Then another steel arm rotated and a label was glued to the bottle and more wheels smoothed it flat against the glass. A plastic safety seal covered the cap and the bottle passed through a heat tunnel to shrink the seal in place. A rotating table accumulated the bottles and scooped them into boxes two dozen at a time. Finally, a human being sealed the box and carried it to a waiting pallet.

The labels on the assembly line gave the brown liquid some glamour. There was Madagascar Bourbon, Royal Bourbon and Organic Bourbon. Mexican and Tahitian Pure, and Sugarless Bourbon. There were blends of Bourbon-Mexican, Bourbon-Tahitian and Bourbon-Indonesian and all in a variety of strengths. There were jars for whole beans, jars for vanilla powder and jars for vanilla bean paste.

'Why so many different varieties?' I asked.

'Vanilla is an application-driven product,' said Craig. 'It depends on what you want to do with it. Take a cookie, for example: it has a very low mass so when you bake it the internal temperature rises very quickly. Madagascar Bourbon is the highest quality vanilla extract, but it doesn't respond well to quick high heat. Indonesian on the other hand has a harsher aroma as an extract but it's more heat-stable. And, as it heats up, the sharp Indonesian bite will mellow out in the cooking process.'

'So what about ice cream – presumably because it's cold you can use the Bourbon?'

'Not necessarily.' Craig pulled a face, realizing how little I knew about the food industry. 'Good ice cream products have a high butter-fat content, maybe fourteen per cent. The mixture is very creamy and the Bourbon notes compete with it and get masked. Again, if you mix Bourbon and Indonesian you get the harsher notes cutting through the butter-fat but as the taste swirls around your mouth you still get the Bourbon notes rounding out the flavour. That means you get an initial "vanilla" impact but you can also still taste it at the end.'

As we left the production line I spotted a large barrel full of brown dust. Craig said it was the waste matter from the extraction tanks. 'Can you do anything with it?' I wondered.

'Some companies use it to add a bit of extra bulk to vanilla powder – but basically there's hardly any flavour left in it. We do have a customer who mixes it in with wood adhesive as a binding agent, and someone who uses it as a base for deer scent for hunters – they rub it on their hands so the deer can't smell them. You can also add it to the strong solvents they use in rubber factories – that stuff really stinks, and this gets rid of the bad smell.'

'What about the actual vanilla seeds?' I could see millions of them in the waste material. Craig hesitated for a moment before answering. 'You know, after the beans have had the flavour extracted the seeds have no taste to them at all.'

'But I've seen them – those little dark specks you get in vanilla ice cream.'

'That's just cosmetic – we sift them out of this stuff and dry them, but the flavour has been exhausted. If our customers choose to add them to ice cream then that's their business. It's just a marketing thing; sometimes they don't use the seeds, just tiny specks of exhausted beans.'

In his office Craig had a collection of old papers and photographs dating back to the 1930s and 1940s. I was interested to learn that his grandfather Chatfield had been involved in the business since the First World War. The Nielsens had become something of a vanilla dynasty, and Craig's father (Chat 'Junior') had once set up his own vanilla curing operation in Mexico. 'Take a look through this stuff if you like,' said Craig, excusing himself to go back to work. 'See if there's anything interesting in those boxes — I never have the time to sort through them.'

The boxes were full of photographs and company memorabilia, much of it publicity-related material from recent years. Among other things, I learned that Nielsen-Massey supplied vanilla essence to the US team at the world pastry championships. According to one news clipping the American team's 'sugar work was unparalleled in the world, and their chocolate showpieces have revolutionized the art form'. There were old advertisements and company accounts, paperwork from the 1970s that was already beginning to look antique because it had been produced on a typewriter. I found a postcard from Chat 'Junior' written in 1940 and posted to his wife from Mexico. He apologized for the delay in returning home to Illinois: 'Having trouble getting sun to dry the beans. Waited around all morning for the sun to come out and didn't come, so hope to God it comes tomorrow.' There was also a postcard from Papeete showing wooden schooners alongside the town wharf, a faded image from the 1920s that seemed impossibly romantic. In another box there was a patriotic advertisement showing US airmen in Saigon from the 1960s holding up a sign saying: 'To the customers of Nielsen-Massey vanilla many thanks and merry Xmas from the USO and Servicemen in Viet-Nam.'

Later, when I was about to leave, Craig took me back to the assembly line, saying he had forgotten to show me something special. 'Look up there,' he said proudly, pointing to a high metal rack.

'That's a ten-gallon oak barrel. We laid it down in 1997 and we'll open it up in 2007 and distribute it to our customers to celebrate our centenary.'

'Why only ten gallons?' I asked.

'Hey,' he snorted loudly. 'At today's prices, ten gallons of vanilla is plenty to leave sitting around!'

The scent and flavour of vanilla is a complex thing. Food scientists use a bewildering variety of words to describe its sensory qualities, an evocative list similar to the vocabulary used by connoisseurs of fine wine. It includes: sweet, floral, balsamic, woody, nutty, marshmallow, leathery, dusty, smoky, strawy, spicy, animalic, walnut, cheesy, fatty, creamy, phenolic, pruney, rummy, medicinal, weedy, cherry-like, anisic, bacon, cucumber, mushroomy, plastic, cardboard and faecal. This complexity is explained by the fact that chemists have identified more than four hundred different components within the natural vanilla bean. The beans contain protein, sugars, cellulose, wax, resin, gum, tannins and minerals. They also harbour dozens of hydrocarbons, alcohols, carbonyls (aldehydes and ketones), acids, esters, terpenoids, lactones, sulphur compounds, acetals, ethers, phenols, furans and epoxides.

Some of these elements are present in only parts per million, or even parts per billion, but advocates of natural vanilla argue that the sum of the parts is immeasurably greater than the whole. It is hardly surprising that vanilla, and its essence, is one of the most intriguing materials available to flavourists and parfumiers.

The extraction of flavour from vanilla beans is a relatively simple process, even if it varies slightly from factory to factory. The beans release their flavour through percolation and soaking with alcohol and water, and are then filtered and concentrated into various strengths. However, the amount of beans used to make vanilla extract is regulated by law – in the USA under the auspices of the Food and Drug Administration (FDA), and by similar national regulations in Europe.

The recent historic price rise in vanilla beans has thrown vanilla buyers, extractors and flavourists into a frenzy. They argue that in spite of the European and American regulations defining the standards for *pure* vanilla extract they face a crisis. Quite simply, they say, industrial users are abandoning natural vanilla for cheaper synthetic alternatives. Some industry insiders estimate that in the last four years the price rises have resulted in a 30 per cent drop in the use of natural vanilla worldwide. With prices for the 2004 crop nudging $600 a kilogram there are few industrial users who haven't considered abandoning natural vanilla. Ironically, the market for gourmet-grade whole vanilla beans is on the increase, especially in Europe where high-quality food ingredients have been popularized by numerous 'celebrity' chefs and their television programmes.

It is a harsh reality that the volume of processed foods produced in the world is too great to be satisfied by the two thousand tonnes (at best) of natural vanilla available each year. For several decades, almost 90 per cent of the 'vanilla flavour' used in foods has been created by the addition of ingredients containing synthetic vanillin – a naturally occurring component in vanilla beans, but which is also found in the cell walls of other plants. Vanillin has been found in barley, mint and asparagus as well as in rum and whisky. Wine, red or white, that is left to mature in green oak barrels may also develop a distinctive vanillin note, and it is also a factor in the fermentation of certain grapes. But nowhere does vanillin occur in such high concentrations as are found in cured vanilla beans.

The effects produced by the natural fragrance and taste of vanilla are crucial to the overall richness of innumerable products. In 1900 the American flavour manufacturer Joseph

Burnett wrote: 'Let the chemist experiment over his tubes and phials as he will, he can never devise anything in the way of imitation to compare with Nature's own handiwork; the secret formula for the delicate qualities of vanilla, which minister to taste and smell alike, cannot be wrested from her.'

Over a century later we still cannot match or replicate the subtlety of natural vanilla.

2. An Indian Secret

There are more than a hundred different species of vanilla orchid, and they grow all over the tropics with the exception of Australia. All of the vanilla orchids produce fruits containing seeds, but only a few species bear the large aromatic pods which can be used commercially. Virtually all of the cultivated vanilla in the world today comes from just one species, *Vanilla planifolia* (sometimes called *Vanilla fragrans*), a plant indigenous to Central America, and particularly the south-eastern part of Mexico. At least two other varieties, *Vanilla pompona* and *Vanilla tahitensis*, also provide a serviceable culinary pod, although they are not as readily obtainable and they produce a different flavour and aroma to the *planifolia*.

For hundreds of years the secret of the Mexican vanilla species caused confusion and dissent among botanists in Europe. They simply couldn't identify the precise plant from which the beans were collected.

The first known written reference to the vanilla orchid dates from 1552, where it is described in the '*Libellus de Medicinalibus Indorum herbis . . .*', a tome which lay hidden in the Vatican library until the early twentieth century. The authors called the plant *tlilxochitl*, from the Nahuatl language spoken by the Aztecs and still used in Mexico today. Known as the Badianus Code, this herbal was compiled by an Indian convert to Christianity named Martinus de la Cruz and a Spanish scholar, Juan Badianus. They list *tlilxochitl* as an ingredient in a nosegay, a potion to protect against infection and worn around the neck when travelling. The potion includes both the 'black flower' and the 'rope flower' (*mecaxochitl*), which was also sometimes used in flavouring chocolate. A small drawing of *tlilxochitl* in the Badianus manuscript gives a crude impression of the flat leaves and delicate flowers of the vanilla orchid.

The emissaries of the Spanish Empire were ambiguous in their attitude to the Indian cultures in the Americas. While wishing to stamp out native religions and replace them with Catholicism, they were open to learning what they could from them about indigenous medicines and herbs. This was a time when medicines and herbs were indistinguishable, and the

Tlilxochitl *(on the left) was known to the Aztecs as the 'black flower'*

natural world was seen as the repository of a seemingly limitless supply of pharmaceutical possibilities.

At the end of her life, Queen Elizabeth I developed a taste for puddings containing vanilla. Like potatoes and tobacco, the flavour was something from the New World, and Elizabeth is thought to have been introduced to the exotic taste by her apothecary, Hugh Morgan, in around 1602. The English queen discovered the pleasure of the dark pod relatively late, since it had been brought to Europe by the Spanish as early as 1513, after they made their first forays into North and Central America from their settlements in Cuba. Vanilla joined new commodities like indigo, cochineal, cacao and tobacco as they made their appearance in the Old World.

In 1605 the royal apothecary sent some vanilla pods to the French botanist Charles de l'Ecluse, who described them in his *Atrebatis Exoticorum* published at Leiden. L'Ecluse called them *Lobus oblongus aromaticus*, remarking that 'anyone who sniffs them will soon have a headache'. It is impossible to tell if the pods were actually from *Vanilla planifolia*, but it seems likely that if they came from Morgan then they must have been received via a Spanish source, perhaps captured from a Spanish ship en route from the New World. It is likely therefore that they came originally from Mexico, since those were the pods which for some time had been used by the Spanish as an additive in hot chocolate, and to perfume cigars – another habit learned from the Mexicans.

L'Ecluse was also in possession of at least part of the knowledge gathered in Mexico by Francisco Hernandez, physician to King Philip II of Spain. Hernandez travelled in Mexico from 1570–77, rejoicing in the grandiloquent title 'Proto-Medico to the Indies'. Philip sent him there to compile a list of the newly discovered plants and medicines which might prove commercially valuable to the Crown. According to Hernandez:

> a decoction of vanilla beans steeped in water causes the urine to flow admirably; when mixed with mecaxuchitl, vanilla beans cause abortion; they warm and strengthen the stomach; diminish flatulence; cook the humours and attenuate them; give strength and vigour to the mind; heal female troubles; and are said to be good against cold poisons and the bites of venomous animals.

Hernandez called the vanilla pods by their Nahuatl name, *tlilxochitl*, but his work was not published in Spain for many years after his return, in part because Philip II was unhappy with the amount of purely scientific, rather than commercially valuable information contained within it. Fragments of Hernandez's work *Rerum Medicarum Novae Hispaniae Thesaurus* eventually appeared in 1628 but it is quite probable that he had made use of some of the material contained in the Badianus Code which already existed when he first reached Mexico. Like the Aztecs, Hernandez never saw a wild vanilla orchid and was content to continue describing the plant as *flore nigro aromatico* – the perfumed black flower. In Spain the rich dark fruits were called 'little pods' or *vainilla*, a diminutive of *vaina* which in turn derives from the Latin *vagina*, meaning simply 'sheath'. Vanilla and orchid share an irredeemably erotic etymology, given that 'orchid' derives from *orchis*, the Greek word for testicle. In the sixteenth century Hieronymous Tragus claimed that orchids did not have seeds, and he postulated a theory that orchids sprang from animals' seminal secretions that fell on the ground. He believed that like created like, pointing to the similarity in appearance of some orchids to certain animals, a development of an ancient theory that bees, for example, sprang from the carcasses of bulls. Orchids that looked like bees must therefore have come from bull semen.

The word 'vanilla', spelled as it is now, was not used until 1658 when Willem Piso published *De Indiæ utriusque Re Naturali et Medica* in Amsterdam. Piso was something of a prodigy, and had attended Leiden University at the age of twelve, eventually serving as a doctor in the service of the Governor of Brazil where he travelled widely. Piso's Brazilian materia medica is one of the earliest and most important texts on tropical medicine, and he is credited with introducing the Ipecac (*Cephaelis ipecacuanha*) plant to Europe as an emetic and potential cure for dysentery. Within a few years of Piso, Francesco Redi, a talented Italian scientist and physician to the Medici court, published *Experimenta*, a work on 'diverse natural matters, in particular those carried to us from the Indies'. Redi's work contains a detailed illustration of a vanilla pod, and what is certainly the first microscopic view of a vanilla seed.

By the late seventeenth century the use of chocolate was well established in Europe, and vanilla as a flavouring was reasonably well known, although the Spanish Empire still jealously guarded its source of supply. Along with coffee, tea and cacao it was specifically named in a royal edict issued at Versailles in 1692, the first French law relating to the sale of those commodities. Trading in vanilla was restricted to those merchants who had paid the Crown a monopoly fee. Anyone found selling vanilla without the royal warrant would have the beans confiscated and had to pay a fine of a thousand livres. Unless it had been grown on French territory, and carried aboard a French vessel, vanilla could only be brought into France via the ports at Marseilles or Rouen, where customs officials could verify the cargoes. Anyone found adulterating the product also faced corporal punishment.

AN INDIAN SECRET

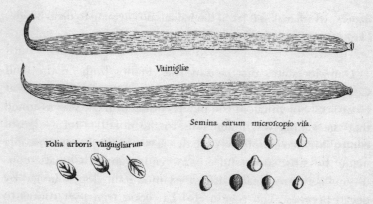

Francesco Redi's microscopic studies of the vanilla fruit

William Dampier, the English buccaneer and adventurer, gives the first truly interesting description of the value placed on vanilla pods in his *New Voyage round the World*, first published in 1697. Recording a visit to what he calls Guatulco and the Capolita River (modern day Huatulco and Copalita in Mexico) he describes seeing the vanilla pods – which he calls 'cods' – drying in the sun:

The Vinello is a little Cod full of small black seeds; it is four or five inches long, about the bigness of the stem of a tobacco leaf, and when dried much resembling it, so that our Privateers at first have often thrown them away when they took any, wondering why the Spaniards should lay up tobacco stems. This Cod grows on a small Vine, which climbs and supports itself by the neighbouring trees; it first bears a yellow flower, from whence the Cod afterwards proceeds. It is first green, but when ripe it turns yellow; the Indians (whose manufacture it is, and who sell it cheap to the Spaniards) gather it and lay it in the Sun, which makes it soft, then it changes to a Chestnut colour. Then they frequently press it between their fingers, which makes it fat. If the Indians do anything to them beside, I know not; but I have seen the Spaniards sleek them with Oil.

Dampier states that he saw the vinellos both on the Gulf Coast of Mexico at Campechy, and on the Pacific coast at Huatulco. For much of the nineteenth century it was assumed that the vanilla was indigenous to the north-eastern edge of central Mexico simply because this is where the Totonac people made the most successful commerce in vanilla. Climatic conditions here are ideal, with moist mountain slopes fanned by ocean breezes. The region also has good transport routes to the capital and to the major port at Veracruz, from where the beans were shipped to Europe. However, Dampier also clearly identifies vanilla growing in the southern Mexican states, now known to be part of its true biological range which also extends into Guatemala, Honduras, Guyana and Brazil. The English adventurer also describes trying to collect and cure vinellos, and failing:

The Indians have some secret that I know not. I have often askt the Spaniards how they were cured, but I never could meet with any could tell me. One Mr. Cree also, a very curious Person, who spoke Spanish well, and had been a Privateer all his Life, and seven years a Prisoner among the Spaniards at Portobel and Cartagena, yet upon all his enquiry could not find any of them that understood it. Could we have learnt the Art of it, several of us would have gone to Bocca-toro Yearly, at the dry season and cured them, and freighted our Vessel. We there might have had Turtle enough for food, and store of Vinello's. Mr. Cree first shewed me those at Bocca-toro. At or near a town also called Caihooca, in the Bay of Campeachy, these Cods are found. They are commonly sold for Three pence a Cod among the Spanish in the West Indies, and are sold by the druggist, for they are much used among chocolate to perfume it. Some will use them among Tobacco for it gives a delicate scent. I never heard of any Vinello's but here in this Country, about Caihooca and at Bocca-toro.

With luck, Dampier might have found his vinellos elsewhere in Central America since the aromatic species occur from eastern Mexico southwards to Costa Rica. Nonetheless, *Vanilla planifolia* (the so-called flat-leafed variety and the one which has become the predominant species in agriculture) is not a common plant in the wild. In pre-Hispanic times the Totonac people of Veracruz regarded their vanilla orchids as a blessing of Nature, something that they would find occasionally in the forest, and use in trade and exchange. Knowing where to find a mature vine, heavy with fruit, was a valuable secret. Even today, it is almost impossible to find genuinely wild *Vanilla planifolia* specimens in the forest, and Mexican botanists have classified the plant as critically endangered. In Veracruz State it grows so readily that it seems certain that all of the plants found near human populations are cuttings transplanted from cultivated specimens. When the Spaniards and other visitors from the Old World first reached the Americas they were reliant on the indigenous peoples' knowledge of the local flora and fauna. It is not easy to tell one vanilla species from another by appearance alone, and perhaps a third of the vanilla family produce fruit which is more or less aromatic. Even so, the specific chemical qualities so sought after in the cured pods of *Vanilla planifolia* are not found in any of the other vanilla orchids. It is a plant which has guarded its secrets well, and still retains much of its mystery.

Under the right conditions, an established vanilla vine is capable of long life in the wild, perhaps a thousand years. In

Seychelles I have seen vanilla vines in the forest, seemingly at home on the humid green slopes of Mahé's steep hills. To the casual eye they seem perfectly natural in the luxuriant jungle. In fact, like every other specimen of commercial vanilla outside Central America they are an exotic invader, escapees from man-made plantations. These long green alien vines rarely flower, and never produce seed pods, since like most orchids they have a highly specific system of pollination. The vine itself is relatively easily grown if the temperature and soil conditions are right, but the flowers can only be reliably fertilized in nature by a particular tropical bee, found only in Central America.

Given that each vanilla pod contains thousands of tiny black seeds, it seems reasonable to ask why these can't simply be planted. Like many orchids the seeds need a specific symbiotic fungus to be present for healthy germination. This fungal association, which botanists call 'mycorrhizal', seems to be beneficial to both plant and fungus. The plant gives the fungus a home, while the fungus assists the plant by breaking down nutrients in the soil, converting them into simpler chemicals such as glucose and fructose which are nutrients to the orchid. Botanists speculate that one reason for the scarcity of *Vanilla planifolia* in the wild is that this mycorrhizal fungus may be highly specialized and restricted in its own range. None of this was known by the Aztecs, the Totonacs or of course the Spanish invaders. They relied on Indian knowledge, and the ability of the indigenous people to cultivate the orchids they found in the forest.

When Spanish ships began taking the riches of the New World to Europe the value of the scarce vanilla pods escalated, in part because drinking hot chocolate became fashionable. The recipes for the production of chocolate received from Mexico were highly variable, and the necessary sweetening ingredients not always available. According to Bernal Diaz, Cortés's historian, the Aztecs consumed their *xocoatl* cold, whipping it into a froth so thick 'it must be taken with the mouth wide open'. Understandably, the Spanish nobility were initially highly dubious about the beverage, with one conquistador claiming it 'so odd a taste, it is more fit to be thrown to Hogs than presented to Men'.

However, with the addition of sugar and milk, the energy-promoting drink became popular with the aristocracy and spread gradually from Spain to other European capitals. In France the beverage was popularized in about 1615 by the daughter of Spain's Philip III, Anne of Austria, who married Louis XIII. By 1657 London had its first chocolate house and the drink was soon being sold in the famous coffee houses where men met to discuss all manner of business. In his diary for 1664, Samuel Pepys mentions drinking 'very good Jocolatte' at a coffee house in the company of Peter Pett, the Navy Commissioner.

Spain's foremost colonial successors, France and England, vied with each other to dominate the trade in valuable commodities brought to the markets of Europe. Tea, coffee and chocolate were sought-after luxuries, being described by John Chamberlain in 1685 as 'those three Drugs, chiefly wherein Heaven has shewed itself liberal to Men'. Chamberlain's work on *The Manner of Making of Coffee, Tea and Chocolate* relied heavily on translations of French and Spanish publications, especially a work by Antonio Colmenero fifty years earlier. Colmenero warned that the new drink, chocolate, is believed by many of its advocates 'to make them fat'. However, even those people who 'take it in the Dog-dayes find themselves well on it'.

Although he is aware that cacao is the principal ingredient of drinking chocolate, Chamberlain states that the 'Indian word chocolatl signifies a confection composed of very many ingredients which hold great commerce with the Mexicans'. Chamberlain gives a recipe for chocolate using seven hundred cacao nuts, white sugar, Mexico Pepper, aniseed, cloves and water of oranges. He adds: 'Everybody uses this confection and puts therein Three little Straws or as the Spaniards call them Vanillas de Campeche. Our Vanillas are used in making the Chocolate, the which are very pleasant to the sight, they have the smell of Fennel, and perhaps not much different in quality, for all hold that they do not heat too much, and do not hinder the adding of Annis seed.'

Recipes for chocolate gradually became simpler, and Spanish society often relinquished vanilla in favour of cinnamon, while the French and English maintained their preference for the 'little straws'. Writing his *Natural History of Chocolate* in 1730, again largely a translation of a French work, John Brown lists vanilla as an essential component of the beverage, unlike so many others which had already fallen out of use. Of the original Mexican ingredients, he remarks, 'only cinnamon and vanilla are spices of general approbation. Vanilla is a Cod of brown colour and delicate smell; it is flatter and longer than our [French] beans, it contains a Luscious Substance, full of little black shining Grains. They must be chosen fresh, full and well grown, and care must be taken that they are not smeared with Balsam, nor put in a moist place.'

While acknowledging the value of the Luscious Substance as an ingredient in drinking chocolate, Brown introduces a note of caution:

The agreeable smell, and exquisite Taste that they communicate to Chocolate, have prodigiously recommended it; but long experience having taught that it heats very much, its use is become less frequent, and those who prefer their Health more than pleasing their Senses, abstain from it entirely. In Spain and Italy, Chocolate prepared without 'Vanilla' is called at present 'Chocolate of Health'; and in the French Islands of America, where 'Vanilla' is neither Scarce nor dear, as in Europe, they do not use it at all, though they consume as much chocolate there as in any other Place in the World. However a great many people are prejudiced in favour of Vanilla, and that I may pay a due Deference to their Judgements, I shall employ 'Vanilla' in the Composition of Chocolate in the best Method and Quantity as it appears to me, one two or three Cods, sometimes more to a pound, according to Everyone's Fancy.

The idea that vanilla might be a 'heating' element – something that would inflame the passions – was soon added to its repertoire of side effects. In the eighteenth century, Casanova is said to have enjoyed a recipe for mulled wine which included vanilla as one of its special ingredients. In his memoirs he also relates saving a lock of a lover's hair and asking a Jewish confectioner to grind it to a fine powder and mix it in a paste with various ingredients including 'amber, sugar, angelica and vanilla' which he kept in a sweetmeat box of fine crystal. Casanova's contemporary, the Marquis de Sade, allegedly supplied dinner guests with a rich dessert of chocolate flavoured with vanilla and Spanish fly which caused the men and women to be 'seized with a burning sensation of lustful ardour'. De Sade also included vanilla chocolate pastilles in the list of foods he wished sent to him during one of his sojourns in gaol. Madame de Pompadour, the mistress of Louis XV, who in many ways defined the height of contemporary French taste, had chocolate served to her at dinner, 'flavoured with vanilla and ambergris, accompanied by celery soup and a handful of truffles'.

In 1762 the sensual appeal of vanilla was given some kind of scientific basis when Bezaar Zimmermann, a German physician, published his treatise *On Experiences* in which he claimed that, 'No fewer than 342 impotent men, by drinking vanilla decoctions, have changed into astonishing lovers of at least as many women.'

Like so many natural products vanilla acquired a curative reputation, seemingly effective against dyspepsia, melancholia, hypochondria and lymphatic disorders but according to one pharmacopoeia was not recommended for 'young people of an ardent and irritable nature especially those whose temperament is prone to over excitement'.

Notwithstanding its aphrodisiac potential, England and France – Spain's colonial rivals – were determined to grow vanilla in their own overseas territories. The aristocracy were acquiring a taste for it, and vanilla pods were worth their weight in silver. If only someone could solve the mystery of how to grow the vines successfully outside Mexico, and then induce them to bear fruit, they would break the Spanish monopoly. They would also make themselves rich.

3. The City that Perfumed the World

In Mexico City's ancient and enormous central square, the *Zócalo*, the tourists filed through the old wooden door leading into the National Palace. Inside the courtyard a troop of young soldiers in green uniforms were preparing to carry the national flag out into the zocalo and raise it to the top of the central flagpole. Few of the visitors glanced at the massive emblem rolled up like a giant carpet on the ancient flagstones, so large that it took a dozen soldiers to carry it.

The tourists, like me, had come to see Diego Rivera's murals painted around the central staircase and the galleried balcony of the colonial building. Parties of Mexican schoolchildren, foreigners and their competitive tour guides mingled in the stairwell, mostly concentrating on the giant triptych around the alcove. With arms raised and fingers pointing, the guides' commentaries overlapped, bouncing Spanish, English, German and Italian words off the walls. It is one of those sights to be ticked off on any decent tour of the great capital, though the political scope of the mural is too vast to be taken in on a single visit.

There is a lot to gawp at. Rivera's epic contains every imaginable icon of Mexican history, from the terrifying gods of the pre-conquest creation myths to the heroes of the revolution, and at its very centre the Aztec eagle, still the central symbol of the nation. According to legend the wandering Azteca founded their great city of Tenochtitlan in the valley of Mexico at the spot where they found an eagle atop a cactus bush devouring a serpent. It was the sign promised to them by the sun god Huizilopochtli. In Rivera's other panels there are noble indigenous peoples going about their business, farming, trading, dancing and worshipping their respective deities. Hairless dogs lie at the feet of the nobility, cocoa plants are tended in the fields, floating gardens surround the city of Tenochtitlan, and of course there are sacrificial victims being led to the altar. The great figures are there too, including the Conqueror Cortés, his Indian mistress La Malinche and the revolutionaries, Emiliano Zapata and Pancho Villa.

Rivera gives his communist philosophy full rein, with many anonymous heroes of the proletariat bearing banners proclaiming their connection to the land and its produce. Closer inspection of the main panels reveals his denigration of those who exploit the workers, the evils of capitalism and foreign interference in Mexican politics. The Catholic Church doesn't get off lightly either; a priest is shown embracing a whore and the Inquisition is just one of the horrors visited upon the indigenous Mexica by the Spanish conquerors. The main panel is magnificent in its scope, but it was one of the less obviously dramatic scenes further along the corridor which grabbed my attention. Here, in great detail, Rivera depicts the cultures of Mexico's tropical Gulf Coast.

In subtle earthy tones, with a backdrop of mountains, an Aztec trader resplendent in feathered dress faces a Totonac tribal chieftain, recognizable from his artificially flattened forehead. In pre-conquest Mexico the Totonac would strap wooden boards to a newborn baby's skull, moulding the bones to emulate the shape of their totem, the jaguar's head. Elsewhere in the panel, which is ten feet high and at least as wide, I spotted other clues to the culture depicted. There is the great stepped temple of El Tajin, a relic from a little-known civilization that flourished in about 100 AD. In the middle ground of the painting is another potent Totonac symbol, a high wooden pole from which men in bird costumes are suspended by their ankles on ropes, so that they 'fly' down to the ground from a hundred feet above. These 'fliers', known as *voladores,* are enacting a powerful religious rite, a symbolic link between the tree of life and the heavenly powers. At weekends I have seen them putting on their flying demonstrations in Mexico City's Chapultepec Park for visitors queuing to enter the magnificent anthropology museum.

The Totonac chieftain in Rivera's panel wears padded body armour and a magnificent headdress. Attendants shade his face from the sun with fans and he proffers a basket of fruit towards the Aztec. At his feet are pineapples, melons and papaya, a slain deer, rolls of tobacco leaves and baskets of beans – all commodities gathered from the tribal land. And between the Aztec and the Totonac there is a dark green vine, its flat leaves immediately identifiable as the crop which formed a crucial part of the region's special tribute to the emperor. The snake-like creeper hangs between the two men, and there, beside the chieftain's face are the small pale flowers, with just a tint of yellow that I recognize: vanilla orchids.

The Totonac land is still fertile, and it is where most of Mexico's vanilla crop is grown and cured. On the narrow tropical plain, between the high eastern peaks of the Sierra Madre and the Gulf Coast, the rolling landscape hides tiny villages where peasant farmers rely on the crop for much needed cash. Sandwiched between the coastal resorts of the Costa Esmeralda and the mysterious two-thousand-year-old ruins of El Tajin there is a small town called Papantla. A hundred years ago fortunes were made here from the black bean, and it produced so much vanilla they called it the 'city that perfumed the world'.

The drive to Papantla from Veracruz city took me half a day, a long run along Highway 180 past the places where Spanish explorer Hernando Cortés made his first stops along the route to the interior. His journey and eventual encounter with Emperor Montezuma Xocóyotl has been romanticized over the centuries. When he entered the Aztec capital Tenochtitlan in 1519 he was greeted by thousands of richly dressed noblemen wearing pearl necklaces and golden earrings. Believing the Spaniards to be in some way divine, the emperor chose not to make war upon them. Warriors dressed as eagles and jaguars and clothed in ornaments made from thousands of hummingbird feathers stood back as the men in steel armour rode their horses into the city. Crossing over causeways built across a great lake, and passing floating gardens, the Spanish invaders were met by Aztec aristocracy who touched the ground with their hands and kissed them before they entered the city. A broad avenue three miles long then led into the centre of the capital where hundreds more nobles waited with flower-filled gourds to welcome them. Finally, more than an hour after entering Tenochtitlan, they were in the presence of the emperor. 'This is your house,' said Montezuma, presenting Cortés with a fine necklace. 'Eat, drink and rest from your own journey . . .' It was a defining moment in history, the moment of contact between the ruler of the greatest civilization in the New World and the conquering power of Europe.

At Antigua I saw the old stone custom house enveloped by

banyan roots where it is said the conqueror stayed. It is just a ruin, but there is a spreading tree close to the wide brown river to which local people believe Cortés may have tied his ship. It was here, at the mouth of the River Huitzilapan, that he took the momentous decision to burn his ships to prevent his troops deserting him. Cortés had no royal warrant to establish a colony in Mexico, and his original mission was supposed to have been merely an exploratory sortie on behalf of the Cuban Governor Diego Velázquez.

Avoiding the half-dozen souvenir stalls near the tree, I walked across the wire rope bridge over the river and saw wooden pirogues drawn up on its muddy banks. Further along the route I stopped at the ruins of Cempoala, where Cortés made a crucial alliance with a local chief, the famous *cacique gordo*, who was so obese he went everywhere on a litter carried by his bodyguards. The fat cacique was crucial to the eventual success of Cortés's mission. Like many of the Aztec subjects he was resentful of the emperor's power, and he offered both men and advice on how best to deal with Montezuma.

Cortés headed inland from here towards Jalapa, guided by Totonac nobles and with several hundred Cempoalan warriors provided by the fat *cacique*. Then I took the road northwards, across flat green plains, the land given over to citrus farms and cattle ranches.

I drove over countless bridges spanning small rivers and past Mexico's only nuclear power station at Laguna Verde. *Zopilotes* – big brown vultures – circled in the thermals above the tarmac keeping an eye out for squashed frogs, rabbits, or if they were very lucky, dogs. In the fields there were cowboys on horses and plantations of bananas, papayas and mangoes. On one of the cattle ranches I saw a small bull ring, a white cement circle of death in a field. Further on, a man stood by the road with his arm outstretched and holding an armadillo by the tail, offering it for sale, either as food or as a pet to the passing motorists.

For mile after mile a steady stretch of billboards tried to entice me to the hotels built between the highway and the beach. The Palacios and the Marymar Paraiso, an El Doral, a Copalar and a Casa Blanca, some shabby, some smart, but none good enough to deter me from reaching the interior. At Nautla the river leading to the sea was a hundred yards wide, and beyond it the highway veered inland away from the plain. As the road climbed into the hills a mist came down and the windscreen clouded over with fine spray. Huge lorries laden with sugar cane laboured upwards, scattering leaves and straw in their wake. Past the narrow road to Tecolutla and through the town of Gutierez Zamora I drove on, until just before dark I saw the sign for Papantla.

The town square was greasy with rain and outside the Hotel Provincia I could smell candyfloss in the air. There were street vendors on every available spot on the pavement and at least four competing open-air disc jockeys were filling the night with a mixture of rap music, folk tunes on the guitar and the tinny sound of poorly amplified Christmas carols. Christmas was just two weeks away, but before that all of Mexico would be celebrating the Festival of the Virgin of Guadalupe, patron saint of Mexico and all of the Americas. The Papantlecos had yet another reason to party. Tomorrow was the official date for the beginning of the vanilla harvest.

The receptionist gave me a room overlooking the town square and told me that there was just one other guest, another foreigner, also looking for vanilla. 'A gringo?' I enquired, wondering if it might be one of the traders from the United States on a buying trip. 'No, no, Señor, he is a man like you.

He is from Guatemala, and we give you the room next to him.'

My only contact in Papantla was through the *Consejo Veracruzano de la Vainilla* (Veracruz Vanilla Council), a state-funded body set up to improve communications between the Totonac planters and the buyers in the main towns to whom they sold the green beans for drying and curing. Victor Vallejo, a local landowner and businessman, was in charge of the Council, and I had spoken to him by phone from London. Speaking to him from the Hotel Provincia proved more difficult. The line crackled and buzzed and frequently cut out entirely, but Victor said he would collect me from the hotel at eight the next morning and take me with him when he went into the hills officially to notify the vanilla planters that the season was open. I wanted to ask him if he knew anything about my Guatemalan neighbour, but the line was too poor to chat.

The rain had not stopped completely, but it was soft and light, what the Mexicans onomatopoeically call *chipi-chipi*. It didn't seem to be dampening the enthusiasm of the DJs in the square, so it seemed a good idea to explore the town. From my balcony I could see the parish church perched on a steep slope overlooking the square, and behind it, higher still, a grey shape illuminated from below and standing out against the night sky. It was the statue of a man playing a flute and I knew it represented the musician who calls the Totonac fliers to their dizzying posts on top of the sacred tree represented in the Rivera mural. Once upon a time the Totonacs would scour the forests of Veracruz for a suitable tree, a search led by the piper. During the build-up to the ceremony the fliers stuck to a regime of fasting and sexual abstinence. Today the fliers use a man-made podium, and there, beside the church, I spotted it: a steel pole with a circular platform at its tip, the platform no more than three feet square where the *voladores* and their piper would sit while incantations to the gods were offered before they flew. The pole stretched up into the rain to what seemed an unfeasible height, which a local flier told me later was 125 feet.

There were no fliers tonight, but in the square there were children playing in the rain, and women in shawls scurrying from last-minute visits to the shops around its perimeter. The market stallholders had food and trinkets for sale, though the busiest trade was being done by the man selling plastic farm animals and Holy Nativity families. Close to the hotel, the man from the Discoteca Brillante was pumping out his rap music and a new acoustic competitor had joined the square. A small red van disguised as a train, with a carriage behind, was now broadcasting an appeal by megaphone. It was Santa's postbox, decked out in logos for Coca-Cola, whose corporate colours fortuitously echo those of the great man's costume and beard. To escape the cacophony I walked towards the church. Mass was going on inside and I veered away, walking onwards and upwards on the steep streets hoping to find my way to the statue I had seen from my balcony. Up here it was dark and the sounds from the market square were barely noticeable, muffled by the press of the rain.

The view from the hill was disappointing. Close-up, the statue was ugly and the rain obscured all but the bright lights of the town square immediately below me. The floodlights at the feet of the piper attracted a massive cloud of flying ants, which seemed impervious to the rain, and I was about to leave when two armed soldiers in dull green anoraks appeared at the foot of the plinth. One was slim and smiled a lot, the other quite fat and he didn't smile at all. The cheerful one asked me what I was doing, saying they wanted cigarettes, and I found myself apologizing for not smoking. I made to leave, but the fat one blocked my path and held up his weapon. Now they wanted money for beer. I had very little cash to give, and it irritated me that I was alone up there in the rain at their mercy, but I stuffed a few coins into his hand. He didn't budge and I didn't know what to do. As we eyeballed each other I noticed that he had very smooth cheeks. The rain made them shine in the naked glow of the spotlights. Eventually the other soldier gave an order, and the fat one turned sideways just enough to let me go down the stairs at the base of the statue. I retreated to the companionship of the noisy square.

The next morning the rain had stopped. Victor Vallejo was running late, and called to tell me that he had official documents to prepare before we headed into the countryside. 'Tim, forgive me, I'm so busy this morning. Please wait for me at the café next door to the hotel, and I'll be there as soon as I can.'

As I handed in my key at reception, the hotel's only other resident emerged from the room next to mine. I guessed he was 'the Guatemalan', a stocky man with large pale eyes and a neat beard. He was a carrying a video camera and wore a baseball hat emblazoned with the logo of a well-known European vanilla importer. I introduced myself in faltering Spanish, and he gave me a firm handshake. He told me his name was Dario Fontana, but didn't smile. '*Inglés?* All English are pirates, yes?'

'Not all of us, no. I see from your hat that you are in the vanilla business?'

He stared at me for several seconds before replying.

'Me, I am a poor Indian from Guatemala. I care only for one thing. The Truth, and Vanilla.' He pronounced it the Spanish way – *by-nee-ya*. 'I am not a spy. That is all I have to say.' With this declaration Dario was gone. I watched him leave the hotel, clacking down the steps to the street in his metal-tipped cowboy boots. It was already 25°C outside but apart from the baseball hat he wore tight jeans, a long-sleeved shirt and a quilted jacket.

In the Ristorante Sorrento I was the sole customer. The owner was installed in front of a television watching a soap opera, the volume so loud it distorted the soundtrack. Papantlecos seemed to like things noisy. I drank tea and waited for Victor, who eventually drew up in a mud-splattered pick-up which bore the lettering *CO.VER.VAINILLA*.

After Dario's strange outburst it was a relief to meet Victor in the flesh, a slim pixie of a man, a charmer with a neat white moustache and a sun-tanned complexion. He spoke good English, and at high speed. 'Tim, we are so *honoured* to have you in Papantla. You must forgive this poor *simple* farmer for being late. I have so much to do today but I really wanted you to witness the start of the vanilla season. But we have a long way to go and I am already behind schedule!'

Victor drove like he spoke, rapidly and with a tendency to veer from one topic to another. It was a two-and-a-half-hour drive to the mountains and he was in expansive mood. He was keen to discuss the work of the Vanilla Council, but equally keen to find out where I stood on matters of global alliance. 'It is so nice to have a visitor from Europe; there are many things we must discuss before you leave. But tell me, will the war come in your lifetime?' he asked eagerly.

'Which war?'

'The one between Europe and the USA! Don't you agree with me it is only a matter of time?'

The countryside flashed by, and I tried to concentrate on asking about the work of the Vanilla Council. We passed cowboys on their horses and barefooted peasants in their traditional white trousers, tunics and straw hats. The landscape was green and gentle, and I was telling Victor how much it reminded me of the vanilla regions of Madagascar, when he suddenly slewed the van to a halt beside the road.

'Shit! Shit!' he exclaimed. And then again, 'Oh shit! Mother of God. I am a stupid old man of sixty-nine years old. Oh my God, how could I do such a thing?' Victor leaned against the wheel, shaking his head in dismay. He had left the all-important vanilla documents behind, the very things he said he had to collect before he picked me up from the café.

Eventually, Victor calmed down. He made a call on his cell phone to his secretary in Papantla asking her to fax a copy of the papers to the mayor's office in the town where we were headed. Then we drove in silence for a time, all the while heading south-west on smaller and rougher roads. There were low hills and hummocks in the fields on either side as we drove, and around the hills I saw striations in the earth where cattle hooves had worn narrow terraces in the soil.

'We need to encourage the vanilla growers,' said Victor, recovering from his embarrassment at forgetting his documents. 'You see what damage the cattle do to the land. And the ranchers cut down the forest for grazing for the animals, and then we get less rain. Even I notice how much hotter it is here now compared to when I first came from California forty years ago. But vanilla doesn't harm the land like this, no, no, no.'

We reached the steep cobbled main street of a village. A large crumbling church took up one side of the central square, and there was a small formal garden in front of the municipal offices opposite. 'This is Coxquihui,' said Victor with a grin. 'Don't you love the sound of the word – "*kush-kee-wee*" – it's a type of bamboo they use hereabouts for thatching the houses.'

Mayor Juvencio González Juaréz was a busy man, and there

were at least twenty people waiting outside his small office for an audience. But for Victor and the *Inglés* he would make time.

'We welcome you,' said the mayor as we were ushered into his small bare office. 'Because you will tell people outside the district that we want tourists to come here. And you, Don Victor, because you bring the documents to allow us to harvest this year's vanilla.'

It seemed that one of Victor's main achievements as head of the Vanilla Council was convincing the farmers that without official documents from his own office they should never, ever cut their vanilla beans. After years of argument the growers had only recently agreed that no one would harvest vanilla before Victor delivered the council's permission, on paper bearing the State seal. Having left the papers in Papantla, Victor now had to explain the complicated plan he had to circumvent his own regulations, and as the conversation became heated I studied Coxquihui's coat of arms on the plaque on the mayor's office wall. There on the carved wooden shield was the vanilla vine, pendulous with beans.

'Why is the paperwork so vital?' I asked the mayor.

'Because of banditry and theft,' he explained. Out of the corner of my eye, Victor looked relieved that I had decided to intervene. 'If the buyers agree,' continued the mayor, 'not to buy any vanilla before the official date, then thieves cannot sell it to the *beneficiadores* – the curers – before that day. We need this protection. The price of vanilla is high now, and there have been killings in the countryside. Outsiders, you understand.'

It was time to move on. Victor's final destination was another village, and again he delighted in rolling its name around in his mouth. 'Here is Zozozolco,' he declared with a grin, as we bumped along the tiny and seemingly deserted main street.

The road flattened out at the top and steep steps led down to other narrow streets clinging to the side of the hill. Here there were even more men in peasant dress gathered outside the slightly less grand *municipio*. Victor was immediately surrounded by the farmers who clustered about him, short men in bare feet with gnarled toenails and sun-beaten faces. They doffed their white hats and reached over one another to shake him by the hand. 'My God, this is so embarrassing,' Victor muttered to me in English. 'Why did I have to forget those damned papers?'

Many of the farmers, or *campesinos*, were clutching canvas bags containing a few kilos of green vanilla. They wanted their paperwork so that one of their number, a kind of foreman with access to a van, could take it by road to Papantla or nearby Gutierez Zamora and sell it to one of the curers. It became clear that part of the foreman's skill included speaking good enough Spanish to deal with the curers. Growing the beans is relatively simple, but the drying and curing is more complex, and labour intensive. A few farmers experiment with curing their own beans but in general the process requires a skill which takes many years to perfect, and secure premises in which to store the crop as it increases in value.

In Papantla and nearby Gutierez Zamora there are just four local buyers, or *beneficiadores*, who dry and package the vanilla for export, though once there were many more. Today the Papantla region produces around 250 tonnes of green vanilla, which equates to about 40 tonnes of dried beans. (As they are cured they dry out and lose weight.) For much of the nineteenth century the figure was more than ten times as great, around 600 tonnes of dried beans, some of it for export to Europe, but most of it going north across the border for the huge American baking and confectionery industry. In villages like

Zozozolco many of the farmers now produce just a few kilos of beans, but in their subsistence economy it is a valuable source of desperately needed cash. If they have a piece of land on which they can grow vanilla, then it is worth picking a few beans when they ripen.

I could tell that the farmers were curious about me, and I asked Victor what they were saying. 'You are a foreigner, they say you must be a rich buyer from America, and they are asking me to tell you to pay more for their beans!'

'*No soy gringo*,' I said to some of the farmers nearby, '*soy britanico!*' It was one of the first things I learnt to say in Mexico, and it usually produced a smile. In Zozozolco it was met with total silence.

'Does anyone know where England is?' Victor asked the crowd. Almost everyone shook their heads, and there followed an explanation about the speed of aeroplanes and how many hours it would take to get to Mexico City from here, and then to England. The farmers nodded slowly as it became clear how far I had come. I couldn't tell if the distances involved meant much to people who had never been more than a few hours on foot from their home villages. To the *campesinos*, Papantla was a big city. At the end of Victor's geography lesson there was further silence. Then one of the farmers spoke up: 'Even if he has slept one whole night on an aeroplane he must still give us more money.'

There was a lull in proceedings while Victor went to use what appeared to be Zozozolco's only telephone, in the post office cum mayor's office. His cell phone was no good here and he needed the fax from his office in Papantla in order to authorize the official harvest. There was tension in the air and nothing to do but wait. I asked one of the farmers if I could take his photograph. Several of the men decided they too would like to be included, and a debate erupted about who should be first. Then one of the foremen decreed that it would not be fair unless everyone was in the picture. And it seemed that there were more farmers waiting somewhere else in the village. They too must be included, or he would not be doing his job of representing the community.

The foreman took charge, and led me off down the steep steps behind the town hall to a street which eventually brought us to the village church. On the way we filed past a barber's shop with a bad-tempered horse tied to a hitching post outside. It flattened its ears and raised a hind foot as I walked by. The church was set into the side of the hill, and on the terraced stairs outside there were at least another eighty farmers and about fifty women, whom I took to be their wives. The men arranged themselves in rows upon the steps, some of them brandishing a fistful of vanilla beans in front of them as I prepared to take the photograph. The women shielded their faces or looked away and there was some surprise when I asked if they too would line up for the picture. One or two of them smiled shyly as they joined the men, but mostly they averted their eyes and showed no expression. The deed was done. I wanted to thank the farmers, and asked for the correct word in Totonaca. The foreman provided the answer — 'pashte katini', which sounded like *pashtee katz-eeny*, when spoken. I repeated the phrase and was rewarded with a murmur from the crowd that I hoped was approval.

Now that we were well away from the mayor, and from 'Don' Victor, the foreman and the farmers were more relaxed and answered my questions about how they hoped to sell the crop. Many of them had walked for three or four hours to bring their beans into town today, and once the paperwork was in order the foremen would drive the crop into town to the curers and sell it for the best price possible. How much did they hope to earn from vanilla this year?

'Well,' said one man, 'the *beneficiadores* have told us they will only pay 150 pesos [about $15] a kilo, so that is what we must accept.'

The figure surprised me, as in the 2002–3 season the wholesale value of good quality dried beans was more than thirty times that. In Madagascar the farmers expected more than ten times that amount for green beans, and if anything they were even poorer than the Mexicans. Given that this low price was for green beans which would lose most of their weight when cured, you could multiply that price by five or six to get the dry weight price. In other words, it takes approximately six kilos of green beans to produce one kilogram of dry. The *beneficiador* has other costs of course: the staff to prepare the beans, the premises in which to store them, security precautions, and obviously the time it takes for the drying and conditioning to be completed – between three and six months. He will also have to sort and pack the beans into uniform bundles and ensure rigid quality control to meet the demands of foreign buyers. Even so, there was a healthy profit to be made between green and black.

By the time I returned to the main street Victor was ready to leave. The fax had never arrived and he couldn't reach his secretary by phone. He had hatched another scheme; the mayor and the foremen would make a list of each farmer's name and the quantity of beans he was selling. Victor would meet the foremen at the buyer's offices in Papantla and collect a copy of the list as a record of which farmers had sold vanilla, and how much. I couldn't see how this would work, since I understood that the idea of the Vanilla Council issuing papers was to ensure that the buyers didn't buy any beans from anyone unless they produced documentation. 'Never mind,' said Victor, 'I will straighten it out with the buyers.'

The problem with vanilla beans is that once they are ripe on the vine they are easy to pick, and hence to steal. They grow on supporting trees in forest plantations where it is difficult to guard every vine. To get around the problem there have been various schemes, at various times, to try to ensure that no one picks beans or deals in them before a certain date. Beans offered to a curer before this date are likely to have been stolen, and should therefore be refused. However, this system depends on the curer being honest, since if he buys 'illegal' beans he can get them at a very low price – like any 'fence' dealing in stolen goods he will pay a fraction of the true value. In a subsistence economy where even $15 is worth having, then desperate thieves are prepared to kill for vanilla. Peasant farmers in Madagascar and Mexico mount armed guard on their crop as harvest time approaches, and in both countries the police and the army will set up roadblocks to check who is carrying vanilla. Supposedly, they will stop anyone transporting vanilla without paperwork, and before the harvest date. In many places it is also forbidden for anyone to transport green beans after dark.

If you look closely at dried vanilla beans from Madagascar you can sometimes find little raised bumps, resembling a Braille symbol, somewhere along their length. The bumps are a unique tattoo, which individual growers brand upon the beans with pins or a piece of bamboo to mark their own crop. It is one more safety measure against theft, allowing stolen beans to be identified and allowing buyers and rural collectors to verify that the vendor is also the grower.

The problems of regulating the market in green vanilla are not new. Henry Bruman, an early American historian of the

Totonac region, discovered documents in the Mexican national archives relating to the problems of regulating the vanilla trade as early as 1743. At that time Don Franco de Cagicipajo, the mayor of Papantla, had issued a decree prohibiting the cutting of beans before 8 December, although his motive seems to have been to ensure that he had a personal monopoly on the crop. At the time, farmers objected to the mayor's decree on the grounds that it didn't allow any leeway for those Totonacs who relied on picking 'wild' vanilla. In one contemporary letter a local nobleman, the Count of Fuenclara, writes to the State governor on behalf of the 'poor Indians who walk in the forest looking for vanilla, to relieve their poverty'. The count claims that the Indians have always picked wild vanilla, and are now being excluded from the market by the unscrupulous mayor. He also appeals against the potential fine of 500 pesos which the mayor wants to impose for early picking, a sum clearly unaffordable to the Indians who are being paid one peso for twenty-five vanilla beans. Another letter, twenty years later, discusses the plight of the peasants who are being impoverished by vanilla thieves and also prevented from gathering vanilla on land which has recently been sold into private hands. Interestingly, this complaint stems from the fact that the Indians say it is land on which they have 'always planted vanilla vines, with much labour and repeated journeys. Here, we have no other means to trade or to maintain ourselves and to clothe ourselves or pay our tribute to the King or tithes to the Church, except for vanilla and a little fishing.'

No one can be certain when vanilla was first formally planted. It seems likely that the Totonacs practised some form of systematic cultivation of the vines during the Aztec period, and that such methods were refined and developed in response to increased demand from Spain following the conquest. Perhaps at first it was merely a case of protecting a wild vine in the forest so that when it produced fruit they could be reliably gathered. The Totonacs, and other Indian tribes, may even have known that the vine could be transplanted and grown from cuttings, but it is by no means certain that they knew how the vanilla orchid was fertilized. Studies on the few remaining wild specimens of *Vanilla planifolia* prove that the plant is endemic to the evergreen tropical forests of eastern Mexico, and also in Guatemala, Belize and Honduras. It seems that individual vines are generally found growing some distance apart, and that they can live for hundreds of years. As with so many organisms, from elephants to sharks, long life tends to go with a low rate of reproduction.

In the thick forests of central and southern Mexico the work of fertilization would be done naturally by the small, metallic-coloured insects sometimes called 'orchid bees'. These fast-flying species are common in lowland forest areas, exactly where vanilla thrives, and it is probable that one particular Mexican species of bee, *Euglossa viridissima*, is the one which does the work of transporting the pollen of one vanilla orchid to another. Another species, *Eulaema cingulata*, is also suspected and at one time *Melipona beechii* was thought to be responsible, but has since been accused of inefficiency by entomologists.

Euglossine bees are known to be responsible for fertilizing at least a thousand orchid species, and it is only the male bee that does the work. Although vanilla orchids are not strongly fragrant to the human nose, these bees generally favour aromatic flowers. They collect scent from them which they are then believed to modify by chewing and masticating and then transferring the mixture to special pouches on their hind legs. This scent is then used as a territorial marker. Female bees are attracted to a male's territory by this scent, and have been observed landing near a 'scent marker' and immediately adopting the requisite mating position. Clearly, the sex life of the bees and the sexual habits of the vanilla orchid are closely connected.

Orchids have a reputation for lewd sexual display. Their intricate and erotic petals and lips are often unavoidably reminiscent of human female pudenda. But, alluring as they may appear to the human eye, they guard their own sexual parts away from view. While 'ordinary' flowers will happily display their breeding organs at the heart of their open petals, the orchid is generally more discreet. One of the special features of orchids is that the sexual parts of the flower are fused into a single structure known as the *column*. Opposite the column, usually on the lower side of the flower there is the orchid 'lip', in fact a modified petal known as the *labellum*. At the tip of the column, and often hidden by the lip, is the *anther* – the part of the flower that produces pollen – which is separated from the fertile *stigma* by a flap of tissue. It is the stigma that must receive the pollen and on which it will eventually germinate. The tissue flap is called the *rostellum*, and it needs to be lifted out of the way for a flower to be fertilized. The rostellum probably serves to prevent the orchid fertilizing itself, and also presents the sticky tips of the pollen masses, called *viscidia*, to the bee. The pollen grains themselves are sticky and adhere together into a ball. When a male bee visits the flower he finds the labellum a useful landing platform, which leads directly to where he wants to go, drawn in by the scent he needs for his own courting strategy. During the collection of the ingredients for making his scent marker a certain amount of this sticky pollen ball will attach itself to the bee's 'back'. This happens as the bee retreats from the interior of the vanilla orchid, when he is forced to climb over a tiny hump of raised tissue on the surface of the labellum known as the *callus*. As the bee climbs out of the flower he pushes against the anther collecting a cargo of pollen.

The scent particles that the bee is searching for have nothing to do with the pollen balls, and neither is he rewarded with food for his visit. Instead the bee scrapes his perfume ingredients from the surface of the flower lip and attaches them to pockets on his hind legs. And, when the bee visits the next vanilla orchid to repeat the process, he will leave a proportion of the pollen behind on the other flower's fertile stigma. When the pollen from one flower eventually reaches the stigma of another, pollen tubes germinate and grow downwards to reach the ovaries which in the case of vanilla lie within the stalk, behind the head of the flower. Then the ovaries develop into the fruits we call beans or pods. In the wild, the vanilla beans are fed upon by bats, and possibly some birds. Once eaten, the beans will spill their seed into the animal's gut, to be excreted elsewhere in the forest. If conditions are right, they will germinate into a new plant.

Vanilla planters cannot rely on natural pollinators to fertilize their orchids. They must do the job themselves.

4. Mexican Money

On the road to San Rafael we stopped at the orange plantation owned by Macario Jimenez. At sixty-eight, he is still strong, with a farmer's firm grip and a thick head of dark hair brushed straight back off his forehead. He has scary teeth, every one of them banded and rimmed in metal which flashed and glistened with saliva when he spoke, transfixing me with morbid fascination. Victor hadn't brought me to see the farmer's teeth. He told me that Macario was experimenting with vanilla, and that he seemed to have hit upon something remarkable. And he was happy to take us into the orange groves and reveal his secret.

It was muddy underfoot on the way to the plantation, clay-like soil which stuck to our shoes in clumps which grew bigger and bigger so that our feet seemed to be growing like a cartoon character's as we walked. The orange trees were larger than I had imagined, big bulbous forms fifteen feet apart. Every one of them was covered in vanilla.

'Isn't this amazing?' said Victor. 'Look at the size of these vines!'

He was right, I had never seen cultivated vanilla bearing so many seed pods. They hung in bunches like swollen fingers about a foot apart along the vines, which themselves seemed to be in rude good health. In the hills around Papantla the farmers reckon on a crop of around two hundred kilograms per hectare, or between two and five kilos of fruit for each mature vine. Macario told me that he could easily expect ten kilos of green beans from each orange tree, and this year he thought he might get twelve. What was his secret?

The teeth flashed. 'There are five commandments in growing vanilla,' explained Macario. 'Number One is water – the vines must drink when they are growing, but they must not get too wet, and the roots must never stand in water. Second: the man who grows them must understand them and watch them every day like they are his children. Number Three: the plant must be strong. The Fourth Commandment is the compost – I have my own recipe. And finally, the tutor, the plant that supports the vine, must be strong and allow just the right amount of shade and light. The orange tree is a good tutor. One more thing: if Number One or Number Two fail, then you can forget the rest!'

'You see,' Victor interjected, pumping his fists up and down in his enthusiasm. 'No one else has tried using the orange trees as the tutors. This is so exciting: you see we have 100,000 hectares of orange trees around Papantla – imagine if we could grow vanilla on them all!'

The sums are attractive. Macario told me that he had four hundred orange trees, and if each carried ten kilos of green beans he alone would have four tonnes of vanilla. If he could cure the crop himself – and the farm certainly had space for it – then at the top of the market he might make a quarter of a million dollars. By the same reckoning, just 2 per cent of Papantla's orange groves could produce 1,000 tonnes of vanilla – the equivalent of Madagascar's total annual production. There are two serious flaws to this plan: first, the resultant glut of vanilla would cause the market value to tumble, and second, growing vanilla and curing it to an acceptable standard are not the same thing. It also occurred to me that if the orange growers took over the vanilla crop on a large scale then the peasant farmers in the hills would be out of a job.

Victor's desire to restore Mexico's vanilla crop to its former glory was well meant, but I couldn't help feeling it was unrealistic. Without an efficient processing industry, growing the beans is simply not enough, and for most farmers the crop is just too labour intensive, and the price too volatile to make it worth a long-term investment. Macario, for all his success, admitted he wasn't an expert in vanilla, and he was happy to grow it as an adjunct to his oranges. In the long term it might be a useful source of extra cash if the citrus market crashed.

However, the visit to Macario had injected Victor with a fresh dose of vigour. We headed back to Papantla at speed, with Victor babbling excitedly about how many millions of dollars the vanilla crop might bring to the region; if only he could get the curers to pay a fair price to the farmers. That was Victor's mission, to give the *campesinos* a fair wage for their efforts. I told him that I had been surprised at how little the farmers were getting for green beans – exactly a hundredth of the amount the curers could expect from foreign buyers.

'You're right,' he said. 'We must confront the buyers with this figure! Otherwise you never know what could happen in the future. Our poor farmers could become terrorists, driven to do terrible things by poverty!' He said it as if it had never occurred to him before.

It was just getting dark as we reached Papantla, and drew up beside a high whitewashed wall on the edge of town. 'Here is the warehouse of Don Pedro Heriberto Larios Rivera,' said Victor, 'the most important *beneficiador* in town.'

We squeezed through a narrow side gate, stooping below a bougainvillaea overhanging the path leading up to the warehouse. Below us to the right was an open yard protected from the street by the high white wall. Outside the doorway to the warehouse there was a queue of farmers and their helpers, waiting to be admitted. They all had sacks of vanilla at their feet.

Victor walked straight through, and led me into the cool interior of the building. More farmers sat inside, occupying a row of plastic chairs opposite a large metal weighing scale onto which sacks of vanilla were being hauled. It reminded me of the big red weighing machines they used to have at English railway stations. It was very quiet, all eyes on the scales while a man with a clipboard noted down the weight of the sacks and called out the totals to an elderly man sitting behind a desk several feet away. The desk was covered in scraps of paper, and the man wrote everything in a dog-eared ledger, occasionally stopping to tap numbers into a rotary adding machine at his elbow. Against the far wall, and with his video camera trained on the activity at the scales sat Dario, the Guatemalan.

Victor nodded his greetings at Larios and we sat and watched as farmer after farmer presented a delivery note to Larios who signed and stamped it with the amount of beans he had purchased. As the last light faded from the sky Larios sat back in his chair with a sigh. The final sack of vanilla was carried to the back of the storeroom and the day's work was done. Dario fiddled with his video camera, packing it away before striding across the floor and shaking Victor and Larios by the hand. They exchanged a few words and then he approached me and again shook hands before bidding us all goodnight and disappearing down the path to the road.

Larios and Victor exchanged information about the day's trading, and it soon became clear that Larios was unhappy at my presence. Although I could follow much of what they were saying in Spanish, it was Victor who made things clear. 'Tim, it seems you have cost Don Heriberto some money!'

I couldn't imagine how, but Victor was grinning from ear to ear as he explained. 'The *campesinos* have been coming here all day telling Larios that a foreigner has been into the hills and he will pay them 200 pesos [$20] a kilo for green beans – so they won't accept 150 any more. And you are that foreigner!' Victor slapped his thighs with amusement.

Larios then explained that the other curers had telephoned him that afternoon with the same story. They all wanted to know who this foreign buyer might be, and they all wanted to know if any of the other curers were paying the 'new' price. Eventually, according to Larios, one of the buyers in the town of Gutierez Zamora had cracked, and agreed to pay 175 pesos a kilo. The other buyers had been forced to follow suit, or risk not getting enough green beans to fulfil the contracts they might have with foreign buyers for export.

'So, do you all cooperate and collaborate to fix the price of green beans?' I asked.

'This is the big problem!' exclaimed Victor, without giving Larios a chance to reply. 'The curers fix the price – the farmers have no leeway at all, unless one of the curers is desperate and offers more. But *they* operate like a cartel, and I want the farmers to get a better deal out of this whole process.'

'How much do you think the farmers should get for a kilo of green?'

'I think $50 or $60 would be fair – then the curers will still make a profit when they sell to the buyers for $150 a kilo.'

Larios shook his head. 'I have my costs to consider too,' he said calmly. 'I have the risk of curing the beans, the cost of security while they are in my charge and of course I need the skill and the experience to get them dried to the very best quality.'

I asked Larios how many beans he would buy this year. 'Compared to when I was a young man, hardly any — about ten tonnes of green, which' — he made the sign of the cross — 'will give me two tonnes cured.'

I did the sums in my head — for two tonnes of premium quality he could earn $300,000. Even if only half of the beans were premium grade he would still expect to make about $200,000. The *campesinos* in Zozozolco and Coxquihui had told me that, with careful spending, a family of eight could live on less than one thousand dollars a year.

I left Victor and Larios to talk business and headed back to the hotel, falling asleep to the sound of *El Buzon de Coca-Cola* as it trundled around the square collecting letters to Santa Claus.

The following morning was clear and bright and in spite of my influence upon the price of beans, Larios had invited me to watch the curing of the vanilla he had bought the night before.

It's not easy to get away from vanilla in Papantla. As I set out across the market square I noticed that the benches around it were decorated with tiled mosaics showing scenes from local life. One bench panel showed a view of the church, and another depicted the *voladores* flying from their pole. There was also a mosaic of the magnificent temples of El Tajin, but the prettiest was of a Totonac woman in traditional white dress, holding a flowering vanilla vine.

In the centre of the square there was a hexagonal bandstand. Like many Mexican bandstands it consisted of an open-sided platform raised to first floor height from which the musicians could serenade the audience below. Between two of the columns at ground level there were vanilla vines tethered to the cementwork, their roots in large earthenware pots at the base of the bandstand. Several of the plants had been woven together and strung into an arch above a trestle table set up below.

Behind the table stood a man in the regulation straw cowboy hat wearing a shiny jacket emblazoned with a Pepsi-Cola logo. The stall-owner had a long sad face, and very short stumpy fingers with sharp pointed nails. He told me his name was Juan Castaño Parra, and that he made everything on the table himself. There were bottles of vanilla extract and packets of cured vanilla pods, vanilla scented cigarettes and cigarillos, and a range of figures made from woven beans. There was a dog, a butterfly and a hanging basket. He had also made a little peasant couple, the man with a sun hat and tunic, with a machete strapped to his belt. The woman wore a tabard dress and had her hair in two long plaits hanging below her waist. The faces were featureless, but somehow Juan had imbued the little figures with life. There were rosaries, small and large, a crucifix – complete with Jesus and crown of thorns – and several varieties of flowers. We talked for a time, and I told him I was on my way to see the curing process at Larios's yard. 'Ah. Don Heriberto,' Parra nodded sagely, but his doleful expression didn't change.

Gradually I worked my way towards Larios's place, paying a brief visit to a shop which proclaimed itself '*El Mundo de la Vainilla*'. It wasn't much of a world, with just a few bottles of extract for sale and most of the shop given over to ornaments made from shells and cheap Taiwanese knick-knacks.

In a side street I came across a man with a small van loaded to the brim with cowboy paraphernalia. He had whips and spurs, blankets and bridles and a magnificent handmade saddle in fine-tooled leather which he was selling for two hundred dollars. On the pavement nearby, a boy of eight or nine was practising with a new lasso, repeatedly spinning the loop in circles at ankle level while trying to step into it and out of it without getting entangled.

The queue into Larios's yard stretched into the street. The double gates at street level were also open and a large canvas awning had been stretched across one section of the yard to protect the green vanilla from the sun. It lay in a heap, thousands upon thousands of beans piled on top of one another to form a green mountain with seven men sitting on low wooden stools around its base. The pile was almost four feet high and at least twenty feet across. In one corner of the yard there were two more men feeding a fire from strips of old packing crates and kindling which they broke by stamping on it with their boots. At its centre was a blackened tin cauldron filled with water which was just beginning to give off steam.

The men around the green bean mountain were pulling handfuls from the pile and measuring them by eye, then stacking them in loose bundles on hessian sacks laid out on the cement floor of the yard. Dario was there too, still wearing his quilted jacket and training his camera on the beans and on the men as they worked. He put the camera down and beckoned me over to where he stood. We shook hands and he showed me a clipboard on which he had a piece of paper with lines marked upon it one centimetre apart.

'Look!' Dario said with a slight smile. He reached into the pile of beans and began to select the longest vanilla pods he could find. He laid them against the paper lines, showing me that many of the beans were twenty-five centimetres long.

Long, thin elegant beans as green as Irish grass. He produced two more beans, shorter and curved like a banana. They were much fatter in girth, and as they grew they twisted, showing prominent edges making them look more like mini-courgettes than the other beans. 'You know this?' asked Dario.

'*Vanilla pompona*?' I guessed, though I knew the variety only from books.

'Yes, *pompona*!' he nodded excitedly, at my recognition of the variant species. Dario urged me to take pictures of his measuring chart and enthused about the quality of the beans we could see in Larios's yard. He seemed less aggressive than on our previous meetings, and had obviously decided that I was no longer a pirate.

A shout from the far corner of the yard told the men around the bean pile that the fire was ready. The men doing the sorting abandoned their little stools and stood up, carrying their small piles of sorted beans over to the fire. The water was giving off steady wisps of light steam and a large wooden box had been dragged close to the fire. One by one the men began twisting the squares of hessian, in which they carried their beans, into bundles and began dipping them into the hot water. They shielded their faces from the heat of the flames with one hand, holding the bundles at arm's length for as long as they could above the almost boiling water. For a minute at a time, perhaps longer, they extended an arm above the fire and the water, squatting back on their heels to get away from the heat. '*Ayee!*' Woodsmoke and steam billowed into their eyes making them wince, and occasionally grunt with pain.

One man stood by the wooden box, a giant red coffin into which the steamed beans were hurled and immediately covered with sacking. Again and again the sacking was peeled back and another load of hot beans dumped onto its growing cargo, all of it steaming and throwing clouds of mist into the air around the box.

After an hour or so the box was a third full, and it was time for *almuerzo*, the men's mid-morning snack. I watched as they retrieved their small bags of food from a little storeroom in the corner of the yard, and placed a large metal kettle on the edge of the fire where they had been steaming the beans. I was offered tea as they produced little bags of tortillas and meat and began to argue good-naturedly about football. The man who had been tending the fire was happy to talk, and he told me that they would expect to fit all of the beans on the floor that morning into the red box – about 800 kilograms in all.

Steaming the beans is an essential first step in the curing process; the heat in effect 'kills' the bean, preventing any further photosynthesis, or growth, and stimulating enzymes within the bean which will eventually make it smell like 'vanilla'. By wrapping the beans in sacking immediately after dipping they are kept warm, and consequently begin to 'sweat'. They remain under wraps for twenty-four hours. However, to prevent moisture accumulating on the beans and making them rot they must be unwrapped and exposed to sunlight every few hours, depending on the weather conditions, and then wrapped again. Next they will be stored away from direct heat and sunlight for several more months to develop their full aroma and flavour. It is the careful drying process which will ensure the beans have the correct moisture content – between 20 and 30 per cent. The curing will also affect the beans' vanillin content, one of the key flavour components which will determine their ultimate commercial value to the overseas buyers. Various attempts have been made to speed up the drying and conditioning process – which can take as much as eight months – sometimes with ovens, especially in Indonesia where vanilla production has increased dramatically in recent years. Such efforts always result in a lower quality bean, one which may have sufficient vanillin but usually with a low moisture content making it unsuitable for premium food grade applications. The best quality vanilla beans are dark skinned, soft and pliable.

Someone switched on a radio as the workers took their break, and the yard was filled with the sound of Bing Crosby singing 'White Christmas'. I saw Dario sitting alone at the other end of the yard, scribbling notes and measuring beans from the pile against his clipboard chart. Together we enthused about the length of the beans, and I plucked up the courage to ask him whether he had come to Papantla to buy vanilla.

'I come only to learn,' he said gravely. 'I will return to Guatemala and create my own plantation. There I will produce the best vanilla in the world. That is my dream.'

Dario became emotional as he talked about his plans, and at one point I thought I saw a tear in the corner of his eye. 'Do you have dreams, Señor Tim?' he asked. 'Men can only be men if they have dreams.'

In spite of Dario's poetic stance I couldn't help being sceptical, especially as Victor had given me another version of why Dario was there. On the car journey from Zozozolco he had told me that the Guatemalan was related to one of the best known vanilla dealers in the world, a company with offices in Europe and North America and significant interests in Latin America. In part, Dario's version was true; he was hoping to have his own plantation in Guatemala but according to Victor he was also being paid to keep an eye on Larios. It seemed that the previous year the European importers had paid the *beneficiador* a large amount of cash to secure a specific amount of cured premium quality vanilla. However, when the time came to deliver the contract, Larios revealed that he had no vanilla. In fact he had found another buyer who would pay more than the Europeans had offered, and he had simply sold them the beans. Naturally, he had already used the European cash advance to pay for the green beans, and could not afford to repay it. And, because the price for vanilla had also risen since he had received the down-payment, he could not afford to buy replacement beans for those he had given to the other buyer. It was a common enough tale in the commercial world of vanilla dealing, a market which to this day operates on handshakes and cash advances. Every foreign buyer knows they take a risk if they hand over an advance, but they sometimes do it in order to secure their line of supply. So, this year Dario had been despatched to sit in Larios's office and quite literally count the beans. His presence would guarantee that what had been paid for didn't simply disappear if someone else made a better offer. In the process, he was also learning what he could about how to cure vanilla, and hoping to realize his dream.

In the 1850s the vanilla was carried into town on mules. In small places like Papantla, Teutila, Gutierez Zamora and San Andrés Tuxtla it came in long trains of pack animals tethered together nose to tail with hoofs slipping on the streets as they went. The curers laid out the pods on the streets to dry and the cobblestones were stained black with the juices that ran out of them. That was when Mexico produced half of the world's vanilla beans, before the oil was discovered, and before much of the land was given over to cattle.

Today's *beneficiadores* are descendants of the men who grew rich on vanilla. Larios's father began his business in 1906, after the first wave of curers had set up their estates in Papantla. Many of them were foreigners, especially Frenchmen and

Italians, men like Don Dominico Gaia Tossi, an Italian immigrant who came to the area in 1873 and whose grandson Orlando opened the Vai-Mex vanilla extract factory seventy-five years later. Immigrants like the Gaias (who now call themselves Gaya) were encouraged to settle in Mexico under the presidency of Porfirio Díaz, when foreign businessmen and settlers were given land in return for exploiting commercial opportunities in the rural areas. During his presidency, Díaz zealously promoted any enterprise that would modernize the Mexican economy, and great social inequalities sprang from the policy of confiscating land which had traditionally belonged to Indian communities. German industrialists, French planters and Texan oilmen were welcomed to the wild 'untamed' territories like Veracruz, which was then mostly forest.

Victor had recommended that I meet someone he knew with a collection of photographs of Papantla. In a small house on the outskirts of the town I found Javier Carreira Dueñas. Javier is in his sixties, and no longer in the vanilla business, but he remembers the old days, when his father-in-law Don Raul Del Cueto Decuir made enough from his vanilla to buy an elegant three-masted schooner to carry his beans to New York. Carreira has gathered together as much information as he can about his family's connection with vanilla. He showed me old family photographs of the time when Don Raul's father, Ramon Del Cueto Linaje, had been at the very forefront of the industry.

'He was ahead of his time,' Carreira told me, producing a picture of a distinguished man wearing a suit on the verandah of a colonial hacienda. Crescent-shaped birdcages hung from the balcony ceiling and there were men in peasant dress laying out the neat bundles of vanilla in the courtyard beside the house.

Don Ramon did so well from vanilla that he went into

banking too, and Carreira proudly handed me an old pen, still in its cardboard box, with the company logo embossed on the side: *Don Ramon Del Cueto e Hijo, Exportadores de Vainilla, Corresponsales Bancararios, Papantla 1940*. He turned it over and over in his hands, as if it were a religious relic.

'The business today is nothing,' Carreira lamented. 'I remember the days when the beans we had here were forty centimetres long. No' – he shook his head sagely – 'the planters have lost the secret of growing good beans, and the *beneficiadores* are not what they were.'

Carreira showed me his grandfather-in-law's notebooks and letters going back a century to the time when Papantla vanilla was widely acknowledged to be the best in the world. The notebooks recorded that it was in 1860 that the *beneficiadores* first used thermometers to monitor the temperature at which they dried the beans. Ten years earlier the first custom-built drying oven was built in Papantla, an adaptation he said, of technology that had been used in Italy to kill silk-worms. The names of other curers surfaced in his journals, many of them with Italian or French roots: Arzani, Fontecilla, Perrotet and Tremari.

According to Carreira, Don Ramon (his wife's grandfather) had set out rules for the quality of the vanilla pods to be exported, laying down a standard which they hoped would ensure Mexico's pre-eminence in world trade. In 1915 he wrote: 'Mexico can, and should, recuperate its place. By 1960 we can predict that Madagascar will produce a thousand tonnes of vanilla. We in Mexico could produce twice that much if only we develop our industry along scientific lines.'

It was not to be. Don Ramon's predictions for Madagascar were uncannily accurate, but the Mexican industry would go into a steady decline, in part due to the advent of cheap artificial substitutes for natural vanilla, but more crucially because the Mexican workforce would find easier and more lucrative alternatives to this labour-intensive cash crop.

That evening, Victor told me to meet him at the Plaza Pardo café on the town square. 'You'll find me with Larios,' he grinned. 'He's always there with the other old men. You know, they call themselves the *pajaros caidos* – the fallen birds – because their dicks no longer rise up!' Victor clearly didn't include himself in the group. In any event he wasn't there, and nor was Larios.

I ordered some food and then noticed that Dario was sitting alone on the balcony overlooking the street. I waved a greeting, and he got up and lurched unsteadily towards my table. 'I will buy my friend the English pirate a drink!' he said, drawing up a chair. 'You will join me, yes?'

I tried to decline but it was one of those conversations that was always going to be one-sided. During the next hour I learnt a lot about Dario, not least that he had been Guatemala's national rodeo champion in 1981. It partially explained the strength of his grip as he held my hand in his own, holding my forearm with his other hand and tugging on my arm every time he made a statement.

'Tell me, *Inglés*. Can I trust an English man to tell me what is in his heart?'

I've never been very good at bar-room confidences, perhaps because I rarely go into bars. Fortunately, Dario's questions were mostly rhetorical. Each one was followed, however, by another test of forearm strength and an earnest request that I look him in the eyes. '*Veme a los ochos*,' he would say, and I feared for the consequences if my gaze wandered. Each time I met the staring-test we had to chink glasses of rum together with a hearty '*Salud!*' – the only time my arm was released from his bear-like grip. Our food lay uneaten beneath our straining forearms as Dario outlined his dream of becoming Guatemala's best vanilla farmer. 'No one can be richer than the man who lives out his dream.'

As the rum disappeared I tried frantically to catch the waitress's eye, so as to summon the bill and escape from the drunken embrace. However, the restaurant staff seemed to be occupied with some unfolding drama of their own. They were clustered at the restaurant door, giggling and shrieking dementedly at something on the other side of the glass. Fortunately, Dario's mood swung swiftly from bellicose to lachrymose. 'I am just a poor Que'Chi Indian,' he intoned tearfully. '*Seriamente.*' Truthfully. '*Salud!*' A toast. And so it went on. 'Look me in the eyes, tell me are you really a pirate?'

Just when I thought I was going to be challenged to some kind of all-out wrestling match, the waitress appeared and Dario said he had to go to the lavatory. I told him I had to meet Victor, and apologized that I might not be at the table when he returned.

Outside on the pavement I found out what had been amusing the waitresses. A very large but somewhat threadbare dog was lying in the entrance to the restaurant with a length of nylon cord knotted tight around its neck. Its tongue lolled from its mouth and by now it had barely the strength to raise its head. No one seemed to find the sight distressing, but a few people stopped and stared at the pathetic sight of the choking animal as I bent over it. I think they were waiting to see if I would get bitten. An old lady in a neighbouring doorway was persuaded to fetch me some scissors and somewhat gingerly I managed to free the cord which had bitten deeply through the skin on the dog's throat. It sagged to the floor, retching and gagging in that whole-body way that dogs do so well. I thought it might die, but after a few minutes it stood up and followed me back to the hotel. I left it on the steps outside, hoping it would survive the night. Once upstairs, I couldn't get to sleep, lying in my bed waiting for any sound of Dario returning to the adjoining room. I half expected him to appear at the door for some more arm wrestling.

The dog was still there the next morning, wagging its patchy tail at me and following me back to the restaurant. Of Dario there was no sign, but Victor decided to show up for breakfast, and apologized for not appearing the night before. He wanted to talk about how successful his efforts at the Vanilla Council had been. 'Once upon a time,' he said, 'all of the vanilla in Papantla went to Coca-Cola, and I think we can bring back those days. You know they've been down here twice this year already.'

It is an open secret in the vanilla business that some of the world's crop eventually finds its way into the world's most popular carbonated soft drinks. Pepsi-Cola readily acknowledge vanilla essence as an ingredient in their drink, but Coca-Cola will make no official comment on any of their ingredients. Victor had no such inhibitions.

'Oh yes, Coca-Cola was here, they sent a lady down in a private jet and she has been twice to see the farmers with me. One day when it was very hot she forgot to drink enough water and became dehydrated and fainted. It was terrible, she cut her head and we wanted to take her to a doctor, but her assistant wouldn't allow her to be seen by a Mexican doctor! Imagine, they sent for the plane to fly her back to the States!'

Victor said that in Papantla the incident had caused ill-feeling, not so much because no vanilla was sold, but because the executive in question had not been allowed to consult a Mexican doctor. 'You see,' Victor muttered darkly, 'what we have to put up with from our neighbours across the border.' He reminded me of the saying coined by Porfirio Díaz at the turn of the nineteenth century: *pobre Mexico tan lejos de Dios y tan cerca de Estados Unidos* – poor Mexico, so far from God and so close to the United States.

Victor told me that as far as he knew none of the *beneficiadores* had signed a contract with the American company. The recent launch of a new brand – Vanilla Coke – had given the Mexican growers high hopes that once again they might benefit from supplying the giants of the beverage industry. It was a story I had heard before, and newspapers in Uganda, India and Tahiti had reported similar hopes for their own vanilla growers. In fact industry insiders say that *if* vanilla is still a vital ingredient in Coca-Cola it is in very small, very dilute amounts, and that Pepsi and Coke probably only buy around forty tonnes of vanilla each per year – just a few per cent of the world market between them.

No one at Coca-Cola will confirm that vanilla is an ingredient in the world's most popular soft drink. I telephoned the lady at Coca-Cola whom Victor named, but she told me that she could not even confirm that she had ever set foot in Mexico. Vanilla dealers all say the same thing – 'even if we sell vanilla to Coca-Cola we can never admit it'. One man, who has been in the industry for forty years, told me an anecdote that he said was widely believed in the vanilla world. 'Remember New Coke? Back in 1985 they introduced "New Coke" and a few months later they went back to the old formula because it was so unpopular.' Indeed, how could anyone forget.

'Well, let me tell you they tried to sell off the vanilla they had stockpiled because they didn't need it in "New Coke", and I believe that's why people didn't like the new brand – it had no vanilla! So, guess what? They brought back the original flavour.' He also said he knew that the company had been forced to buy back the vanilla they had sold off, but at an inflated price from a canny broker.

Another version of the story is that the company reformulated its product with the express purpose of removing vanilla as an ingredient, not wanting to be dependent upon an ingredient that could fluctuate widely in price and availability. Whether the story about vanilla, and its role in the debacle, is true or not, the fact remains that original Coke was reintroduced after three months, relabelled as 'Classic Coke'. According to this man, Coca-Cola was originally planning to phase out 'original Coke' completely, and sell only the 'new' version. The company therefore no longer needed to keep any vanilla in stock. Like urban legends, rumours about Coca-Cola and vanilla abound. What is certain is that no one who does business with the big players in the food and beverage industry dares talk about what they do or do not supply to them. However, 'Vanilla Coke', introduced in May 2002, does contain a certain amount of natural vanilla flavouring, and according to Coca-Cola it has been a huge success, reputedly accounting for a rise in profits in the company's 2002–3 accounts. According to official figures from Coca-Cola the vanilla flavoured drink sold almost a hundred million cases in its first year and 'brought in eight million new consumers who were not drinking Coca-Cola'.

Victor Vallejo was equally happy to tell me that he had been entertaining other high-profile figures from the vanilla world in recent months. Buyers from the big vanilla import-export companies like Aust & Hachman, Zink & Triest, Shank's Extracts and Vanipro had all passed through on buying trips. With no more than six or seven significant players in the world vanilla trade it isn't difficult to find out who is buying beans, although the quantities and the price they pay are closely guarded secrets.

For Victor, and the Vanilla Council, the obstacle to securing a fairer price for the farmers is not the foreign buyers; it is the Mexican curers. Not only are they reluctant to pay a higher price for green beans, but they also find it difficult to stick to the rules governing the official harvest date. 'We know they buy beans at an even lower price before the harvest day,' said Victor. 'They are businessmen, and they won't turn down a good deal – but cheap beans are often stolen beans, and if people know the curers will buy them then they have the incentive to steal.'

Mexico, the home of *xa'nat*, now produces just forty tonnes of vanilla each year, whereas sixty years ago it was exporting ten times this amount. The oil industry has displaced the vanilla crop as the main source of income for Totonac wage earners, and with it the rural way of life is changing too. Like many other Mexicans, young Totonacs are forced away from their villages to work in the cities, or across the border in the USA, in order to send vital cash back to their families. Farming is not an easy or profitable option, though many Totonac people are proudly defensive of their traditional way of life. For them, growing vanilla is something they have done since time immemorial. They say it is part of them now, in the same way that the dark green vines they tether to the trees become part of the forest.

It seemed a long way back from Papantla to Mexico City. The road inland makes it possible to retrace the route Cortés followed when he made his epic trek towards Tenochtitlan in 1519. I passed through Cempoala again and made my way to Jalapa, where at the recommendation of a friend, I dined at La

Sopa. The chef 'Negro' Ochoa gave me chickpea soup spiced with *jalapeños,* the city's eponymous peppers. Negro is the first Mexican chef to be awarded the Medal of Honour by the French Institute of Gastronomy, but he is better known in Jalapa as an exuberant advocate of nourishing food provided at minimal cost. He joined me as I ended my meal with a small *natilla*, a peach and vanilla custard compote. 'Don't worry, it's not fattening,' Negro pronounced. 'I'm keeping the people of Jalapa slim.'

He and his hand-picked team of model-handsome waiters flitted between the tables like a troupe of unemployed ballet dancers. 'Surely, you're not worried about being overweight?' I said, in deference to his narrow hips and tight trousers.

'No,' he giggled. 'I'm terrified of developing diabetes. I've heard it stops you getting it up!'

From Jalapa I continued towards Tlaxcala. Cortés was guided here by three Totonac nobles and his journey took thirteen days, up, up and away from the humid coastland and through the high pass between the cloud-covered peaks of Orizaba and Nauhcampatepetl. At Tlaxcala the conqueror made another alliance, boosting his small army with thousands of troops supplied by the Indian chiefs who, like the fat *cacique* of Cempoala, had long-held grudges against the Aztecs who forced them to pay taxes and restricted their own trading ambitions. There, in the Cathedral of the Ascension I tiptoed past a wedding party to see the stone font where Cortés stood as godfather to four Tlaxcalan nobles who were baptized following the conquest of Tenochtitlan. On this spot, Maxixcatzin, Xicohtencatl, Tlahuexcocotzin and Zitlalpopocatl became Lorenzo, Vicente, Gonzalo and Bartolomeo. 'Here was begun the Holy gospel in this New World,' ran the inscription on the original stone pulpit nearby.

I drove on across the flat scrub plain dotted with maguey cactus and fields filled with strange miniature haystacks no more than four feet tall. I skirted the desert and the last pockets of wet swamp where Cortés lost all of his Cuban porters to exposure. That night I slept in a cold bedroom at an old family hacienda on a dusty road some way from town.

The owner was Javier Zamora, a young man with grand plans to turn his grandmother's home into a modern hotel. He had a face straight out of a Velázquez painting, thick ringlets of onyx-black hair framing his linen-white skin and dark Spanish eyes. The main house had an enormous dining room and a log fire, but because I was cold, and the only resident in the hacienda – apart from granny who had the upstairs floor – I was allowed to eat at the family table in the kitchen. Javier gave me *mixiote*, a bag made from a boiled maguey cactus leaf tied at the neck with cord and filled with lamb marinade in a rich scarlet sauce concocted from more than twenty ingredients, including garlic, cumin and several types of pepper. He told me the lamb and the cactus leaves all came from his own land. There were also strips of fried *nopal* cactus, fresh guacamole and an old china teapot filled with hot strong tea. Fortified against the cold, I slept deeply, and had violent spice-fuelled dreams.

Cortés entered Tenochtitlan four months after he left the Veracruz, but by early afternoon the next day I was there, installed in one of the crop of new designer hotels which have reinvigorated the metropolis. If legend is to be believed, Cortés became the first European to taste vanilla, an ingredient in *xocoatl*, which Montezuma presented to him in a gilded goblet carved from tortoiseshell.

I had come to the great city in search of Miguel Soto, a somewhat reclusive botanist, who knows more about vanilla than any man alive. After several conversations by telephone from London, he had at last agreed to meet me, though he said he could not reveal too much of his specialist knowledge about vanilla since it was as yet unpublished.

After several days in town, we eventually met on the Avenue Masaryk, one of Mexico City's smartest streets with shop-fronts decked out by Cartier and Bulgari, Burberry and Alfred Dunhill. Roadside kiosks offer the well-heeled businessmen a quick shoe-shine for a few pesos or a hot tortilla for the office workers hurrying into the banks and car showrooms that line the avenue. Miguel arrived late, and given how hard it had been to make contact I was becoming nervous that he was not going to appear. He walked into the lobby of my hotel, a slim youthful figure in a denim jacket and faded jeans, explaining that his reluctance to meet was partly due to problems with his car, but he had made the two-hour journey from home by public transport. At first Miguel was shy, and reluctant to talk about his work except in a very general way, but gradually he relaxed and began to enthuse about his research. Another factor in his reticence on the telephone had been that he was having problems at the university, some kind of conflict with a junior academic who happened to be having an affair with Miguel's supervisor, the head of department. It was a common enough tale of the in-fighting and petty rivalries which blight academe, and it reminded me of why I had abandoned my own ambitions of writing a PhD.

There was a winter chill in the air as we drank tea on the terrace of the fashionable Habita Hotel, a frosted glass cube of a building with a thin rooftop pool overlooking the vast spread of the city. The heated water sent steam into the sky. Miguel was patient, and explained his own research in a way that led me to believe I understood it. He also said he had difficulty funding his research into the genetic and molecular structure of vanilla orchids. 'I love this plant, it's an amazing survivor,' he said. 'I believe it's quite possible that every cultivated *Vanilla planifolia* specimen in the world today has come from just one specimen taken from Mexico in the eighteenth century.'

For more than twenty years, Miguel has travelled widely around southern Mexico looking for wild uncultivated specimens of commercial vanilla. He has camped out in the mountains of Chiapas State, and across the border in Guatemala for weeks at a time, hoping to locate vanilla orchids in the thick jungle. In all that time he has found fewer than thirty plants which he believes are truly wild and may have spread naturally – rather than having been transported by human beings. Miguel seemed in awe of the vanilla plant, breathlessly listing its special qualities: 'I've never seen a seedling in the wild – this is a clonal plant, highly specific in its habitat. It has survived even though it has been the victim of uncontrolled extraction by human beings.'

He said he knew at least fourteen species of vanilla orchid within Central America, several of them as yet undescribed. To the naked eye, many of these species look identical to *Vanilla planifolia* when they are not in flower, something which has led to confusion among botanists for centuries. I had been puzzled to see vanilla specimens in Madagascar which local growers said were *planifolia* but with different shaped leaves, and great variation in stem sizes. Miguel was quick to explain how these specimens could still be the Mexican species.

'Look, I am made up of my father and my mother's genes,' Miguel said, rolling up his shirtsleeve. 'But, see here on my arm – these freckles, they are mine, not my parents'. These are just somatic differences – a variation in my individual form caused by how much sun my skin has been exposed to. My phenotype – the genetic form my body takes – is very clearly "Mexican", with a little Chinese from my grandfather! So the "strange" vanilla you have seen may well be *planifolia*, with differences in the leaves caused by soil or heat: without genetic markers it is impossible to be sure.'

The sky darkened as we talked and I watched the aeroplanes descending through the orange haze over the capital as they came in to land at Benito Juarez airport. Miguel is an articulate man, a clear thinker with an understated passion for his work. Gradually he told me more about the difficulties involved in his research. He told me how a well-known international organization refused him access to their extensive collection of vanilla specimens when he wouldn't reveal the location of a self-pollinating variety of *planifolia*. The commercial value of a vanilla plant that didn't need to be fertilized by hand would be enormous, but he didn't want the specimen he had found in the forest to be disturbed. Miguel also described the dangers in locating vanilla orchids in southern Mexico, not just because they grow in remote mountainous terrain which can only be reached on foot. It is the kind of landscape that bandits and drug traffickers favour too, and they are understandably wary of people, even innocent botanists, invading their territory.

To identify the true spread of naturally occurring *Vanilla planifolia* within Mexico, Miguel needs more funds and more time. He works as a consultant to the government, and to various botanical organizations, activities which take up time and prevent him publishing his definitive research. He is certain that *Vanilla planifolia*'s natural range is a more or less straight line from Mexico's Oaxaca State extending south through Guatemala and Belize. For this reason, he doubts that the plant is truly native to Veracruz, and to the Totonac lands. Miguel believes that pre-Hispanic cultures were probably responsible for its spread northwards from Oaxaca towards the Gulf Coast. However, he is also quite confident that the Totonac would not have relied on natural pollination to produce the vanilla pods they gave to the Aztecs. Even so, there is no direct or even anecdotal evidence of manual pollination being carried out before the nineteenth century.

On one thing we could agree, that *Vanilla planifolia* had moved from Mexico to the Indian Ocean via Europe. 'Don't forget,' Miguel said quietly. 'The English were obsessed with horticulture and cultivating exotic species in a way that never happened in Spanish culture. Yes, the conquistadors came from Spain, but they took vanilla back home only as an item to trade. In England you were much more interested in it as a plant.'

5. From an English Garden

Paddington Green is besieged by traffic. To the south it faces the confluence of the Harrow Road and the Marylebone flyover, two of central London's busiest arteries. For much of the day and night the sound of rubber tyres on asphalt fills your ears like the thrumming of a monstrous insect. North and east, the slower-paced but equally congested Edgware Road cuts across Church Street, the green's other main border. These major roads and ugly modern developments have squeezed the remnants of the open space into a triangle of urban dereliction.

On the north-east corner of the green you see a red-brick mansion block in fair condition, and next to it two shabby Victorian buildings housing St Mary's Hospital Department of Child and Adolescent Psychiatry. Tucked behind these buildings and abutting Church Street there is a modern doctor's surgery and beside it a temporary car park soon to be developed as office space beside the Edgware Road. At the edge of the car park, like a set from some gritty crime film a few ancient brick sheds blackened by age and soot lie in disrepair behind a derelict snooker hall. It takes a leap of imagination to picture the area as a village whose residents once sought it out as a retreat from the metropolis.

The green is not all ugliness. If you can shut out the noise of the traffic, the view of the tower blocks behind and the shabby strip of buildings that lines its edge, then it is just about possible to see traces of a noble past. Church Street still leads to St Mary's, where Sarah Siddons, the great tragedian and star of Drury Lane, is buried. A statue of the actress, serene in her marble skin, faces the Harrow Road, a cool effigy that reveals none of the passion which a contemporary said 'emanates from her breast as from a shrine'. There is still greenery, with more than a dozen London plane trees each well over a hundred years old guarding the paths criss-crossing the grass. And a plaque at one edge of the green commemorates the fact that the first London bus ran from here to the Bank of England in 1829. What the plaque does not reveal is that Paddington Green is at the heart of a botanical mystery.

At the end of the eighteenth century Paddington Green attracted minor members of the gentry, men and women of quality who could not quite afford to live in the smarter squares within the city. The Chirac family, jewellers to Queen Anne, had a decent sized house here, and there was open land not yet filled with buildings. Residents took advantage of several streams which made the area around Paddington ideal for gardening. In 1797 John Symmons of Paddington Green published a list of the plants he had grown there, including fifty-eight varieties of rose, various grasses, alpines and flowering shrubs as well as pears, cherries, plums and quinces. Symmons also boasted of exotic plants, listing among his collection the Forked Marvel of Peru, Spanish Gold of Pleasure, Job's Tears and something he called a Toothache tree.

This was a time of intense interest in gardening, a time when all manner of new plants were coming to England from abroad. Great rivalries sprang up among the aristocracy who wanted to own them and keep them in their extravagant gardens. Having a well-planted country estate was as important as the quality of the paintings and objets d'art inside your stately home. The first great English landscape designer 'Capability' Brown had just died, having already transformed many of England's most prominent estates including the gardens at Blenheim Palace. His successor, Humphrey Repton, would soon publish his influential *Sketches and Hints on Landscape Gardening* in 1795 and *Observations on the Theory and Practice of Landscape Gardening* in 1803.

In about 1800 glazed roofs became readily available for the first time, allowing a rapid expansion in the numbers of gardeners able to create 'stoves' or 'hothouses' for keeping exotic plants. The technology of 'forcing' native plants by keeping them warm was already well known, but with the advent of glass roofs there was the possibility of more adventurous projects, and on a larger scale. Within a few years there was a spate of gardening journals, initiated by the successful launch of a publication entitled *Botanical Magazine, or Flower-Garden displayed* in 1787.

One of the key features of the magazine was its attempt accurately to depict the plants described, and it made a speciality of greenhouse species from temperate and tropical regions. The publisher, William Curtis, had previously tried selling folio pictures of more unassuming plants, and found that people would not buy them. Curtis now commissioned the best-known botanical artists available, men like James Sowerby and William Hooker to illustrate his magazine which proved such a success that early volumes had to be reissued to meet demand.

In 1804 another crucial event was to take place, impelled in part by the growing fascination with gardening as a suitable occupation for the well-to-do. On 7 March, at 'Mr. Hatchard's

House in Piccadilly', seven men held the inaugural meeting of the Society for the Improvement of Horticulture; an organization which half a century later would become the Royal Horticultural Society.

On that March evening the founders of the society included Sir Joseph Banks (then President of the Royal Society), John Wedgwood, scion of the famous pottery dynasty, and William Forsyth, gardener to King George III. Also present were William Townsend Aiton, a landscape gardener whose father had been curator of the Royal Gardens at Kew, and two further botanists, Richard Anthony Salisbury and James Dickson. The seventh man in the room was one Honourable Charles Greville.

The original idea for the society can be traced back to Wedgwood, who had first suggested forming such a body to Forsyth a few years earlier, urging him to ask Sir Joseph Banks to help. Banks was already in his fifties, and one of the pre-eminent scientists of the time, having enjoyed horticultural fame since translating Linnaeus's *Philosophia Botanica* into English in 1760. The Linnaean system revolutionized how animals and plants were classified by giving them a generic (or genus) name and a specific epithet denoting the species. This binomial (two word) method simplified matters considerably, replacing the long and idiosyncratic Latinized descriptions employed hitherto. Banks was also aboard the *Endeavour* on Captain Cook's epic voyage around the world between 1768 and 1771. A few years later he was a key mover in the plan to relocate breadfruit trees from Tahiti to the West Indies as a cheap source of food for slaves, an idea that led to Captain Bligh's notorious expedition to the South Seas aboard HMS *Bounty*. From 1773 Banks became the unofficial director of Kew Gardens and he was instrumental in organizing the activities of many of its first plant collectors. His fame as a scientist (he was

President of the Royal Society for forty-one years) and botanist, as well as considerable personal wealth, also gained him membership of the Privy Council from 1797 until his death in 1820.

Among the notable names that met at Hatchard's on that evening in 1804 to form the Horticultural Society, it is Charles Greville's which is first recorded. At that time he was living on the corner of Paddington Green and Church Street where he rented the 'new built dwelling house, coach house, stables and the gardens thereto belonging'. In the archives of London's Guildhall I found Greville's original lease on the house, a large handwritten document with his own finely executed signature upon the paper. The lease is between Greville and the trustees of the estate to which the land belongs, namely, Sir John Frederick of Bowwood in the County of Surrey, Baronet Arthur Stanhope of Tilney St., Mayfair, Frederick Triese Morshead of Trenant Park, Cornwall, and Henry Frederick Thistlthwaite, an Ensign in his Majesty's First Regiment of Footguard. It is a fairly standard document for the time, specifying that among other things Greville may not use the land to carry on the trades of 'Catgut Spinner, Hogskinner, Boiler of Horseflesh, Slaughterer, Soapmaker, Melter of Tallow or any other offensive or noisome trade'. The rent payable is '£20 of lawful British money', a third of which was to go directly to the Bishop of London since the lands were also Church of England property.

The Hon. Charles Francis Greville was the second son of the Earl of Warwick. Like many second sons, Greville was not wealthy, and with no prospect of inheritance he was hoping to make a suitable marriage with someone from another aristocratic family, preferably a girl with a decent fortune. What Greville lacked in cash, he made up for in connections, and he had a long-standing friendship with Sir Joseph Banks who was of a similar age. Through Banks, Greville was admitted to the Royal Society, his special interest being the collection of minerals and precious stones. When Greville's father died in 1773, his elder brother George became Earl of Warwick and Greville took over George's seat in the House of Commons.

In the cosy and interconnected world of the eighteenth-century English nobility it is easy to see how social circles perpetuated positions of power. Greville's friendship with Banks was further reinforced by their joint membership of a circle of art lovers, known as the Society of Dilettanti. Charles Greville's other important route to high society lay through his uncle, Sir William Hamilton, the British Ambassador to Naples. Hamilton had been appointed to the post by his friendship with George III, and Greville too was welcome at Court. Hamilton, it seems, relied on Greville to provide him with regular letters informing him of the latest news from Parliament, and at Court. It is Greville's relationship to his uncle that links him, unfortunately and ignominiously, to one of England's greatest heroes.

Greville was unmarried, and although he had a salary as a Member of Parliament and an annual allowance of family money, it was hardly sufficient to maintain the lifestyle he led with his society friends. It seems that as a Member of Parliament, Greville was asked to help a poor mistreated serving girl who had been made pregnant by a gentleman, possibly someone of Greville's acquaintance. Greville employed the young woman, who called herself Emy Lyon, in the role of 'housekeeper' at his London residence. Emy, along with her mother and Emy's illegitimate child, lived with Greville from around 1781. Once in London, Emy changed her name to Emma Hart, and Greville gave her money for the upkeep of the child, who was eventually sent away to relatives. Under Greville's protection and tutelage, Emma underwent something of an Eliza Doolittle transformation, becoming a real 'lady'. Her face was her fortune, and she was so attractive that she became a favourite subject for portraiture by the celebrated artist George Romney. In 1783 Greville's uncle, Hamilton, paid a visit from Naples, and was similarly struck by Emma's beauty. Knowing that Greville was short of money and needed to find a wealthy bride, some kind of scheme was hatched whereby Emma was persuaded to travel to Naples for further education – including singing lessons.

Emma duly travelled to Naples, accompanied by her mother, believing that Greville would follow later, and that together they would return to London at some future date. It is clear that Emma had become deeply attached to Greville, and probably hoped to marry him at some stage. It also seems clear that Greville passed Emma to his uncle in return for financial assistance. Several years later, Emma married Sir William Hamilton, and then went on to achieve well-documented fame as Admiral Nelson's mistress.

Greville's place in history has been rather overshadowed by his connection with Hamilton, and the 'Emma affair' has branded him as something of a cad. In fact, it seems that Emma and he enjoyed perfectly good relations after her departure for Naples, and later, Greville even became friendly with Nelson too. However, when Greville was re-elected to Parliament in 1795, Emma wrote to him, congratulating him on his success, adding: 'I don't know a better, honester or more amiable and worthy man than yourself . . . and I am not apt to pay compliments.' Greville never did marry, but when Hamilton died in 1803, he left him £7,000 and an estate in Wales.

In the midst of all this, Greville indulged a passion for

gardening, and as a result of his involvement in the Horticultural Society his name was given to the genus *Grevillea* – a member of the protea family mostly found in Australia.

The attraction of the house at Paddington Green was that it had a large garden – roughly a hundred and twenty feet long and twice as wide. There, in the greenhouse, he was able to grow numerous rare plants. At least eight species are thought to have been introduced to England by Charles Greville, including *Adina globifera* from China, and *Diapensia lapponica* from Labrador. The *Journal of the RHS* records that Greville and Sir Joshua Banks were in regular correspondence about gardening matters, and discussed the recruitment of suitable gardeners for their respective properties.

Sometime in 1806, or perhaps early 1807, something remarkable happened in Greville's greenhouse at Paddington. For the first time ever in Europe, a *Vanilla planifolia* orchid came into flower.

The appearance of Greville's vanilla flower was such an event that it was recorded in two of the foremost botanical works of the time. The first published, Richard Salisbury's *Paradisus Londinensis* (1807) was a comprehensive catalogue of interesting plants contained in London's gardens. The illustration was executed by William Hooker, official artist to the Horticultural Society. Within a year, the same plant featured in Volume XVIII of H. C. Andrews' *Botanists' Repository*, an important work which provided hand coloured etchings of beautiful and interesting plants.

Unfortunately, these two botanical works have added greater confusion to the story of the vanilla plant. In *Paradisus Londinensis*, Salisbury calls the plant in Greville's garden *Myrobroma fragrans*, while Andrews calls it *Vanilla planifolia*. Salisbury rejects the term 'vanilla' as a vulgar and inaccurate description, hoping to claim the generic classification *Myrobroma* as his own. Unfortunately, Salisbury also confused what we now call *Vanilla planifolia* with a separate species (*V. phaentha*) when he decided that it merited a new genus name. Under the international rules of plant nomenclature this made Salisbury's genus *Myrobroma* illegal and defunct.

Andrews named the plant *Vanilla planifolia*, preferring to accept the commonly used generic term derived from the original Spanish 'vainilla' (first used by Plumier in 1703). However, because Salisbury was technically the first to identify the variety in Greville's garden, some botanists then continued to call the plant *Vanilla* but stuck with the species epithet *fragrans*. To add to the confusion, both Salisbury and Andrews wrongly decided that the vanilla orchid in Greville's garden was not the 'Mexican orchid of commerce'. Relying on earlier inaccurate information about the origins of the plant which produced the valuable scented fruits, they chose to assume that vanilla pods came from another species. Both Salisbury and Andrews agree that Greville's plant came from a specific source – the extensive private plant collection of George Spencer Churchill, the Marquis of Blandford.

Charles Greville's precise connection with Blandford remains unclear. However, both men knew Sir Joseph Banks, and while Blandford's interest in gardening was probably less scientific than Greville's, he certainly had more money with which to indulge it. Blandford (who later became the fifth Duke of Marlborough) created an enormous and well-stocked garden at White-Knights, his estate at Reading.

The marquis was a fanatic when it came to acquiring plants, so much so that his debts to nurserymen were a contributory cause of his eventual bankruptcy in 1819. The scale of his spending can be judged by a bill from one of his creditors, the Vineyard Nursery in London. His unpaid account with them came to more than £15,000, a fortune at a time when a domestic servant might be paid £1 a month. On one occasion, Blandford had a wall of magnolias planted in his garden – some twenty plants each costing five guineas – the equivalent of a hundred thousand pounds in today's money. The marquis's pride in his plants was immense, and he commissioned a book detailing the extent of the collection as well as a description of his manor house in which we learn there were 'chandeliers suspended by golden chains, containing Grecian globular lamps placed upon glass plates surrounded by rich gold flowerwork, from which descend a deep fringe of pendant crystals of most exquisite lustre'. The curtains were of 'purple silk intermixed with peach-blossom coloured sarcenet and tassels of gold-coloured silk'. On the walls were paintings by Caravaggio, Holbein, Rembrandt, Rubens and Titian.

Outside, White-Knights covered almost three hundred acres, and between 1798 and 1819 Blandford created a Linnaean garden with formal botanical planting, a Striped Garden with variegated foliage, the Duchess's Garden and a formal terrace garden. He also had 'a splendid and elegant greenhouse . . . filled with rare and exquisitely beautiful exotics . . . in jars and bowls of scarce, costly and elegant china'.

In addition there was also a Long Greenhouse (stretching for more than a hundred feet), an Orangery and a Cinnarean House, a Greenhouse aquarium and Hothouse aquarium, an Elm Grove, a Cedar Grove and an Oak Grove as well as a 'Rustic Orchestra' – a trellised enclosure 'large enough to accommodate his Grace's complete band'. Blandford, by several accounts, was a talented composer as well as a gardener.

Somewhere among all this, there was a vanilla vine, though

no records revealing its provenance exist today. Many of Blandford's personal papers were later destroyed to avoid family embarrassment, since he attracted a variety of scandals over the years, including a court case for adultery.

It is impossible to say how the Marquis of Blandford acquired his vanilla orchid. Several contemporary sources refer to the plant as originating in the West Indies, and for many years it was assumed that Blandford's vanilla came from Jamaica. This seems likely to be a simple mistake, since many English botanists continued to confuse several species of vanilla with the Mexican variety. However, it is also possible that *Vanilla planifolia* had been transplanted to the island from Mexico, perhaps when it was under Spanish occupation in the first half of the seventeenth century. Blandford certainly had a supply of plants from the West Indies, many of them sent to him by Dr Thomas Dancer, the island botanist of Jamaica. In 1798 Blandford wrote to a fellow collector that he had just 'had notice of between 200 and 300 plants having left Jamaica from Dr Dancer; a great many new genera. I shall be happy to show them to you, as well as all my others.'

Although the Marquis of Blandford is now credited with bringing *Vanilla planifolia* into England for the first time, it may be fairer to say that he reintroduced it. There were vanilla plants listed in the collections at Kew Gardens as early as 1765, but they did not survive. Another early reference to vanilla species occurs in the second edition of Philip Miller's *Gardener's Dictionary*, which appeared in 1740. Miller describes the plant as having a 'horned soft fleshy fruit filled with seeds . . . called by the Spaniards in America, *Vanilla*, or *Vinello*, and much used by them to scent their Chocolate'.

In 1819 Blandford moved to Blenheim Palace having inherited the dukedom from his father. Although he continued gardening at his new home, it was without the enthusiasm and passion that had created the collection at White-Knights. A visitor to the estate in 1829 remarked that all of the greenhouses, hothouses and aquariums were by then standing empty. After a tour of White-Knights that same year, John Claudius Loudon writes in his influential *Gardener's Magazine* that 'it must grieve a gardener to look at the ruins of so much splendour'.

To clear the duke's considerable personal debts much of White-Knights was sold at auction, and in succeeding years the land was divided and the house itself was eventually demolished in 1840. The eventual fate of individual specimens of other rarities in Blandford's plant collection remains unknown.

Sometime between 1798 and 1800, Charles Greville obtained a cutting from the vanilla orchid in Blandford's glasshouse. The importance of Greville's orchid is that once in Paddington it thrived and blossomed, leading other collectors and horticulturists to want cuttings from such a healthy specimen. No reference to the plant ever bearing fruit while in Greville's care exists. However, more than twenty years after Greville's death, another illustration of his vanilla orchid appeared in John Lindley's *Illustrations of Orchidaceous Plants*. Lindley's artist, Franz Bauer, was the same man who had provided the artwork for H. C. Andrews' *Botanists' Repository* in 1807, and the painting in Lindley's book was drawn from the same specimen. This time, not only was the orchid shown in bloom, but Bauer also drew a ripened seed pod which some botanists believe he must have seen growing on Greville's vine.

Bauer's paintings for Lindley are delicate representations of nature drawn with a meticulous eye, part of an enormous body of work carried out during a career at Kew Gardens which lasted more than fifty years. Employed directly by Joseph Banks, the honorary director at Kew, Franz Bauer was paid

£300 per year to paint examples of the plants in the botanical gardens. His time at Kew coincided with a massive growth of interest in orchids. When Bauer arrived in London from his native Austria in 1788 there were just thirty-six orchid species at Kew, and only three of them were from the tropics. Fifteen years later the gardens had more than a hundred orchids, a quarter of them tropical species. In large part this was due to changes in the technology used in greenhouses. The original dry air-flue systems for heating the tropical houses were unsuited to orchids and had been replaced by hot water circulating through cast-iron pipes – a method which allowed finer control of humidity. Now that orchids could be kept alive more reliably, orchid collecting reached epic proportions. So great was market demand that one private collector had four thousand trees cut down in Colombia so that he could collect ten thousand epiphytic specimens of one picturesque variety to sell in Europe.

Bauer's skill was not confined to merely depicting the plants as objects of beauty, and he developed a keen interest in botanical theory and in the use of the microscope to study them. He painted thousands of species, many of them orchids never before seen in Europe. Gold and yellow Foxtails speckled with black dots arrived from the Himalayas, and blue-green Creeping Lady's Tresses from Japan. Czechoslovakian Lizard orchids with a perfume reminiscent of the scent of a male goat came to Bauer, as did rich purple Wax Lips from Australia. The bright delicate lines of his work are still vivid today.

Bauer's depiction of Greville's *Vanilla planifolia* is no less detailed than any of the more obviously decorative species he documented. He paints the elegant pod with its cargo of tiny black seeds, and then with the aid of his microscope reveals the seeds in various stages of ripeness. Alongside are the ovaries and transverse sections of the seed pod, their intimate structure exposed and immortalized in ink.

The dissection and analysis of rare or newly arrived plants was crucial to their proper identification and classification. Orchids were also sought after by private collectors, and it became something of a cult to own a species which no one else possessed. Plant nurseries became big businesses, in part propelled by the success of the Horticultural Society's annual 'fête' which began in 1827 and eventually became the Chelsea Flower Show. The gentry would flock to the shows, eager to add the latest and most unusual plants to their own gardens. In the scramble for ornamental plants the vanilla plant was not a star. Its small pale flowers did not have the allure of other richly coloured tropical orchids with their blatant ornamental charm. The orchid's value lay in its fruit, the scented seed pods with their unique and seductive aroma.

When Charles Greville died in April 1809, he had not made a will. His impressive collection of almost twenty thousand minerals went largely to the British Museum, but his collection of plants was purchased by Thomas Jenkins of the Portman Nursery in London. Fortunately, cuttings from his flowering vanilla had already been taken, and sent to the botanical gardens at Liège in Belgium. Although he never knew it, Greville's skill in keeping the tropical vine alive would spawn an industry.

6. Ile Bourbon

Eight hundred miles east of Africa, the island of Réunion heaves its flanks out of the dark blue expanse of the southern Indian Ocean. Basalt cliffs take the weight of the water as it rolls in, carving and splitting the rock in places, tumbling and beating it into fragments that cannot resist the sea. It was here that I first heard about a slave-boy named Edmond Albius, a few sparse details about a life repeated in varying forms, though scarcely with any pride. There is a souvenir shop beside one of the beaches which calls itself Albius's Grotto, and a secondary school in one of the small towns bears his name. Yet, I was later to discover, without him the modern trade in vanilla might never have begun.

At the centre of Réunion there are mountains rising ten thousand feet into the clear unpolluted air. Here, steep ridges surround Cilaos, Salazie and Mafate, extinct volcanic calderas lined with thick tropical vegetation. It is wet in the mountains, and the stunted trees of the high slopes are hung with wispy beards of green moss as thin and stringy as angel-hair pasta. So inhospitable is the approach to these craters that in the eighteenth century they were a refuge for slaves, desperate to escape the harsh conditions of the spice and sugar plantations which thrived along the coastal plains. Many were never recaptured, and lived out their lives on the high precipitous slopes, carving out tiny patches of farmland to feed themselves and the families they created with other runaways. From time to time, bounty hunters would venture into the mountains, fierce men with guns and savage dogs who would spend weeks in the forest tracking the slaves, bringing them back to town to face trial. Persistent escapees might be put to death; others received a branding with a hot iron in the shape of a fleur-de-lis on the shoulder. A second escape would earn manacles and a neck chain for life. Sometimes an ear or a couple of fingers would be lopped, or the hamstrings of one leg neatly cut to show the others what to expect if they too tried to run.

Cilaos, Salazie and Mafate sit side by side, like the chambers in a heart, and there is a fourth crater too, the active volcano Piton de la Fournaise, but it is displaced towards one end of the island where it periodically spews molten lava towards the east coast. Only a few roads trace their way inland towards the interior, curving and twisting like veins across an eyeball, and to this day there is no road into Mafate. This crater is a lost world reached only on foot or, in case of a medical emergency, by helicopter.

This island has sheltered beaches too, protected by coral reefs, and long stretches of sand, a modern beach-chic world of surfers and poseurs where beach bums and playboys, college kids and civil servants rub bare bronzed shoulders.

Réunion seems to fight with the elements. Cyclones sometimes visit and there are days when the volcano spits fire into the air and lava tumbles towards the sea cutting the coast road in two. Men have tried to tame this place, and beside the modern dual carriageway leading southwards from St-Denis they have even bound the cliffs with chain-mail nets a hundred yards long, tethering the rock face so that boulders will not crush the speeding Renaults and Citroens below. The cars that rush in and out of the capital are mostly made in France, like the islanders. Their bread comes in baguettes and they can buy yesterday's newspaper from Paris in dozens of small *tabacs* dotted around the coast. And around the irregular circle of coast the towns are almost all saintly. In the west and south-west they are St-Paul, St-Gilles, St-Louis, St-Pierre and St-Joseph. Go east from the capital, St-Denis, and the saints change sex, albeit briefly: Ste-Marie and Ste-Suzanne are just a few miles apart, and then the men take over again, with St-André leading on to St-Benoît. In the sparsely populated interior the towns have earthier appellations, names with a creole past: Cilaos, Salazie and Hell-Bourg.

The mountains are my favourite place. Up there, I have tasted the sweet white wine they make with grapes grown in sheltered valleys. I have heard the jangling notes of a banjo echoing beside mountain streams while villagers in their Sunday best celebrate one of their saint's days. Above Cilaos I have climbed the steep rock paths towards Kerveguen Ridge on the approach to Piton des Neiges and stopped to rest at six thousand feet while rain clouds traverse the face of the peak. Tiny finches, the *tec-tecs*, flit between the branches and wild strawberries poke from the grass at the edge of the path.

Near Cilaos I once met a very small man carrying a shotgun. He had a speech impediment, and hardly any teeth. From his heavily accented creole I could make out that he wanted me to follow him back to his small wooden house. He was neither friendly nor unfriendly, and I couldn't be sure if he needed help, but I decided to follow him anyway. He led me to a typical mountain house made of neat white painted clapboard panelling fringed with daintily carved fretwork around the eaves. Masses of bright red geranium plants grew around the gate and pressed in against us along the narrow path leading to the front steps.

I remember a verandah stuffed with china ornaments, many of them life-size dogs of various breeds, and a sitting room crammed with heavy dark nineteenth-century furniture. I wondered how these treasures had been safely transported around the two hundred hairpin bends up to Cilaos from the coast. Inside, it was cool and dim and there were framed needlepoint panels embroidered with sayings from the Bible upon the walls. In the dining room there was an enormous heavily carved table with a dozen high-backed chairs arranged around it. The little man leant his shotgun up against the wall and disappeared under the table, from where I could hear him making great efforts to drag something heavy across the floor. A moment later he reappeared with a large plastic tub in which dark red liquid swilled and sloshed against the sides, threatening to spill on the parquet floor. It was home-made wine, and he wanted me to buy a bottle. An equally tiny old lady appeared from the kitchen, bringing wafts of home-baked dough in her wake. Her sleeves were pushed back and she seemed hot and flustered, wiping her hands on her apron and explaining in slightly more comprehensible French that the wine was for sale. A small glass was produced, and after a little polish on the matron's apron, I was handed a sample. It tasted like vinegar.

The pair waited expectantly. I stared at the glass, running my tongue around my teeth to remove the taste and wondering what I could say without giving offence.

'Too sweet?' she enquired.

'Yes, too sweet,' I replied. She and the impish man both stared at the tub and shook their heads, nodding in agreement.

'Too sweet,' they chorused, as he once again laboured to

push the tub back under the table. I didn't know what to do. I was tempted to buy a bottle of wine just to reward the little man for his effort, but I really didn't want any. The old lady said goodbye and went back to her kitchen, and the man escorted me to the door, smiling and mumbling his incomprehensible patois all the while. I left him there on his little geranium-framed porch in the company of the china dogs.

The mountain creoles are a French creation. Like Seychelles and Mauritius, its Indian Ocean neighbours, Réunion had no indigenous inhabitants when the first European adventurers arrived in the seventeenth century. At first the island appeared on the sea charts as *Mascarin*, after the Portuguese explorer Pedro Mascarenhas who first visited it in 1516. The French East India Company claimed the island for itself in 1642, renaming it Bourbon seven years later in honour of the French royal family. In the battle between France and Britain for domination of the trade routes to India, Bourbon became an important addition to the French colonial collection. This was the era of the titanic struggle between Britain, France and Holland for domination of the seas — and for control of the spices and commodities which were essential to the growth of European power. Following the defeat of the Spanish Armada in 1588, England had been able to break the Spanish and Portuguese monopoly on all manner of valuable commodities, including cinnamon, ginger and cardamom. Unhampered access to India would bring trade in tea, cotton and silks, indigo and saltpetre. All of these things lay across the Indian Ocean, sometimes called the Sea of Spices.

The French were initially slow to formalize their mercantile claims in the Indian Ocean. While the English and the Dutch East India Companies were formed in 1600 and 1602 respectively, the French *Compagnie des Indes Orientales* did not receive its royal charter until 1664. It owed its creation to Louis XIV's Finance Minster, Jean-Baptiste Colbert, a man desperate to improve the size and power of the French Navy. The trade advantage that first the Dutch and then the British gained from superior ships, and access to the Cape of Good Hope, were a source of frustration to Colbert. Without a base in the south-west Indian Ocean his ships would be vulnerable to attack by his rivals. When he proposed the creation of the French East India Company, Colbert had high hopes that Madagascar might eventually become a viable rival to the Cape as a staging post for French ships en route to India. At first, Bourbon was simply a useful satellite of Madagascar, but the bigger island proved difficult to tame, its early settlements decimated by fever and massacred by the natives. Five hundred miles east, the tiny colony of Bourbon was mercifully free of troublesome native inhabitants. Meanwhile, the French East India Company was attempting to establish several vital trading bases in India, notably at Pondicherry a hundred miles south of Madras.

The prize of a safe and secure route from Europe to India was great. Merchants and investors could expect a minimum 100 per cent profit on voyages to the spice routes, and as the seventeenth century progressed, bigger and bigger ships were making the voyage eastwards to India from Europe via the Cape. With a return voyage lasting at least six months, the sailing ships depended upon the trade winds, and the timing of a voyage was crucial to its success and duration. Owing to the seasonal winds, French ships had to leave home before April if they were to take the fastest route to the Indies. Above the Equator the winds blow north and east between October and April, carrying sailing boats towards India, while between May and October the prevailing winds go south and west. Once clear of the Cape of Good Hope on the outward voyage the trading ships would head northwards up the Mozambique channel and then across the Indian Ocean. However, if they left France later than April it was better to avoid the channel and go east of Madagascar to cross the ocean via the island of Bourbon.

Bourbon could serve as a victualling port for French ships en route to India, but only so long as it could provide food or commodities both for visiting ships and for export home to the motherland.

The island has changed its name along with its political fortunes. Only in 1793, after the French Revolution, did Bourbon acquire the less elegant if more politically acceptable label *île de la Réunion*. The name commemorates the alliance, or union, between the Marseillais and the National Guard who joined forces to storm the palace of the Tuileries in Paris. Generally aristocratic in their aspirations, the island's wealthy plantocracy were never fond of the new name, and for a brief interlude between 1806 and 1810 they named their island Bonaparte to show solidarity with the Emperor Napoleon. After being captured by the British in 1811, that name would no longer do, and it reverted to Bourbon. Although France regained possession of Bourbon from Britain after the Treaty of Paris in 1815, it was not finally renamed Réunion until the establishment of France's Second Republic in 1848.

After winning the Napoleonic wars, Britain cared little for this small rugged outpost, since she had gained possession of wealthier Mauritius and the more strategically placed Seychelles. More importantly, the British had long since disposed of the threat from France in India, where Pondicherry had fallen fifty years earlier. Small rugged Bourbon, with its smouldering volcano and inhospitable coastline, could be left in the hands of the French planters and their slaves.

Today's population, all of whom have full French citizenship, has evolved from a mix of settlers, soldiers, civil servants and slaves. In Réunion, many of the original French settlers had little money when they arrived, hoping to make their fortunes in the colony by growing any number of agricultural products which were in vogue at the time.

In spite of its slightly less obvious strategic value, all kinds of fruits, spices and staple commodities were imported to Bourbon under the direction of various French governors, and with the help of one remarkable man, Pierre Poivre. Trained as a missionary, Pierre Poivre travelled widely in China, the Philippines, India and Indonesia. In 1745, at twenty-six, his missionary career was cut short after losing a hand to a bullet when his ship was attacked by the Royal Navy in the Far East. Forced to convalesce in the Dutch colony at Batavia, he became obsessed with horticulture and in particular the cultivation of spices. When he was recovered enough to return to France, his ship stopped at île de France (now Mauritius), and Poivre realized that this island, and nearby Bourbon, might make ideal nurseries for any spices he could gather in the Indies. Such plantings would doubtless be valuable.

In 1753 Poivre returned to île de France with a small collection of cloves and nutmeg, plants he had quite literally stolen from under the noses of the Dutch in the Moluccan islands. It was Poivre's audacious efforts that ended the Dutch monopoly in the precious commodities of cloves and nutmeg. Until then, the Dutch exported nutmeg kernels from the islands only after they had been dipped in lime to stop them sprouting, and they went to great lengths to prevent anyone growing cloves anywhere except on a few small islands where they maintained a military guard on the crops. Agricultural 'espionage' of this type was punishable by death, but Poivre was determined that France should not be left behind in the mercantile duel with Holland and England. However, most of these first imports died, and it was later discovered that they had been deliberately poisoned – killed off by a man in the pay of the Dutch East India Company. But Poivre would not give up, and in 1772 he returned to the Moluccas where he succeeded in buying a few more of the jealously guarded spice plants on the island of Patani. His success with nutmeg gave France a ten-year lead on the British, who eventually began growing the spice for themselves in Grenada. As a reward for his efforts, Poivre was made *Intendant Général* for île de France and Bourbon, and between 1767 and 1773 he set about turning the islands into a spice repository. Cloves, nutmeg, peppers, cinnamon and allspice were cultivated under his direction, as well as breadfruit and almonds.

Throughout the eighteenth and early nineteenth centuries, French ships from India and the Middle East, from China and Indonesia, would pass by Bourbon and île de France, her sister island further north. Island governors, eager to prove their worth to the French East India Company and the Crown, would gratefully receive anything that might have commercial value. The cornucopia of tropical fruits grew and grew as mangoes, lychees, papaya, pineapples, coconuts, bananas and tamarinds were imported in turn. Red peppers from Brazil, coriander from China and saffron from India came too. Later, as in the Caribbean colonies, coffee, tobacco, cotton and sugar would eventually be the most important cash crops, and their cultivation would shape and alter the very landscape of Bourbon. The island's moist warm climate also made it suitable for the production of spices and exotic essences. Ylang-ylang, vetiver, indigo, geranium essence and eventually vanilla too, would all become essential exports for the island, products vital to the French perfume and toiletry industry. In all, some sixteen hundred plant species were introduced to Bourbon from around the tropics, some purely decorative, but most with a view to commercial exploitation. An additional benefit for planters in Bourbon or île de France was that exports from French colonies were less heavily taxed than the same goods originating elsewhere. But the sheer physical effort of harvesting these crops would require another foreign import — slave labour.

Like modern-day Réunion's impressive collection of plant life, the mountain creoles have their origins in the colonial developments of the eighteenth century. Ironically, as agricultural plants were imported and blossomed, life for the planters became increasingly difficult. According to French custom at the time, land was inherited equally by all children in the family. What had been a large estate when granted by royal decree at the beginning of the eighteenth century would gradually become smaller and smaller, divided and sub-divided until poorer and poorer descendants of the original proprietor were gradually displaced to the remote and inhospitable interior.

The system resulted in the creation of a new social class, *les petits blancs des hauts* — poor highland whites — as they became known. Inevitably, these *petits blancs* would eventually intermarry, or at least reproduce, with Africans, Indians and other races creating another sub-class, the half-castes or *métis*. All of them lived in a different world from the land-owning plantocracy, *grands blancs*, many of whose families are still dotted around the Indian Ocean today. These were the families who prospered enough to buy land for their heirs, making strategic marriages to expand their estates wherever possible. They lived in large houses surrounded by furniture imported from France, and they danced quadrilles on parquet floors made of mahogany. They were waited upon by servants and ladies' maids, and took coffee from silver pots on their spacious verandahs. They had their portraits painted in oils, and rode around the island by barouche, while slaves tended to the crops on which their fortunes were built.

Modern Réunion tends to hide its slave memories, and heap them onto the name of Bourbon. Local historians claim that conditions here were never as harsh as in the French colonies of the Caribbean, and that the *grands blancs* of Bourbon had a more relaxed attitude to their slaves. Bourbon, they say, was a place where masters would often grant freedom to their slaves, and women who bore children as a result of liaisons with their masters would have their offspring recognized, and granted a surname. Freed slaves could own land, and even acquire their own slaves. By 1815, Bourbon's population had grown to over 70,000 people, of whom around 12,000 were classified as 'white', with almost 3,000 'coloured freemen', but slaves now numbered more than 50,000. As the racial mixture of the island increased it became difficult to know who was a slave and who was free – the colour of one's skin was no longer a reliable guide. One of the neat distinctions between a slave and a freeman was that slaves were forbidden to wear shoes or hats.

On the high ground above the modern resort of St-Gilles-les-Bains are the remains of one of the grandest slave-estates on Bourbon. It has been preserved in a lacklustre sort of fashion as the Musée de Villèle, although few of the surfers and swimmers from the holiday resort ever make the journey to see it.

At Villèle there are the broken down ruins of the old sheds where the sugar cane was crushed and rinsed to release its syrup. Surrounded by large shade-trees, a grand house sits at the end of a driveway with a circular approach suitable for turning carriages. Mary Anne Thérèse Ombline Gonneau Montbran, later known simply as the widow Desbassyns, lived here from the time the main house was built in 1788 until her death in 1846. She produced thirteen children with her war hero husband, Henri Paulin Panon-Desbassyns, whom she married at the age of fifteen. After being widowed in 1800 Madame Desbassyns set about managing the estate herself, amassing more and more land and benefiting from the boom years of sugar production for the last forty years of her life. When she died the estate covered 180 hectares of forest, and more than 1,000 hectares of open land suitable for crops. To service it all, the widow had almost 500 slaves.

There were no other visitors the last time I visited Villèle, and the air was damp and cool after the rain. The main house is square, and built along the lines of an Indian colonial mansion, a style that Henri Desbassyns was familiar with after spending time in the French colony at Pondicherry. Upstairs, two verandahs give a choice of views: at the front of the house you see the mountains to the east and, at the rear, the distant sea to the west.

Inside, the house was dim, shrouded in gloom which emanated both from the dullness of the day, the lack of modern lighting and the dark panelling on many of the walls. In spite of the sepulchral shade the trappings of opulence were all there: heavy cabinets ordered from the celebrated Parisian *ébèniste* Magnien on the rue du Faubourg Saint-Antoine, and a gilt and marble clock made by Berthout. There were marquetry card tables, and side tables bearing blue East India Company porcelain. Heavily carved crucifixes adorned many of the door lintels, and in one room there was a large-bore hunting rifle, a gift from Louis XV to a man named Mussard, a bounty hunter famed for his ability to track down and retrieve escaped slaves in the mountains.

The brightest part of the house was the dining room, lined with golden panels of jackfruit, lychee and tamarind wood which shone in the light breaking through a pair of half-glass doors leading out onto a terrace.

Like all houses of the period, the kitchens were located outside the main house. A simple cement roof covered the enormous open oven fed with firewood and charcoal. Against the walls stood the accoutrements of a farmhouse kitchen: pestles and mortars, burnished copper cauldrons and wicker baskets for storing grains and lentils. Here the servants and slaves would prepare the meals and scurry across the flagstone terrace into a small pantry area, where the food could be served up onto porcelain dishes and plateware before it was carried into the fine dining room.

A hundred yards from the main house there is a row of whitewashed cement outbuildings, slave quarters where many of the household staff would have slept. It is close to the administration offices for the museum, and as I passed by I could hear a gaggle of men and women chattering inside to the accompaniment of a transistor radio, and the unmistakable whiff of marijuana. In the shade of an aged tree a set of crumbling and mouldy coral cement stairs led to an arcade of cool brick alcoves twenty feet deep. This was the slave hospital. Outside, a stone plaque records a copy of the slave-census of 1842. There, known only by their Christian names, is the list of men and women, old and young, fit and infirm, held by Madame Desbassyns. Against each name is their age, and a single word describing their allotted workplace, or status on the estate.

Constant	68	garden
Guillaume	41	fields
Celestin	21	fields
Barbé	23	invalid
Marie	48	housemaid
Bonaventure	30	fields

The list goes on and on. It also records runaway slaves who nevertheless 'belong' to their owner. Bastin, aged seventy-two, is listed simply as *marron* – 'escaped', twelve years earlier. Slaves might also be on loan to others. Madame Desbassyns' census shows two sixteen-year-old girls, Euphonie and Hortense, 'working for my brother Charles'. Elsewhere in the slave records I learn that seventy-one-year-old Veronique had an estimated value of five hundred francs, slightly less than the cost of three cows from Madagascar. It was into this world that a slave-boy named Edmond was born in 1829.

7. Creole Hearts

The small town of Sainte-Suzanne sits on the north-east coast of Réunion. I came here in search of slivers of the past, a glimpse of the world where Edmond lived. Here, the landscape rolls gently towards the sea against a distant backdrop of jagged peaks. They call it the 'windy coast', and between April and October it bears the brunt of the moisture-laden south-east trades. On this side of the island there are places where three hundred inches of rain may fall in a year, a tropical deluge that fills the mountain streams to bursting point and gives birth to cascades of fresh clean water through the gorges leading to the sea. It is humid here, the sticky enervating heat that saps the strength, but the soil is good, rich and fertile. This is where the planters settled in the early days, and where the great estates of sugar cane and coffee were most profitable. It is the part of the island where vanilla thrives.

At first, in spite of their fertile soil, and their skills in nurturing tropical plants from around the world, the planters of Bourbon were no more successful with vanilla than anyone else outside Mexico. Like European botanists and collectors, the planters were confused as to which vanilla species would produce the correct fragrant seed pods. However, as coffee

1. The vanilla vine features in Diego Rivera's monumental mural in the Palacio Nacional in Mexico City

2. Below: A crocodile woven from vanilla beans in Madagascar

3. Crucifix made from Mexican vanilla

4. The young Edmond Albius became a constant companion to his master, Ferréol Bellier-Beaumont

5. Below: Mexican vanilla being dried in the sun in Papantla, 1910

6. In the 1930s almost all first-grade Mexican vanilla beans went to the USA

7. Young boys help the men to sort a mountain of green vanilla in Papantla in the 1950s

8. Mexican vanilla farmers in Zozozolco, in the hills of Veracruz

9. Some farmers sell just a kilogram of vanilla

10. Plump green vanilla will lose four-fifths of its weight during curing

11. Dipping the beans in scalding water by hand

12. Tahitian vanilla drying on the slopes of Taha'a

13. The vanilla orchid is a small flower

14. On the road to Antalaha, Malagasy farmers trade vanilla cuttings

15. The dried beans are lustrous, dark and moist

16. Graded by length and quality, the bundles of pods are sorted by workers at the Ramanandraibe warehouse

prices were threatened by cheaper imports from Brazil and Central America, the planters of Bourbon were keen to experiment with new crops.

The idea that vanilla might be grown outside the Spanish dominions of Central America was tantalizing, but not new. Sixty-five years before Charles Greville's vanilla orchid flowered at Paddington, the commercial prospects for vanilla growing were already well known. In his *Gardener's Dictionary* of 1740, Philip Miller laments the lack of enterprise which prevented English colonists from exploiting the scented pods. Miller was a member of the Royal Society, and rejoiced in the title of 'Gardener to the Worshipful Company of Apothecaries at their Botanic Garden at Chelsea'. He was also a great collector of plants and when he published his first edition of the dictionary in 1733, he had never seen vanilla. Seven years later, in a supplementary volume, he was able to describe accurately 'an anomalous flower, consisting of six leaves, five of which are placed in a circular order, and the other, which occupies the Middle, is concave. The Empalement afterward becomes a horned soft fleshy Fruit, filled with very small seeds.'

Miller's dictionary lists only three distinct species: one with a greenish white flower with a dark fruit, one with a violet flower and a reddish fruit, and the third with a white flower and coral-coloured fruit. Correctly, in spite of the confusion over species which would set in among later botanists, he identifies the first variety – with the greenish white flower – as the one from which the Spanish obtain their beans. Miller reports that the Spanish expect 'thre'pence a fruit' for the beans, a figure he clearly takes from William Dampier's account more than forty years earlier. Similarly he repeats the buccaneer's assertion that the fruits are cultivated by the Indians, and sold cheaply to the Spanish who go on to profit from trading them in Europe. He complains that the vanilla is rarely found in any of the English settlements in America: 'though it may be easily transported, because they will continue fresh out of the ground for several months. I had some branches of the plant, gathered at Campechy and sent over between papers, by way of sample: they had been at least four months gathered, when I received them; and upon opening of the papers I found the leaves rotten, with the moisture contained in them, and the paper also perished with it; but the stems appeared fresh.'

Miller may have been the first European to import a living vanilla vine into Europe. Intriguingly, he was able to plant the vanilla vines, and keep them alive 'with difficulty'. It seems likely therefore that the Marquis of Blandford was in fact reintroducing the plant to England when he grew it in his collection at White-Knights. Miller advises planting vanillas in a hothouse, watering them copiously and providing them with shade. He is also aware that the vines need to be at least six years old before they reliably fruit. What surprises him is that the English have not tried to take this profitable monopoly away from the Spanish: 'it is a commodity which bears a good price, and is well worth cultivating in several of the English settlements, especially as the vanilla will grow in moist places, where the land is not cleared for timber.' Noting that in England vanilla is only used as an ingredient in chocolate, he says that the Spanish in America have long used it medicinally, repeating the claims made by the earliest writers that it was helpful to the stomach and the brain, that it could expel wind and cure poisoning. In his estimation, vanilla is a horticultural treasure waiting to be exploited:

As this Plant is so easily propagated by Cuttings; it is very strange, that the Inhabitants of America should neglect to cultivate it, especially as it is an Ingredient in Chocolate, which is so much drank all over America, but as the English have in a manner quite neglected the Culture of the Cocoa, it is no wonder they should neglect this; since the former was cultivated in great Plenty by the Spaniards in Jamaica, while that Island remained in their Possession; so that the English had an Example before them, if they would have followed it: whereas the Vanilla was not found growing there, and therefore it is not to be supposed, that the Persons who were so indolent, as to quit the Culture of many valuable Plants then growing on the Spot, should be at the Trouble of introducing any new plants.

Miller's achievement in keeping his vanilla plants alive was a short-lived success. When Charles Greville's vanilla vine flowered in his greenhouse at Paddington it was a celebrated botanical curiosity. In the 1800s the only commercially available vanilla beans were arriving from Mexico, with the total production no more than one or two tonnes. Vanilla was still a rare gourmet treat, something reserved for a select minority.

For a few years prior to the French Revolution the American statesman Thomas Jefferson served as minister to France, a period in which he acquired a reputation for good living and liberal politics. Among other tasks, his diplomatic mission was to establish a market for American tobacco and to negotiate an agreement for American whaling ships to deliver their catch to French ports. When he left Paris in 1789, Jefferson had travelled widely in Europe, and developed a taste for fine wines and new foods. Later, as President of the United States (1801–9), his guests in Washington were treated to recipes he had collected for French sauces, fruit tarts and French-fried potatoes. A succession of French chefs and butlers imported from Paris allowed Jefferson to continue dining in the style to which he had become accustomed.

In July 1791 Jefferson wrote from Philadelphia to William Short, the US chargé d'affaires in Paris, concerning the shipping of various goods from France. Jefferson encloses a cheque, drawn on a London bank, to pay for wines from Champagne and Bordeaux. His expense accounts were complex, a mix of private and official transactions which Short was to help sort out. A postscript is added to the letter:

Since writing the above, Petit [Jefferson's French butler, Adrien Petit] informs me that he has been all over town in quest of Vanilla, & it is unknown here. I must pray you to send me a packet of 50 pods (batons) which may come very well in the middle of a packet of newspapers. It costs about 24 sous a baton when sold by the single baton. Petit says there is a great imposition in selling those which are bad; that Piebot generally sells good, but that still it will be safe to have them bought by some one used to them.

It took Jefferson's letter exactly two months to reach Paris, but William Short wrote his reply the next day, giving prominence to the supply of the vanilla, reassuring Jefferson that: 'A person in whose skill I have confidence is to chuse the vanilla, and it shall be forwarded to you by way of Havre.'

A subsequent letter, in October, gives further details: 'You will receive in the gazettes sent the 50 batons de Vanilla you desired. It cost 20 sous the baton. It was chosen by Madame de Flahaut who says it may be relied on as excellent. Besides Piebot seemed so well satisfied with your remembrance, that I am persuaded he has given only the best in hopes of a continuance of your practice.'

Among his papers stored at the Library of Congress, is Jefferson's own handwritten recipe for vanilla ice cream, thought to be the first in America. He records 'a stick of vanilla' in the ingredients, and he recommends that the frozen dessert should be accompanied by Savoy biscuits, for which he also provides his own recipe.

As late as 1821, Jefferson was still struggling to obtain reliable supplies of vanilla, though by then he was sending money for their purchase from his home in Virginia to Browze Trist, a student in Philadelphia. By then, Jefferson was expecting to pay 10d for a hundred vanilla pods. The price was rising, a consequence of instability in Mexico where the Wars of Independence had been simmering for a decade, and which would cause a serious decline in the amount of vanilla reaching Europe. As Mexico freed itself from Spanish rule, its internal divisions and subsequent war with the United States over Texas would add further pressures to the already beleaguered peasantry. The time was ripe for vanilla to leave home.

After cuttings from Charles Greville's plant were gradually circulated around the botanical gardens of Europe, vanilla became a mere curiosity, something to include in a respectable tropical collection. The long green creeping vine might on rare occasions flower, but frustratingly little. Just as Greville's orchid had flowered and fruited in his greenhouse in London, transplanted vanilla vines in other locations would occasionally produce a few pods. Like many orchids, the vanilla sometimes produces a flower which is misshapen and capable of self-fertilization. More often, though still rarely, a local insect will accidentally replicate the job of the bee normally associated with *Vanilla planifolia*, and spread pollen to the stigma. More than a quarter of a century after Greville's death, the creeping green vines were still just a curiosity outside Mexico, withholding their luscious fruits from commerce. But things were about to change.

In 1836 there was a flurry of excitement among academic botanists. Professor Charles Morren, newly appointed to the Chair of Botany at Liège University in Belgium, revealed the results of fertilization experiments he had made upon vanilla plants which had been growing without producing fruit for more than fifteen years. In 1837 he published his findings in the Annals of the Paris Horticultural Society, and two years later repeated his claims with further details in the British *Annals of Natural History*:

It was in 1836 that by a peculiar horticultural treatment we had at Liège upon one Vanilla plant fifty-four flowers, which having been fecundated by me, produced the same number of pods; and in 1837 a fresh crop of about a hundred pods was obtained upon another plant by the same methods: so that now there is not the least doubt of the complete success of this new method.

The academic tone of Morren's paper is prefaced with abundant hope that his research will yield commercial results.

I believe I may assert that henceforth we may produce in Europe vanilla of as good a quality (if not better) as that which is exported from Mexico . . . in all the intertropical colonies vanilla might be cultivated and a great abundance of fruit obtained by the process of artificial fecundation . . . proof of the importance of science for improving every branch of industry.

It is easy to forget that botany was, at the time, still a relatively young discipline anxious to prove its commercial worth. Morren himself was an advocate of the theories of the German botanist Christian Sprengel, who had first discovered that the nectar-producing organs of a flower attracted insects with the use of colour. Drawn by the colours, the insects collected pollen and transferred it between flowers thereby allowing fertilization to occur. Sprengel also revealed that some flowers avoided self-fertilization by a process he called 'dichogamy', whereby the stamen (male) and pistil (female) parts of individual flowers mature at different times. Sprengel's work went a long way to explaining why flowers developed different characteristics – their smell, colour, shape and size. In 1793 he published *The Newly Revealed Mystery of Nature in the Structure and Fertilization of Flowers*, but received little acclaim.

The very notion that plants might have some kind of sex-life was controversial, and in some quarters, unpopular. Many botanists remained unconvinced by the study, and Sprengel's theories about the relationships between insects and plant reproduction did not gain widespread acceptance until they were advanced and confirmed by the work of Charles Darwin.

Morren's vanilla experiments confirmed that in order to produce healthy fruits, *Vanilla planifolia* vines needed to be at least five or six years old, and that to produce flowers they needed precise conditions of shade, heat and humidity. The problem with Morren's method of fertilization was that he used a pair of scissors to cut the rostellum, a relatively fiddly technique suited only to greenhouse conditions. His discovery, while academically important, remained a subject for discussion only within the narrow circle of academic botanists. The 'great abundance of fruit from the intertropical colonies' simply did not appear.

Not far from Sainte-Suzanne there is an old creole house set back from the sea on high ground. The narrow coastal road is edged with sugar cane that obscures the view towards the old estate until a break in the foliage reveals a long avenue of spindly palm trees leading up towards the house. Known as Le Grand Hazier, it is one of the oldest wooden houses left on Réunion. The tropical climate is hard on buildings, and among other things the humidity is an excellent environment for termites. When I arrived there were men on the roof, replacing some of the old timber, under the supervision of the owner Joseph Chassagne. It was his ancestor, Albert, who travelled here from Bordeaux and bought six hundred hectares of land in 1801. The family estate is tiny now, little more than a large country garden, but the current generation have reached an agreement with the government, and among themselves, to maintain it as part of Réunion's heritage.

Although I had never met him, I had seen Joseph Chassagne's face before. The white skin, wrinkled and freckled with sun, his gentle French accent modulated with its creole sing-song, and his piercing blue eyes reminded me of men I had seen in Seychelles, Mauritius and Madagascar. The names may change but the gene pool they come from is unmistakable. I had met them on old plantations, in government offices and in bars. In Seychelles I had seen them barefoot and bare-chested in ragged shorts, and in Mauritius I had seen them dressed to the nines as they inspected their horses at the Turf Club. Something about the climate keeps them skinny.

Joseph had a crew cut, neat silver spikes of hair protruding from a tanned scalp. He welcomed me to the estate and apologized for the presence of the workmen on the roof. They would be hammering and sawing all day.

'We have no choice,' he explained. 'When the weather is good we must do what we can, or soon there will be no roof left. And without the roof, you cannot have a house.'

As we climbed the short flight of steps at the front of the

house I saw an old lady sitting in a wheelchair on the wide verandah. She was very pale and had snow-white hair neatly brushed away from her smiling face. Joseph explained that she was his aunt Marie, and she had been born in the house in 1919. She shook my hand without speaking, two bony hands emerging from the blanket that covered her lap. Her grip was as light as a child's and she met my gaze with steady pale eyes. Joseph ushered me into the study at one end of the verandah and closed the door. 'I must try to keep the humidity out,' he said, shaking his head as if he knew he was wasting his time.

The room was extraordinary. In places the plaster had almost completely fallen away, revealing the wattle strips behind. Portraits of the Chassagne family hung on the walls, cracked and rippling oils which seemed to be in danger of peeling from the canvas at any second. A large mahogany desk dominated the centre of the room, its surface strewn with family papers and mementoes that Joseph was in the process of cataloguing. As we talked he produced items from the collection, enthusiastically revealing details about the way his family had lived in the old days.

'Look, look. Here is a letter from my grandfather to Monsieur Berthelot, his shoemaker in Paris. You see, he is very concerned about the shoes he ordered in 1910 which still hadn't arrived when the First World War broke out. See here, he says they are "*en forme Roosevelt*" – he wanted the style made popular by the American president!'

There were deeds and maps showing the Ste-Suzanne district throughout the centuries, a patchwork of neat lines showing the extent of the various estates and the names of the plantations. Joseph chuckled as he showed me a letter from the governor's office in the eighteenth century confirming that the tax payable for the Grand Hazier estate was an annual contribution of twelve chickens and twelve turkeys. 'My new zinc roof alone will cost 30,000 euros!'

Joseph led me back onto the verandah to see some of the other rooms, passing Tante Marie again, who was now being fed some mush from a bowl by a maid. In one of the front bedrooms I could see that a modern hospital-style bed with a metal frame had been pushed between two old wooden beds, and Joseph confirmed that this was the old lady's room. 'Those wooden beds are made of *bois de fer* – you call it iron-wood,' he said. 'Try to move one – feel the weight! My great-grandfather had them made here, but copied from a design he saw in a catalogue from Paris.'

There were holes in the ceiling and more old furniture as we passed towards the back of the house. Joseph's fragmented image was caught in an ancient mirror, so old that most of the silver backing had peeled away. In the simple kitchen there was another maid, a large dark-skinned woman chopping up a palm heart on a wooden board. Two still life paintings of tropical fruit decorated the walls. They were drawn with skill, and the colours seemed fresh. 'Tante Marie did those when she was in her twenties.'

More steps led down to the work area at the back of the house, and a collection of old sheds made of weathered coral cement. Weeds grew in profusion along the base of the walls and there were large pieces of rusting iron embedded in the undergrowth. Joseph said that they were cauldrons once used for evaporating sugar, which would be heated over an open fire and stirred with a giant wooden spoon. I wanted to see the garden, though Joseph was apologetic at its current state of neglect.

We walked through the grounds, and passed a vegetable garden where marrows and tomatoes poked from the beds. Off to one side of the property was an overgrown area stocked with every variety of fruit tree. The mosquitoes were bad, and I was soon scratching at my calves and ankles in the long grass. Even in its untended state the Chassagnes' land still boasted jackfruit, oranges, pineapples, cashew nuts, breadfruit, camphor, coffee and cacao.

We carried on through the trees, occasionally squelching over-ripe fruit unseen in the long grass beneath our feet. It was clear that Joseph loved the garden, and knew a lot about what grew there.

'Do you have any mangosteen?' I asked. I hadn't thought about the fruit for years, but something about Grand Hazier gave me hope that it might be found there.

'Ah, how does an Englishman know this fruit?' Joseph's eyes sparkled.

I had once tasted it in Seychelles, a pale succulent orb with an indescribably subtle sweetness which completely envelops the taste buds but is at the same time unbeatably refreshing. The only mangosteen tree (*Garcinia mangostana*) left in all of Seychelles grows in the president's garden at State House, and I had once been given a fruit by the head gardener. In the mid-1990s the same tree was badly damaged in a suspicious fire, having the misfortune to grow close to an office block where the government stored its accounts. An independent auditor was about to go through the balance sheets when the whole place burnt down, and the last I heard it may not still survive. Like nutmeg, this tree once came from the Moluccas and was gradually transplanted to the Philippines and beyond in the eighteenth century. It needs high humidity and heavy rainfall to survive, and produces circular purple fruit with firm white flesh on the inside. The French still call it the 'King of tropical fruits', and apart from having an exceptionally complex and gentle taste, it is reputed to reduce fat in the bloodstream. Joseph led me through the trees until we came to a noisome-smelling tortoise enclosure close to a small house some way from the main building. The giant tortoises were a magnet for the mosquitoes and the only consolation for the smell and the discomfort was that the tree shading the reptiles was a mangosteen. Joseph plucked a darkening fruit about the size of a tangerine from a branch above his head and split the skin between his palms. Neat white segments in a ball glistened slightly in the sun. He gave me half of the fruit and once again I tasted its sweet juice.

Joseph winked at me. 'Horrible, *non*?'

As we moved back towards the main house I spotted a familiar shape against the bark of an old tree. The dark green vine.

'*Vanille*,' Joseph muttered dismissively as I hurried towards it.

'Is it *planifolia*?' I asked.

'No, not this one,' he said shaking his head as I caressed the long green stem. 'This is one of the varieties that they planted here by mistake, and we just leave it to grow in the forest. We did have *planifolia*, but there is a fungus in the soil here that kills it. I need to treat the ground but it costs money.'

Back at the main house, Joseph returned to supervising the workmen on the roof. As I said goodbye, Tante Marie was still there, watching the proceedings from the verandah with her watering artist's eyes.

The planters of Bourbon long dreamed of being the first to break the Spanish monopoly on vanilla. Like the horticulturists in Europe who struggled to identify the plant which would deliver the sweet-scented pods of commerce, the island's colonists had already made their own mistakes with vanilla.

In 1819 the first vanilla plants arrived on Bourbon, carried aboard *Le Rhône* from the French colony at Cayenne in French Guiana. The *Rhône*'s captain, Pierre-Henri Philibert, was a white creole, proud to bring this potential treasure back to his own island. He had personally collected the plants from Cayenne's governor, Carra Saint-Cyr, who said they were samples of 'great vanilla', probably *Vanilla pompona* – since they were described as banana shaped. At the time, Philibert apologized to Bourbon's governor, Pierre-Bernard de Milius, lamenting that he had only managed to bring back a handful of vanilla plants, because 'at Cayenne they grow it little'.

The following year, Philibert made another voyage in search of vanilla, this time to the Philippines. After an expedition lasting four months, the expedition botanist, Perrotet, reached Cueva de San-Matheo, where he reported, 'to my utmost joy, in the middle of a virgin forest I saw vanilla vines, climbing among the branches of an enormous bamboo thicket'. Perrotet brought Philibert to the spot, and together they collected as many specimens as they could, describing the plants as 'more slender and fragrant than the "great vanilla" from Cayenne'.

Philibert was excited at the prospect of returning to Bourbon with the precious vanilla, hoping that this time he had found the right species to produce the precious fruit. Once again, he wrote to Governor Milius: 'I believe that you will consider the introduction of vanilla to our colony a great benefit. It may become a source of prosperity, and in future years we may use it as an object of trade – especially with Asia. Our colonists can only profit from its cultivation.'

The governor's reply was equally hopeful, and congratulatory but with a sting in the tail:

We have long awaited the introduction of this precious plant. And, we will not forget that it was one of our own children that finally brought it to the island. It is a pity that you did not donate all of the plants from your last visit to Cayenne to the botanical gardens — thus delaying the cultivation of the crop by several years. The individuals to whom you gave these plants can hardly expect to take as good care of them as the experts at the Jardin du Roi.

Philibert's defence was that the vanilla plants from Cayenne were few in number, and that he had indeed brought back numerous other plants for the botanical gardens. He had entrusted his small stock to planters whose reputation and skill could not be in doubt, hoping they would succeed in keeping them alive.

It is just possible that the plants Philibert brought back from the Philippines were indeed *Vanilla planifolia*, even though they were found in 'thick virgin forest'. According to Philibert the plants were only about thirty miles from Manila, and it is conceivable that they were specimens transplanted there from Mexico by the Spanish two hundred years earlier.

Records in Réunion's *Archives départementales* reveal that the new arrivals were planted at several properties, including the gardens of Madame Fréon at Rivière de Pluies, and on the estate of Hubert de Montfleury at St-Benoît. Once again, Philibert did not want any single planter to have all of the plants in case something went wrong. However, none of the vines flourished, and a few months later they were all dead.

The third consignment of vanilla plants to arrive on the island was to be more successful. In 1822 specimens that were identifiably *Vanilla planifolia* arrived from Paris, this time donated from the collection in the hothouses at the Jardin des

Plantes. These were plants grown from cuttings taken from the vanilla orchid which grew in Charles Greville's garden at Paddington. Imported by another creole, David de Floris, these plants did finally survive. However, the planters of Bourbon, like the Spanish in the Philippines, the British in India or the Dutch in Java, became resigned to the idea that outside its native Mexico, vanilla would never bear fruit except by chance. There seemed no prospect of getting the vines regularly and reliably to produce the seed pods which were so valuable in Europe. At a plantation called Belle-vue, close to the town of Sainte-Suzanne, Ferréol Bellier-Beaumont succeeded in keeping a vine alive for twenty years. He complained: 'Of one-hundred vanilla vines on our island, we would be lucky to see ten flowers, and even fewer fruits, in a whole year.'

Early one morning towards the end of 1841, and after almost twenty years of sterility, it was little wonder that Bellier-Beaumont was astounded to find two fruits growing on his own solitary vine. He made the discovery while walking through his gardens accompanied by one of his slaves, a young boy called Edmond. To the planter's amazement, Edmond claimed that he had fertilized the vanilla flower.

Years later, Bellier-Beaumont would say that he at first dismissed Edmond's claim as an idle boast. However, a few days later, another flower column showed the unmistakable signs of swelling ovaries. Once again, Edmond claimed the credit. This time Bellier-Beaumont demanded an explanation, and as there were other flowers on the vine, the boy proceeded to peel back the lip of the small orchid with his thumb, and with the aid of a small stick, lift the rostellum out of the way and press the anther and the stigmatic surfaces together.

The planter could not keep the boy's discovery to himself,

Cuttings from vanilla vines in the Jardin des Plantes in Paris eventually found their way to Bourbon

and within days he invited other estate owners to Belle-vue where Edmond was told to show them his trick. Representatives from the largest estates duly arrived: Sarrazin de Floris came from St-André, Patu de Rosemont from St-Benoît and Antonin de Sigoyer from the estate of Joseph Desbassyns at Ste-Suzanne (the same land where Le Grand Hazier sits today). Soon, the boy Edmond was in great demand, despatched in a carriage on a tour of other plantations so that he could demonstrate the art of 'orchid marriage' to other slaves. His sensational trick, *le geste d'Edmond*, was about to make many of their masters rich.

8. The Slave's Crime

The man's body lay face down on the grass traffic island, as if he were sleeping. His head and shirt had been dyed dark red with his own blood. The car that hit him was parked a few yards away, its two occupants crouched at the kerbside staring straight ahead in shock, unable to face the sight of their victim as they waited for the police and ambulance to arrive. Traffic slowed as early morning commuters, myself included, peered at the carnage a few feet from their own vehicles, then curiosity satisfied, gradually picked up speed again for the daily rush towards St-Denis. It was the third fatal accident I had seen in the same number of weeks, on the same stretch of the busy N1 which traces the outline of the coast all the way to the capital from St-Pierre in the south.

Everyone complains about the traffic. It's not what you expect of a tropical island, but the impenetrable bulk of Réunion's volcanoes means there is only one practical route from the west coast to the east. For at least two hours each morning and evening, the *route du littoral* is a dizzying conveyor belt of speeding vehicles all seemingly driven with a dangerous mixture of Gallic bravado and creole joie de vivre. They are all trying to get to St-Denis, the commercial, political and cultural hub of the island, and where I was making use of the national archives. To avoid the excessive heat of the city I stayed at Saline-les-Bains, a small offshoot of the more fashionable resort of St-Gilles where surfing and serious sunbathing are turned into an artform. The drawback of being near the beach was the hour-long drive in each direction every time I had business in St-Denis. Each night, Madame Louvat, my landlady, would look up from her office and shake her head pityingly. 'Bad traffic?'

'Yes, Madame. Bad traffic.'

Things really slow to a crawl at the island's northernmost tip, where everything is drawn into a narrow logjam at the main city esplanade they call *Barachois*. Buses and lorries, cars and vans spill out of the old narrow streets of the city onto the seafront under the watchful gaze of the statue to Roland Garros: the first man to fly non-stop across the Mediterranean who was later killed in an heroic dogfight just weeks before the end of the First World War. Standing beside a large propeller, he is trapped in a concrete suit. On the other side of the road, a line of impressive old cannons faces out to sea defending the heart of the colonial city. Not far away is the smart white edifice of the prefecture where I once attended a cocktail party with no fewer than three uniformed French admirals in attendance. And up there, stretching along the high ground are the grandest of St-Denis's old houses, a cluster of wooden mansions along the Rue de Paris protected from the street by ornate iron railings.

Many of the grand houses are uninhabited, awaiting restoration, with shutters closed and white paint peeling from Doric columns under the fierce southern sun. Fountains stand dry and cracking in their courtyards, and delicate ironwork aviaries with pagoda roofs are empty of ornamental doves. The law says that these houses are part of the island's heritage, and any restoration must be true to the original design. Rather than foot the bill, the families that own them leave them to decay. At the far end of the Rue de Paris there is the old botanical garden now called the Jardin d'Etat, but once Jardin du Roi. Its layout, and some of the trees, date from the days of the French East India Company, and were collected in the Indies by Pierre Poivre himself. Here too, Captain Philibert brought his treasures from Cayenne and the Philippines. The gardens are a little shabby now, battered by cyclones in recent years but still a haven from the traffic of the surrounding streets.

Since 1946 Réunion has been a fully fledged *département* of France, the President of the Republic represented locally by a *Préfet*, but with its own regional council. Five deputies and three senators sit in the French parliament and the island is also part of the European Union. The islanders are entirely free to travel to mainland France, and to live there if they choose. In practice few make the move, unwilling to exchange their tropical lifestyle and sunshine for the cooler motherland.

Much of the island's heritage is stored in the *Archives départementales*, which date back to the early seventeenth century. Now housed in a modernist tower-block at Champ-Fleuri on the outskirts of the capital, the history of Bourbon and Réunion is under the guardianship of a fierce set of librarians and archivists who bring the full force of French bureaucracy to bear on their task. None of them spoke a word of English, claiming my grasp of their own language would be all we needed to communicate. I wasn't quite so confident, and I never quite felt I mastered the arcane cataloguing system within the archives. Card index trays, microfiches, handwritten ledgers and various ring-binders of different colours all contained code numbers which must be written down and handed in to the desk staff in any attempt to locate a particular document. After several weeks of battling the system I could never fathom exactly which catalogue might contain the information I needed. There were also rules to be followed. Only seven documents could be requested before midday, and the same number following lunch. Lunch is from midday until two.

Photocopies of rare documents require that a letter be written to the Chief Archivist, who resides on the fifth floor. This she must stamp and return before the document can be transported the two-metre distance from the issuing desk to the copying machine. After I had spent a month using the archives the novelty of dealing with an Englishman seemed to wear down one or two of the *responsables* in charge of the photocopying machine. Not only would my presence at the issue desk be greeted with a half-smile, but occasionally, very occasionally, I was permitted an illicit duplicate without having to wait for *Madame la Directrice's* imprimatur. Perhaps, they decided, it was easier to just provide a photocopy than to decipher my execrably written French.

In the archives I found many of the original handwritten documents relating to the time of Edmond's discovery, and before. There was Commandant Philibert's neat copperplate handwriting, and letters from Ferréol Bellier-Beaumont in a bold flowing hand. Their signatures lay on faded and cracking paper bound in folders with red ribbons. Once I asked for a photograph of an etching in an old book. After two weeks I enquired when it might be ready. '*Ah!* But the photographer is on leave this week. First thing on Monday . . .'

On Monday, the photographer (whom I never met or spoke to directly) was 'snowed under with work after his holidays'. A week later my request had been marked '*urgent*' and '*priorité*', but alas, it still did not appear. With five days left on the island I asked if a date could be set when I might receive the photograph. 'But Monsieur, you mean you haven't received it? . . . oh la-la, I will ring Madame la Directrice! Indeed, she has your request in front of her, she will make sure it is done this afternoon.' Each false alarm necessitated the hour-long drive in each direction, and the long traffic queues to circumnavigate St-Denis. Finally, on my penultimate day on the island I was told: '*Desolé*, Monsieur . . . there has been a *contre-temps*!'

'How big is this *contre-temps*?' I asked, attempting a strained smile.

'Ah, well, it seems that the photographer has run out of black and white film. Could you possibly provide him with one? Otherwise we will have to wait for Madame la Directrice to order some more. And we really cannot say how long that might take.'

I returned a few hours later with the film. 'If Monsieur could call tomorrow, I'm sure it will be ready.'

'On my way to the airport?'

'Perhaps Monsieur should telephone before making the journey.' Perhaps. Four months later, after a lengthy exchange of emails, the image arrived in London by post.

French historians have uncovered much of the existing evidence about Edmond, and his master, Ferréol Bellier-Beaumont. But there are large gaps in the story, and at times, earlier writers have glossed over the events which followed Edmond's discovery. Sometimes, they have flatly denied that the boy had anything to do with the beginnings of the vanilla industry on the island. In the light of what happened to him in later years, it is hardly surprising. Important and valuable as his contribution would become to the island's economy, he was, after all, still just a slave. Within a short time of Edmond's discovery the rumours and arguments began. Could such a young boy, particularly a young black boy, really have discovered and perfected something as intricate and important as the secret of manual pollination? Such doubts persist today.

In Tahiti, another former French possession, I met a vanilla grower who laughed when I told him what I knew of the story of Edmond. 'Rubbish!' he said, with a scowl. 'In fact, the boy was just a slave – and it is well known that he hated his owner. If he did fertilize the vanilla flower – it was an accident, not any kind of discovery! The truth is, Edmond had been scolded by his master about something, and for revenge he went out into the garden and crushed all the vanilla flowers he could find. Some of them were fertilized that way, that's all.'

Another vanilla grower, this time in Réunion, repeated another version of the legend to me. 'Edmond was in the garden with a creole girl and they were making love. You know,' she whispered conspiratorially, '*les Africains* – they start to have sex very young. Well, to impress this girl, the boy told her he could show her the male and female parts of an orchid. You can imagine – *la fécondation* – it is a very sensual process. Afterwards, Edmond suggested that he could do to the girl what he had just done to the orchid.'

Slavery, and the attitudes to race that it left behind have not been entirely forgotten in the Indian Ocean islands. The modern Réunionnais are proud of their French citizenship, and hesitate to draw attention to each other's bloodlines. But once, when I told a friend that a vanilla grower had failed to keep an appointment with me, she exclaimed, '*Ah oui!* Of course he's *pretending* to be busy, as if he is an important businessman. He's such a *grand blanc*!'

France finally abolished slavery in all of its possessions on 27 April 1848. The news reached Bourbon in June, causing great disquiet among the plantocracy, who feared that economic ruin and social uproar would follow. By now, slaves accounted for 60 per cent of the population of the island and the white landowners knew they were outnumbered. In October a new governor, Joseph Napoléon Sarda-Garriga, disembarked at St-Denis with a copy of the new law among his papers. Knowing that there were great misgivings about the emancipation, and to allay the fears of the planters, he agreed that any slaves not yet freed should remain in service until 20 December. This would give the employers time to plan for the liberation, and also to harvest that year's crops with a full complement of staff.

When the great day for freedom finally arrived, the governor received a delegation of specially selected slaves, to hear the official proclamation.

'My friends,' he began. 'By decree of the French Republic, you are free. All men are equal under the law, and you have no one around you but brothers. Liberty, you will understand, brings its own obligations, one of which is work and respect for law and order.'

Sarda-Garriga seems to have gone out of his way to induce the freed slaves not to desert their masters, exhorting the freed slaves to remember that they should 'respect God's will, and be good workers like your brothers in France. Respect your employers and remember that this colony is not rich: many employers can only pay your wages after the harvest has been gathered.'

The governor was also quite clear that he would not tolerate any misbehaviour or vagabondage. 'We must all work together for the prosperity of the colony. Remember, my friends,' he continued, 'labouring in the fields is not a sign of servitude. You are playing your part in creating the common good. Henceforth, proprietors and workers will form one common family whose members must help each other.'

The final paternal flourish of the decree reminded the slaves how lucky they were: 'Call me father, and I will love you like children. Listen to my advice: always remember that it was the French Republic that set you free! And that your duty is to God, France and Work. Vive la République!'

After this florid proclamation, Sarda-Garriga reported that the eight slaves who were present threw themselves upon the floor in front of him. 'My friends,' said the governor. 'It is only at the feet of God that men should prostrate themselves. Take my hand.'

The previous social rules of the colony were now under assault, but it would be some years before the attitudes of the plantocracy towards its largely black labour force softened. Freed slaves would now be recognized as citizens, their names dutifully recorded on the Civil List, complete with their newly chosen surnames — many of them adopting the name of the family to whom they had belonged, or the name of the estate on which they worked. Occasionally they simply chose a name they liked.

By December 1848, Edmond had already been a freeman for half a year. Ferréol Bellier-Beaumont knew that the official emancipation was on its way, and like many planters he granted his 'favourite boy' his liberty. Edmond was not only free: he also had a surname — Albius. As with so much of Edmond's story, even his name is a curiosity — it means 'white', and various historians have argued that it might be an honorary reference to his free status, or as some kind of ill-conceived joke at his expense by the white men in charge of the registry. Others have claimed that he was simply relatively light-skinned, even though portraits refute this. One writer at the turn of the century even suggested that Edmond may not have been a black person, suggesting that he was of mixed race, and by implication owed any of his genius to his white heritage.

Like all slaves, Edmond had been born without a surname, and his mother's identity is recorded simply as Mélise, a maid in service in the district of Sainte-Suzanne. She died giving birth to Edmond, and he was told later that his father, whom he never met, was a slave named Pamphile. When the boy was old enough to be of some use, his owner, a woman named Elvire, sent Edmond to live at her brother's estate at Belle-vue. There, Edmond became a house-boy to his new master, Ferréol Bellier-Beaumont and his wife, Angelique.

Within Bourbon's small social circle of white landowners Bellier-Beaumont had a reputation as a knowledgeable horticulturist, and he enjoyed experimenting with new varieties of decorative plants as well as with commercial fruit and vegetables. As the boy Edmond grew, he followed his master around the estate, watching and learning as Bellier-Beaumont tended his plants. Years later, his master wrote: 'this young black boy became my constant companion, a favourite child always at my feet.'

The detail of Edmond's childhood is lost, his life at Belle-vue a daily round of household chores at the behest of his master, albeit a kindly man who would later defend the boy's reputation.

A year after his emancipation, Edmond's name is listed in the county register for Sainte-Suzanne. There, he is recorded simply as 'citizen Edmon' (*sic*), the son of deceased slaves, Mélise and Pamphile. The registrar's task was formally to recognize any former slaves within their own community and record their new names for posterity.

Abandoning the rural isolation of Belle-vue, Edmond joined the ranks of the other 62,150 slaves on Réunion released by order of the Revolutionary Government in Paris. Meanwhile, the industry that his discovery seven years earlier had created was beginning to flourish, the vanilla crop an essential part of the new economy. Whether Edmond's success resulted from malevolence, ingenuity or simply a stroke of luck, there is no doubt that a rapid rise in vanilla production followed directly from the events of 1841, when Ferréol Bellier-Beaumont summoned other landowners to his estate at Belle-vue to learn Edmond's technique.

After Edmond's discovery, numerous planters on the northeast coast began cultivating vanilla in earnest. From small beginnings they propagated and planted new vines, so that by 1848 the island was able to export fifty kilograms of vanilla pods to France. Ten years later, Bourbon – now officially renamed La Réunion – was able to send two tonnes of dried pods back to the motherland. The curing process used on the island became known as the Bourbon method, and it is still applied to the beans today. Just as French wine makers from Champagne reserve the name for sparkling wines from their own locality, there are attempts to restrict the term 'Bourbon vanilla' to those beans grown only in the former French possessions of Réunion, Madagascar and Comoros. However, some dealers use the term loosely, applying it to any *Vanilla planifolia* pods cured in the Bourbon manner.

Year by year, cultivation and curing methods were improved so that by 1867 the island could export 20 tonnes, and in 1898 a record 200 tonnes of dried vanilla. By then, Réunion had outstripped Mexico to become the world's largest producer of vanilla beans.

Vanilla as a new resource could not have come at a better time. Coffee, one of the most important products of the island, had already had its heyday, with production affected by pest, and sales damaged by the influx of much cheaper coffee from the Antilles and South America. Cyclones in 1806 and 1807 had also resulted in severe damage to plants, as well as soil erosion and avalanches which badly affected the amount of land available for coffee production. Sugar, which had enjoyed a peak production of fifty thousand tonnes in the year that Edmond first fertilized his vanilla orchids, would gradually also decline. By 1850 production had already halved, and in 1865 the crop would be afflicted by a parasitic insect. More seriously, the tropical sugar-cane grass was being replaced by the temperate sugar beet, which by 1880 would become the main source of sugar in Europe. The opening of the Suez Canal after 1869 would also dramatically reduce the number of ships stopping at the island, and further weaken the strategic value of the colony to France.

With so many threats to the agricultural prosperity of the island, the colonial government was quick to see the commercial advantages of a new crop, and by 1853 they had already imposed a tax of five francs per kilogram on any vanilla exports, money which the official colony bulletin revealed would 'be used to encourage other, local agricultural efforts'.

The archive collection of photographs and engravings of the old estates led me into a forgotten world. In manners and lifestyle the *grands blancs* were keen to emulate the latest fashions of Paris. The colony had its own newspaper, *Le Moniteur*, and there were music and art societies for the upper classes to attend. From 1860–63 a local author, Antoine Roussin, published three large volumes offering a snapshot of life on Réunion. His aim, he said, was to 'represent the most picturesque sites and the principal monuments of the colony'. Describing the city of St-Denis, he asks his reader: 'Do you expect a primitive place at the end of the oceans where people speak in old-fashioned ways? You will be amazed. Our beautiful city knows all the tricks of flirtation: she reveals her charms little by little, and she will not show you her best parts all at once.'

The allure of St-Denis worked its magic upon the young Edmond, enticing him away from the countryside to the hustle and bustle of the city. It was not to be a happy move. When Edmond left his master's estate at Belle-vue he had no formal education, and he was just one of many thousands of agricultural workers who were faced with the choice between remaining on the farm or looking for some kind of paid work in the towns. Although he may have had a *grand blanc* name, Bellier-Beaumont was not a wealthy man, and it was other planters who would take up vanilla cultivation on a large scale after Edmond's discovery. Consequently, he could only afford to give Edmond a small amount of cash when he left the estate to start a new life. Even though the vanilla industry was still in its infancy, Bellier-Beaumont knew that Edmond had laid the foundations of a lucrative trade. As his favourite boy prepared to leave Belle-vue, Bellier-Beaumont wrote to Governor Sarda-Garriga's office, asking if any kind of official stipend could be paid to Edmond for his role in making the vanilla industry a possibility. Although by all accounts an enlightened man, Sarda-Garriga did not reply. The letter was buried in a pile of official correspondence which he did not have time to answer before he was recalled to France.

At eighteen, and with the prospect of a new life away from the narrow confines of the estate near Ste-Suzanne, Edmond Albius was eager to experience the delights of the city. Like any young man, Edmond hoped that life in the capital might offer better prospects than a life of domestic servitude on the farm. Nearby Ste-Suzanne was hardly thrilling, a place described by a contemporary writer as 'neither town nor village, just a collection of homes between two ravines'.

Afterwards, the bulletin of the Society for Science and the Arts of La Réunion would record: 'Edmond left Belle-vue, and ungrateful black boy that he was, forgot all the good things his master had done for him since he was a child. He ran to the city, chasing after who knows what golden dream . . . and ended up in bad company.'

For a time Edmond found menial work as a labourer in St-Denis, before eventually being employed as a kitchen boy at the house of an officer in the city's garrison. One night, there was a robbery at the house and some jewellery was taken. A white woman was injured in the process and although it seems as if there were several men involved in the crime, Edmond was blamed. A trial was held, and Albius would later tell Bellier-Beaumont that the state defender refused to listen to his own version of the events leading up to the theft. Edmond was found guilty, and the court duly applied the harsh discipline that Sarda-Garriga had promised former slaves who failed in their civic duty. On 15 June 1852 the freeman known as Albius was sentenced to five years' imprisonment with hard labour.

Albius's sentence was hardly surprising. The authorities were determined that any breaches of law by former slaves would be dealt with severely, and the assault on a white woman made it a serious crime. Records for the St-Denis assizes reveal that freed slaves accounted for the largest number of prisoners at the time, perhaps unsurprisingly as they were the majority of the population. In the prison there were three Europeans with convictions for theft (and one for bigamy), five white creoles and five black creoles. These were all classified as freemen, while twenty-six criminals were labelled 'freed slaves', their former place in society forever affixed to their name like a badge around their necks. Ranked even lower than the freed slaves were thirty-one Indians, whose main crimes were murder and rape, and finally twenty-six Malagasy whose crime was simply vagabondage.

Edmond Albius did not serve out his entire sentence. Although his former master had not been able to get him a state pension as reward for discovering how to fertilize vanilla, he was at least able to vouch for the boy's previous good character. Bellier-Beaumont also enlisted the support of Ste-Suzanne's local justice of the peace, a man named Mézières Lépervanche, who wrote to the governor on Edmond's behalf within a few months of his detention. 'It is possible,' wrote Lépervanche, 'that if some kind of state pension had been provided, this man would not have turned to crime to satisfy his desires, a taste for fine living acquired when in the service of his original owner.'

Bellier-Beaumont did not give up on his favourite boy. Early in 1855, when Edmond was halfway through his sentence, he wrote again to the governor appealing for an early release. The faded black ink is drawn with a narrow nib, barely legible against the ancient paper, its surface darkened as yellow as vanilla custard. The tone of the letter is formal, but reveals the planter's sensitivity:

Sir,
 I appeal to your compassion, and your sense of justice, in the case of a young black boy condemned to hard labour. For more than two years he has suffered in silence, his conduct irreproachable . . .

 . . . Edmond Albius is just one of many slaves in our

country, who was thrust into the wide world without proper preparation. Left to his own resources after emancipation, he could not resist the temptations of crime, temptations which many of our population find themselves in the midst of – and especially the temptation to steal . . .

Since his condemnation, he has told me the exact circumstances of his crime, and about those who took advantage of his youth and inexperience. I have also learnt that the boy's defence counsel did not take these circumstances into account . . .

. . . Surely, Sir, any just society must take some account of services rendered to that society when considering a person's punishment. If anyone has a right to clemency and to recognition for his achievements, then it is Edmond. It is entirely due to him that this country owes a new branch of industry – for it is he who first discovered how manually to fertilize the vanilla plant.

Bellier-Beaumont recounts the details of Edmond's discovery, and names the other *grand blanc* planters who can verify his story:

. . . these men will recall how they welcomed Edmond to their plantations, so that he could teach their own workers his technique. I, myself, even wrote to a local journal describing what the boy had done, and this will stand as further evidence of his acts. Later, I wrote to the Governor, asking if the boy could be considered for some kind of allowance in recognition of his contribution, a recognition that at least one section of our society feels is due to him.

For these reasons, Sir, I believe this unfortunate condemned man should be considered for clemency, and because of these facts I appeal to your compassion, and dare to hope for your goodwill.

Your humble and obedient servant,

F. Bellier-Beaumont.

The appeal was successful, and by order of Governor Louis-Henri Hubert Delisle, Edmond was released in 1855. He returned to the safety of the estate at Belle-vue, where Bellier-Beaumont allocated him a small parcel of land to cultivate. It is possible that little more would ever have been heard of Edmond, if it had not been for Bellier-Beaumont's determination to exonerate Edmond's character in a copious flow of correspondence with a couple of interested parties. Thanks to these letters a few more snapshots of the events surrounding Edmond's discovery, and his eventual fate, gradually emerge. The planter wrote to Ste-Suzanne's justice of the peace, Monsieur Ganne, who in 1861 had asked for some precise details concerning the circumstances surrounding Edmond's discovery. Bellier-Beaumont reveals that Edmond's vanilla technique was an adaptation of the manual fertilization he had seen him apply to a type of watermelon. 'In this plant,' wrote Bellier-Beaumont, 'the male and female flowers occur on different plants, and I taught the little black boy, Edmond, how to marry the male and female parts together.'

Bellier-Beaumont has no qualms about crediting Edmond with the discovery. 'This clever boy had realized that the vanilla flower also had male and female elements, and worked out for himself how to join them together.'

In April 1862, Bellier-Beaumont was to commit the details of Edmond's discovery to paper once more, this time in letters written to a local historian, Eugène Volsy-Focard. Focard would recount Edmond's story in the third volume of Roussin's

Album de l'île de la Réunion published in 1863. Bellier-Beaumont and Volsy-Focard were at great pains to clarify Edmond's role in the history of vanilla on the island. When shown an early draft of the article which would eventually appear, Bellier-Beaumont writes: 'The paragraphs concerning Edmond's discovery are quite correct. And you add, with some justification, that this young negro deserves recognition from this country. It owes him a debt, for starting up a new industry with a fabulous product.'

In later correspondence it becomes clear that Volsy-Focard had been told that a prominent botanist, identified as 'Mr. Jean-Michel Richard', had denied that Edmond had been the first to discover the secret of manual fertilization. Mr. Richard had apparently claimed that he had been experimenting with vanilla pollination in Paris, and had paid a visit to Réunion in 1838, where he had demonstrated his technique to various horticulturists. Edmond the slave-boy, claimed Richard, must have learned the technique then. Bellier-Beaumont is quick to reply:

My dear Compatriot,

No one could possibly believe that I would be stupid enough or audacious enough to try to pass off [Edmond's] discovery as something new if it were not so. Why would such notable gentlemen as Messr. Floris, Patu de Rosemont, Joseph Desbassyns and others come here in search of a young negro to teach their staff how to do it if the process was already well known?

How could Mr. Richard have taught the young boy this technique in 1838 – when he was only eight years old? And if he did so, why would a botanist of such note keep such a lesson to himself, sharing it only with this young boy and not with myself or other planters? I suggest that the esteemed Mr. Richard's memory is playing tricks with him.

Mr. Richard also claims that it is impossible that an uneducated boy of eleven or twelve could be expected to have the scientific knowledge to make such an important discovery. Indeed, but what Edmond lacked in schooling, he made up for by experience. He had been helping me in the garden for many years, and had seen me fertilizing other plants as we have discussed.

The botanist Richard also claimed to have been manually pollinating vanilla orchids before 1837, in other words, *before* Charles Morren discovered the technique practised at Liège. Bellier-Beaumont is at a loss to explain this discrepancy, suggesting tactfully that the French botanist has become confused over the dates. Bellier-Beaumont apologizes for having to send all this information to Volsy-Focard by letter, saying he is indisposed. He indicates that Edmond will be the bearer of his letter, 'as he is my factotum while I am kept indoors'.

Bellier-Beaumont's correspondence with Volsy-Focard also reveals that he has been discussing the whole issue of the vanilla story with Edmond:

Edmond is more than happy to assist you in getting the facts straight. And he does not mind having his picture appear in Mr. Roussin's album . . .

. . . The best answer to those who contest the truth of Edmond's involvement in this story is that the method of pollination used today is the very same technique that he first demonstrated all those years ago. I will stop here, Sir, at the end of this long plea in favour of the man who discovered the process of vanilla fertilization in our colony.

This was not the end of the matter. In December 1862, Bellier-Beaumont is forced to respond in even greater detail about Mr. Richard's claims. He expresses his sincere apologies for questioning the word of a respected expert, but adds: 'I have been his friend for many years, and regret anything which causes him pain, but I also have my obligations to Edmond. Through old age, faulty memory or some other cause, Mr. Richard now imagines that he himself discovered the secret of how to pollinate vanilla, and imagines that he taught the technique to the person who discovered it! Let us leave him to his fantasies.'

The result of the lengthy exchange of letters between Bellier-Beaumont and Volsy-Focard was that Edmond's role in the history of vanilla was accepted and printed in the third volume of Roussin's *Album*. Volsy-Focard also repeated the detail of the story in a paper for the Academy of Science and Art the same year. He also tried to address the tangled history of who should be credited with transporting the vanilla plants to the island in the first place. Some favoured Captain Philibert, while others preferred Marchant, the man who collected specimens from the botanical gardens in Paris. In the introduction to his third volume, Roussin described Edmond Albius as one of several children who have rendered service to Réunion. 'For this reason,' he writes, 'his portrait appears in this volume. Quite naturally, it goes alongside the portrait of the man who first brought vanilla plants to our island. We trust that it will not be judged inappropriate that his grey linen jacket sits close to the gold embroidery on the uniform of a ship's captain.'

Roussin may have mocked the proprieties of Réunion's class system, but he also asked the plantocracy to examine their consciences. Would it not be possible to reward Edmond

Albius for his discovery? 'Could not our vanilla planters save a few bundles of their harvest for this man?' he wrote. 'Surely it would not take much to build him a house with a straw roof, and a small patch of land to farm.'

Nothing came of Roussin's appeal, and Edmond remained dependent on Bellier-Beaumont's charity. In his final letter to Volsy-Focard, Edmond's former master added a postscript. 'Edmond thanks you for the copies of the drawings of him that you sent. The ingenious inventor of vanilla fertilization has been able to show them to all his friends and family, who like all negroes, are great connoisseurs of drawing and engraving.'

The engraving that appeared in Roussin's album shows Edmond standing beside a vanilla vine. The portrait is an oddly posed thing, with Edmond now in his thirties wearing a pale jacket and black bow-tie, looking for all the world like a waiter. An earlier image also survives, a daguerreotype said to be of Edmond aged about eighteen. Smartly dressed in a frock-coat and white breeches, the boy has a handsome open face.

Edmond remained at Belle-vue until he married. Of his wife, no information survives, other than that she was called Marie Pauline Rassama, and that she was a seamstress. They had no children, and she died before Edmond. Vanilla brought Edmond little reward, except his early release from gaol, and the offer of a return to life as Bellier-Beaumont's factotum. The last contemporary detail of Edmond's life lay concealed in the vaults at the archives. According to the catalogue, the *Moniteur* newspaper of 26 August 1880 had recorded his death. The paper was in extremely poor condition, and had been removed from public view. For some weeks I was told it was impossible to look at it, the document was simply too fragile to be handled. On my last day in the archives I tried one more

Edmond Albius returned to the plantation at Belle-vue after his release from prison

time. Madame Vidal, the head librarian, shook her head sadly. '*Oh la-la* . . . tsk-tsk . . . it's too fragile, Monsieur. We cannot touch it!'

As I tidied my belongings and packed away my notes, I felt a tap on my shoulder. It was Madame Vidal. She beckoned me into a corridor behind the reading room, and wordlessly escorted me to her private office. There on the desk was the bound volume containing the newspaper. It had split horizontally and the paper was as dry as tinder. Gingerly we opened the book as slowly and gently as we dared and found the edition for the last week of August 1880. There, towards the back, was a section entitled '*faits divers*' – the equivalent of a modern day 'snippets' column. I read that the packet boat *Rio* had arrived from Mananzary in Madagascar that week, bringing news that another boat *Louis Rumler* had been lost the previous month on the coast at Mahanooroo. From Mauritius came news that the Turf Club was to launch a new race, the Maiden Stakes. Locally, Monsieur Louis August Hoareau, a farmer from Palmiste Rouge, had suffered a robbery in which he had lost the sum of eighty francs. And then:

Thursday 26 August.
The very man who at great profit to this colony, discovered how to pollinate vanilla flowers, has died in the public hospital at Sainte-Suzanne. It was a destitute and miserable end.

The column repeats some of the detail of Edmond's story, information reproduced from an article by Volsy-Focard, before adding:

We need scarcely add that Volsy-Focard's plea for an allowance has never brought a response.

Edmond was fifty-one years old when he died. His name lives on in a small way in Réunion with a couple of towns naming streets in his honour. Like Pierre Poivre, Sarda-Garriga and the First World War flying ace Roland Garros, he also has his name attached to a school. The Collège Edmond Albius at Le Port, close to St-Denis, is a rather featureless modern set of buildings with almost a thousand pupils.

Just over twenty years ago, a local newspaper, *Ce Matin*, published a short article entitled 'A Great Creol', focusing on the lack of a monument to Edmond. The article urged the authorities to rectify the situation, 'in order that Réunion can prove itself less ungrateful than Bourbon'.

Like the original appeals for a pension to be funded from the vanilla crop, the call went unanswered. However, I learned that some kind of monument had later been built near Sainte-Suzanne. It was Madame Vidal at the archives who first mentioned it, and she used the old-fashioned word '*stêle*'. It wasn't marked on any of the maps I could find, and she had not actually seen the monument herself. No one I asked seemed to have visited the spot, but they said it was close to where the plantation at Belle-vue had been. I wanted to see it for myself.

9. Homage to Albius

The hot city fell behind me as the traffic picked up speed along the Boulevard Lancastel heading east. Once past the tip of the island the road straightened out, running parallel to the old railway line which once carried thousands of tonnes of sugar to the port. To my right, office buildings covered in hoardings for French cellular phones reared up on the outskirts of the city and to my left, the surface of the dark blue sea lay dimpled and glittering in the morning light.

Past Roland Garros airport and onto the eastbound N2 highway the landscape opened out, depriving me of the sight of the water as the road cut inland. Great rolling fields of tall sugar cane spread out on either side of the motorway, and the sign to Sainte-Suzanne drew me onto a promontory just where the curve of the coastline begins to head due south. I followed the signs for the centre of town, and found a small square dominated by a whitewashed church. Close by was a bus stop, and behind it the tourist information office. Inside, there were two sullen youths, an extremely thin boy wearing a football shirt and a chubby girl with rather bad acne. Her jeans were skin tight and his shirt was made of some type of shiny nylon which shimmered when he moved. Neither garment seemed a good choice for the steamy heat. They ignored my presence, barely interrupting their conversation as I photographed a civic shield on the wall above their heads. *Hic Vanillam Albius Fecundavit.* 'Here Albius fertilized Vanilla', said the motto on the scroll beneath the shield. I found this rather exciting, and asked if they could tell me about the monument to the man himself. The fat girl shook her head, looking at the skinny boy for help. She looked slightly amazed when he jabbed a finger onto the map affixed to the wall and pointed to a small road inland labelled D63. 'Up here,' he said. 'Just follow the road and you will see it.'

The road he indicated seemed to peter out at Belle Vue, the modernized name of Bellier-Beaumont's original plantation. I knew from the archives that the original property no longer existed, but its name had remained as a general term for the area.

'Do you have any more information about Edmond Albius, and his connections with Sainte-Suzanne?'

'No.'

'Do you know where the town's old poor-house was situated?'

'No.' The girl let out a long sigh. 'We don't get tourists here.'

'But, there is a lighthouse,' the boy volunteered. 'Built in 1845.'

This was the best the town could offer in the way of sights. It was very much a standard lighthouse: tall round stone column with glass domed lantern on top. A plaque on the wall told me that on a clear night its light could be seen from eighteen miles offshore, and that before it was built the rocks at Ste-Suzanne had claimed a lot of ships. I left the town and crossed under the motorway to find the small road the skinny boy had shown me on the map. It took me inland, due south of the town and began to climb through sugar cane rising ten or twelve feet high and blocking the view to left and right. For several miles there were no houses, and no other traffic.

As the road climbed upwards I caught sight of the mountains in the distance, the irregular rim of the Cirque de Salazie like a fortress wall blocking access to the interior. The land fell away now, sloping back towards the sea and freeing me from the suffocating press of the sugar fields. I spotted a lone harrier, the type they call *papangue*, soaring on thermals high above the fields, a strong dark bird with a three-foot wingspan searching the cane for mice. A breezeblock house and a small church with a red zinc roof stood on a sharp bend in the road. I stopped to take my bearings, parking a few yards in front of a bus stop. There was a bench for passengers to use and I walked towards it, intending to study my map. The sign said the stop was part of the Vanilla Line: and the name of the bus stop was Albius. The sign had a small picture of a vanilla orchid in one corner. And there, tucked under a shade-tree, was the monument to Edmond.

A square of cement had been laid out as a base, and in flaking green capitals it proclaimed 'Homage to Edmond Albius 1829–1880'. In the centre of the cement stood a crude model of his head. Around the base of his neck Edmond wore a painted necklace of vanilla vine. A misshapen Afro coiffure, beetling brows and protruding eyes made him look like a caricature of a Black and White Minstrel. The whole effect was like a giant novelty birthday cake.

A metal sign behind the monument said that the head had been erected in 1980 at the behest of the Mayor of Ste-Suzanne. I could only imagine it had been modelled by children as part of a school project.

I sat down at the bus stop to take in the details of the scene. The harrier was stooping over the cane field and I watched it for several minutes before it was carried downwind on its hunt. After a time two fair-skinned boys in threadbare denim shorts emerged soundlessly from the cane close to where I was sitting. One of them carried some kind of animal trap over his shoulder, and a few seconds after them came a pack of four stringy hunting dogs. The boys nodded at me in greeting and sloped off down a path close to the bus stop, leaving me alone with Edmond again. A little way uphill there was a wide grass verge with a small pond and a grove of banana trees with views of the mountains in one direction and to the Indian Ocean in the other. The air smelt deliciously fresh, wiped clean by its long journey across the ocean. The afternoon sun caught the sugar cane and drew a dozen shades of green within the fronds. A light breeze came up, and made them whisper. It is a peaceful spot, at least.

When the other planters came in their carriages to Belle-vue to watch Edmond pollinate his vanilla orchids they included Sarrazin de Floris from nearby Saint-André. The De Floris name has been linked to the little Mexican flower ever since, and the family still grow some high grade vanilla. Surrounded by a cluster of ugly modern buildings in the centre of town they own a small wooden creole-style house and plantation called Maison de la Vanille. Tourists can visit the grounds and watch the curing process that produces the finest quality *Vanille Bourbon*.

On my way back to town, I stopped at St-André, where Alain de Floris offered me tea made with lemon grass for refreshment in the garden beside the neat wooden house. I had been to the plantation several times on successive visits to

Réunion, but this time I wanted to ask him about the lack of a decent memorial to Edmond.

'You know how these things are,' he said with a shrug. 'Politics.'

'Wouldn't it be good politics to commemorate a man like Albius?' I asked. De Floris shook his head.

'I'm not a politician. I don't have anything to do with such things. And a lot of the past is difficult in Réunion.'

For reasons I couldn't decipher, he also seemed reluctant to discuss his family's connections with vanilla, perhaps disavowing their links with the past. 'Things have changed, you know. Our family's name is still associated with vanilla here but we don't live by it now. Compared to the old days production is small and we hardly export anything, even though the quality is still good. We sell it locally, but remember in 1928 the island sent over a hundred tonnes to Europe, and even after the Second World War seventy to eighty tonnes was a good year. But no one needs to grow vanilla on the island now,' De Floris explained. 'People don't want to work in the fields, and they don't need to. And, in any case, growing and curing vanilla is not so easy, it takes a lot of practice.'

There was a De Floris aboard Marchant's ship when the first vanilla plants arrived from Paris in 1822. Thirty years later, thanks to Edmond Albius's newly discovered technique, he was growing commercially productive vines at St-André. In collaboration with another eminent resident of the town, a lawyer named Ernest Loupy, they began experimenting with a new method of blanching the vanilla beans before they were dried. Traditionally, the Mexican vanilla growers had simply relied on the sun to cure the fruit, but the Loupy–De Floris method was to use hot water to speed up the process. By experimenting they discovered that when the beans were dipped for two to three minutes in water that was between 60 and 70°C, they would start to turn brown almost immediately. It was another important step on the road to producing the perfect Bourbon bean.

After tea, Alain de Floris left me to explore the grounds. This was not the season for vanilla flowers, but there were wooden trays heaped with dark brown pods drying on the grass close to the long whitewashed stone building where the vanilla was cured. The contents of the trays glistened with their familiar oily sheen, the moist signal that the enzymes inside the pods were doing their work. As I stepped into the curing shed, I inhaled the rich sweet scent of Bourbon vanilla. This is what vanilla from Réunion, Madagascar and the Comoros is famous for: the sweet deep haylike notes that we associate with desserts and ice cream.

Inside the shed the air felt cool and dry, with dozens more wooden trays each about three feet long and two feet wide laid out in neat rows on the cement floor. Tall wooden shutters along one wall of the shed had been opened to the breeze, while high doors led out onto the verandah on the other. At the far end there was a simple wooden trestle table, where a man in a straw hat sat sorting loose vanilla beans from a wicker basket at his side. His name was Jean-Patric Baraka and he told me that he was a 'matchmaker', one of the men who fertilize the vanilla orchids by hand between October and December, the flowering season. His features were small and neat, like his fingers, which continually dipped into the basket of pods as we spoke. Each bean was held flat against a ruler affixed to the surface of the table, and then placed in a compartmentalized tray, something like an old sorting box for mail with pigeonholes marked out with numbers. Each number related to the length of the beans it contained. According to the tray, the maximum length could be twenty-four centimetres, though Jean-Patric said fifteen or sixteen was considered good. He spoke in heavily accented creole, and shyly told me he was happiest speaking to people like me, foreigners who didn't mind that his French was imperfect. 'We are in the same boat,' I replied, and his features crinkled into a broad smile.

When Jean-Patric had enough beans in a compartment he would take them and sort them into bundles of one hundred, tying them tightly with cord. These neat bundles would then be placed inside sturdy wooden chests at one end of the drying room and locked tight with a brass padlock.

'This is the best vanilla in the world,' Jean-Patric explained proudly. 'You can keep it in a jar for twenty years and it will be as good as new when you want to use it.'

I picked up one of the biggest pods and ran its length between my fingers. Fully ten inches long, plump, sensual and full of aroma, it was slightly greasy to the touch. Like oiled leather, and almost black in colour, it bore no blemishes or scratches. It was the finest quality I had ever seen.

In the nineteenth century, French growers developed a large vocabulary to cover the different grades of bean they produced. In the same way that people joke that Eskimos have a dozen words for snow, the vanilla dealers have refined the categorization of their beans into an art. First they would break down the beans into first, second or third grade, and fourth grade known simply as 'ordinary'. Size, plumpness and even how straight the beans are all have an effect upon what the buyers will pay. Then they would subdivide those categories according to the appearance of the beans, even though minute cosmetic details might have no relevance to their flavour component. It resulted in a bewildering array of sub-categories relating to the different blemishes the fruits could display. Beans could be described as 'scratched', 'rubbed', 'stained', 'dry', 'split', 'bitten' (by an insect) and 'pitted'. Beans might also be 'pockmarked' or 'musty', and even 'snailed' (*escargotée*) if they showed a fine tracery of lines resembling the tracks of a tiny mollusc. Another category of vanilla is known as *givré*, from the French word for rime, or hoar frost. The term describes the effect produced at a late stage of fermentation, where the vanilla beans sprout fine needle shaped hairs of crystallized vanillin – one of the principal chemicals that produce its flavour. Such beans are among the most valuable in the world, bearing on their skin the evidence that they will have a strong flavour, and that they have been left to mature for at least eight months.

'Look.' Jean-Patric took the pod from my hand and deftly tied a knot in it. 'It doesn't split or tear. That shows it's perfectly cured.'

The wooden chests where the bundles were being packed could each hold 150 kilograms of the very best black Bourbon beans. Filled with gourmet-grade beans the boxes could be worth $75,000. 'Do you lock these chests up at night?' I asked.

Jean-Patric nodded vigorously. 'Oh yes, *le patron* is very careful. And you see, each box has a brass padlock too.'

I was curious to know if Jean-Patric understood why the gourmet-grade beans were so valuable. 'Because of the work involved,' he explained calmly. 'I am over forty years old, but I am the youngest of the matchmakers; it is a dying craft. The young people here are not interested in doing such work. You know' – he lowered his voice as though divulging a secret – 'each bean will be handled perhaps twenty-five times before it reaches the shops. And there are so many steps along the way. There is the fertilization, the picking, then the killing in the hot water. Then we must wrap the beans for twelve hours to sweat. This is where it turns brown, but all the time you have to watch it like a small child. You see, what with the pollinating, the growing and then the curing – it is just like making a baby!'

After dipping, and then sweating for twelve hours, Jean-Patric explained that the beans are laid out in the sun to dry again, a process that has to be carefully monitored – too much sun will dry them too rapidly, while too little will increase the chance of mould. Then they must be brought inside to dry in the shade for a month, being sorted and checked daily for moisture content and health. The French call this the *triage*, just like the term for sorting and prioritizing casualties on a battlefield. Before the beans can be measured and bundled they need to go into drying boxes for another eight months, and all the while they are shrinking as they lose their original moisture, so that five or six kilograms of green beans will weigh just one kilogram when dried. The amount of volume lost is also something that depends on the skill of the curer, and trying to speed up or slow down the process can spoil the whole crop. Beans are sometimes massaged to keep them straight as they dry out, since a curved bean will be less valuable. By the time the finished beans are shipped to the brokers in the USA or Europe it will have been eighteen or nineteen months since they first began growing on the vine.

Not all of Réunion's vanilla growers are as steeped in the history of the plant as the De Floris family. On the southeasternmost corner of the island the coastal road runs directly beneath the slopes of Piton de la Fournaise, one of the world's most active volcanoes. It keeps most people away from farming the verdant soil north of the town of St-Philippe. They call this the Scorched Land, where molten lava has been ejected from the furnace eight thousand feet above, cutting a swathe through the coastal road more than once in recent years. The pumice-strewn scree is a black scar on the island's flank. This is still the windy coast, and savage seas beat against the rocks sending spouts of spray up over the road in places. The combination of the elements and the rocky cliffs beset by the vast southern ocean, gives this part of Réunion a wild, untamed atmosphere.

One day, not far from St-Philippe, with hard rain sweeping in from the east and darkening the skies ahead of me, I spotted a small hand-painted sign at the edge of the road. It was advertising vanilla for sale, and it belonged to a bone-thin man with large marmoset eyes called Aimé Leichnig, whose tiny garage was also his vanilla workshop. We stood in the doorway watching the rain fall and he told me that his grandfather had taught him how to cure vanilla. He used the plant to make perfumes as well, and the garage had been laid out as a miniature laboratory. Vanilla-perfumed toiletries and liqueurs were on display in modest quantities. In common with other farmers at this end of the island he grew his vines in the forest, using wild natural supporting plants rather than planting them in neat artificial rows. The vanilla pods he produced were not as fine as those at the De Floris house, but Aimé Leichnig handled them with love. I wondered if he could earn a good living at his small-scale business. He shook his head slowly, as if he were explaining something to a fool. 'Vanilla is part of me. This is simply what I *must* do, I can't help it.'

Leichnig's words reminded me of something an American vanilla broker once said to me. 'Be careful,' he warned. 'This little plant is addictive. If you start following it around the world it'll get a grip on you and it won't let go.'

I have met obsession and passion more than once on my journey. Although they guard their commercial secrets well, vanilla growers, buyers and dealers are usually happy to talk about their arcane trade. Dealing in vanilla is an intensive occupation. Thanks to the volatility of the world market, the international buyers need to be extremely vigilant, always on the alert for news that might affect next season's price. They also need to juggle the different seasons in their heads – remembering that, for example, in Mexico the vines will flower between March and May, while in Madagascar they flower from October to January, and in Tahiti between July and October. Sometimes there will be two flowering seasons in each location, producing a second crop. In Madagascar the harvest will be in mid-June through to August, while in Indonesia it will run from March until July. And while each region has a different flowering season, there are other variables to consider. In Indonesia the beans will be picked after only three or four months on the vine, as opposed to the ideal eight or nine months' growth in the Indian Ocean. The strength of the flowering season will also affect how many kilograms of dried beans are likely to be available after curing, and the experienced traders must base their advance prices on estimates of supply and demand. Frequent visits to the producing countries are a necessity. At a dinner in Paris one evening the wife of a broker confided: 'He gets that look on his face sometimes. I could be telling him I want a divorce, but I know I'm wasting my breath – he's not really listening because he's off in his vanilla world.'

In Southern California there is a woman who calls herself the 'Vanilla Queen'. She signs her letters 'VQ', and has been known to attend industrial food fairs wearing her Vanilla Queen regalia. In a white dress from Mexico and with a garland of woven vanilla in her hair, she carries a 'vanilla wand' with which she conveys her blessings. Her name is Patricia Rain, and she is a passionate advocate of the plant and its uses, especially in cooking.

Behind her Vanilla Queen façade, Patricia is an anthropologist and a successful cookbook author. Some years ago, and much to the annoyance of some of the larger vanilla dealers, she had the foresight to register her own website address as vanilla.com. The website informs visitors that it is 'an interactive e-commerce business dedicated to vanilla information and education as well as the sale of vanilla and vanilla value-added products'. In addition the Vanilla Queen reveals that the problems of deforestation in the tropics are one factor in promoting harmful climate change. As part of her mission, the VQ wants to encourage people to buy 'natural, consciously grown products to provide more economic opportunities for people living in the tropical band on either side of our Equator'. This in turn may help to slow down the environmental degradation caused by poor agricultural practices, especially the disastrous effects of clear-cutting the forests to create grazing land for cattle. The website also states that the 'Vanilla.Company has a mission to further the expanding renaissance of vanilla.'

While on a visit to Los Angeles, I took the opportunity to fly up to San José for an audience with the VQ. The scenic drive over the hills through thick pine forests to the seaside town of Santa Cruz put me in a suitably mellow frame of mind. It is a surfers' town, and has a large number of resident artists, though the ambience is changing as the creative community is gradually being displaced by computer specialists spilling out from nearby Silicon Valley. Although we had never met, Patricia welcomed me with a Californian hug and led me into her small neat house, ushering me into the dining room where there was a table laid with gleaming china and polished cutlery. There were also plates of sliced Californian peaches, raspberries and strawberries all freshly picked from her garden. Within a few minutes, Patricia had produced tea and warm vanilla scones from the kitchen.

'I just had to bake you something that an English person

would enjoy!' she enthused. The house smelt of vanilla, although Patricia confessed that the scones had been cooked with a ready-made mix from the supermarket. 'I'm sorry, I've been so busy with one thing and another, I meant to mix up my own recipe but there just wasn't time.'

After tea, and the very tasty scones, Patricia brought out her photograph albums and showed me her pictures of Mexico, describing her own journey to the vanilla growing regions and her affection for the people she met there. 'I suppose I'm just an old hippie,' she laughed. 'But I fell in love with Mexico and the farmers down there. Something has to be done to help them get a better price for their vanilla – you know they have an absolutely fabulous product but it's so difficult for them to get organized and market it properly.'

Patricia sells vanilla, mostly through her Internet-based business, but she also has a heartfelt desire somehow to educate the Mexican farmers and the *beneficiadores* who buy the green beans for curing. Eventually, she hopes that a fairer relationship between the two can be established. 'It's so, so difficult,' she sighed. 'But we have to try. I've written to [Mexico's] President Fox several times to try to get him interested in helping the vanilla growers. But' – she shook her head, with what seemed like genuine disbelief – 'he hasn't yet replied.'

All of the big vanilla dealers know the Vanilla Queen, and some of them are wary of her socially responsible attitude to vanilla buying and her campaign to get the farmers a better deal. One of the biggest buyers told me the Vanilla Queen made him nervous because she claimed she could see that he possessed a 'very violet aura'. Some vanilla dealers are more prosaic in their doubts; they say they fear the VQ's social mission will push up the price of natural vanilla by giving the farmers too much control of their own crop.

As we talked, Patricia took me into her vanilla storeroom and showed me some of her products. Somehow, I was soon possessed of the knowledge that in true Californian tradition Patricia had been married three times, and I knew what had led to each of her divorces. The details of her life came spilling out as she led me around the store, pointing out soaps and candles, preserves and potions, all scented with vanilla. And there were boxes of beans.

'These are Mexican. Smell them – aren't they wonderful? Now, here are some of the Tahitian – do you get the floral aroma – it's magical, isn't it?'

I plucked up the courage to ask Patricia about her Vanilla Queen regalia. 'Oh, don't say you've heard about that! Maybe the wand wasn't such a wise idea.' She laughed loudly, colouring slightly. 'But I don't mind what people say, the fact is I get noticed and it's just a bit of fun. We need more fun in the world, don't you agree?'

Late that evening I returned to Los Angeles. Somewhat unexpectedly, and uncharacteristically, the friend I was staying with had driven to the airport to meet me in person. 'I had a phone call from a lady called Patricia,' he explained sheepishly. 'She told me that it wouldn't be kind to let you get a taxi into town on your own. So here I am.'

10. Empress of Tahiti

Above the Tropic of Capricorn the islands stretch in an arc as broad as western Europe from *Henua Enana* — the Land of Men — to *Rapa Nui* — the Navel of the World. Their cultures span the ocean from Hawaii to New Zealand, and ever since Samuel Wallis became the first European to reach Tahiti in 1767, the islands have lured men in search of all manner of treasure from the other side of the globe. Within a couple of years the French explorer Louis-Antoine de Bougainville had also reached Tahiti, and on his return to France word soon spread about these beautiful islands where men and women were seemingly unhampered by narrow morals. The three voyages of Captain Cook (1768–71, 1772–5 and 1776–9) fuelled the western appetite for tales from the South Seas. The myth of an earthly paradise was born, and still endures.

Perhaps Polynesia's greatest prize is the promise of an escape from everyday life, a feeling I entirely understand. It is the same syndrome that led me towards the Indian Ocean. For me, Polynesia is much more a place of the imagination, a cognitive puzzle where I cannot help but mix reality with a score of half remembered cinema and literary images implanted in the brain. Being there never seems quite real; it has become a dreamscape of breadfruit and bougainvillaea, pearl divers and giant clams.

I saw humpback whales close inshore as my aeroplane descended towards Faa'a airport on Tahiti. It was a mother and her calf, nestling side by side and so close to the land that the whalers who flocked to the port of Papeete in the nineteenth century could have picked them off from shore. Herman Melville was one of them, and Americans still come to Papeete by boat, though they arrive on cruise liners, not Boston whaling ships. Melville deserted the clipper *Acushnet* here in 1840, and ended up in gaol on Tahiti for a short time. Fifty years ahead of Gauguin, Melville had fallen for the seductive charms of the remote Marquesas, spending several months there among the friendly natives. His sojourn led to his first major successes, *Typee: a Peep at Polynesian Life* (1846) and *Omoo: a Narrative of the South Seas* the following year, both of which were more successful during his lifetime than *Moby Dick*. The books began a literary tradition that continued with Robert Louis Stevenson's *In the South Seas* (1896), and Rupert Brooke's poem 'Tiare Tahiti' (1915) among many. Brooke's poem was inspired by his own Tahitian love affair with a woman named Mamua, leading him to write of 'whispering scents that stray, about the idle warm lagoon'.

At the airport there were tourists queuing for the short flight to Titiaroa, a relatively undistinguished atoll made famous by its association with another man who fell under the spell of swaying palms. Enamoured with Tahiti after making *Mutiny on the Bounty* in 1962, Marlon Brando acquired the island and lived there for some years with the actress Tarita Terepaia who had played 'Maimiti' in the film. Curiously, his first wife, Movita Castaneda, though not Tahitian, had played the part of 'Tehanni' in the 1935 version of the same film, the rather superior screenplay starring Clark Gable as Fletcher Christian, and Charles Laughton as Captain Bligh.

My own obsession led me by boat to the island of Raiatea, past its sister Taha'a and the seductively named bays of Tapuamu and Hurepiti, then across the three-mile passage of Tearearahi to reach the northern tip of the island. The tiny port of Uturoa is known as the capital of the Leeward Isles, the group northeast of Tahiti, which also includes the honeymooner-friendly Bora Bora. Unlike Bora, Raiatea has no Club Méditerranée, no Bounty Pizzeria, no miniature submarine rides or Nemo's World diving centre. Raiatea is more suited to gods and legends, and it was once the main stopping-off point for the earliest Polynesian navigators, the Maori, whose blue water empire stretched from Hawaii in the north to New Zealand in the southwest. They called it 'sacred Raiatea', and built one of their most important ritual sites here, the great stone meeting place, the royal *marae* of Taputaputea on its shores. It is also one of the most fertile spots in Polynesia, and along with Taha'a, it is home to *Vanilla tahitensis*.

At the Taha'a Pearl Beach Resort and Spa the honeymooners wrapped themselves in their beach towels and frowned as the lagoon surrounding their tiny atoll rippled in the breeze. The wind is called *mara'amu*, the south-easterly that brings Tahiti and the Society Islands, to which Taha'a belongs, their winter. In July and August the *mara'amu* lowers the temperature by a few degrees and gives the vanilla vines the shock to the system that causes them to burst into flower. From the beach I could see the crinkle-cut silhouette of Bora Bora on the horizon, with Mount Otemanu, her mysterious green peak, rising eight hundred metres above the Pacific. They used to grow vanilla over on Bora Bora, but now tourism dominates the economy of the island. Here on Taha'a, thirty miles south, they still grow vanilla, and tourism has yet to make an impact, largely due to an absence of good beaches. The Pearl Beach Resort is the first hotel to offer luxury accommodation to rival anything on Bora Bora, but Taha'a itself has no other specific tourist attractions. Didier Rougé-Biscay, the manager of the new hotel, extended his lips into a French pout when I said Bora Bora looked beautiful.

'Yes, but you already have seen the best of it — the view from here allows her to retain her charm. But the atmosphere over there is not what it was — too many hotels,' he said without irony. 'Too many tourists in general, the islanders are tired and irritable nowadays. But over here Taha'a is like Bora fifty years ago; you still feel something of the real Polynesia.'

The Pearl Resort isn't actually on Taha'a. Its sixty over-water suites have been built on stilts at one edge of a tiny *motu*, or islet, half a mile offshore on the edge of the lagoon that surrounds Taha'a and the almost adjoining island of Raiatea. Neither island has been much developed for tourism, and the Pearl Beach is one of the most beautiful locations imaginable for an hotel. Unlike all the other visitors to the resort, I came here because Taha'a produces more than two-thirds of all the vanilla grown in Tahiti. At the Pearl Resort, Didier was very proud of his new Restaurant Vanille, where the chef, freshly arrived from Paris, had created a menu featuring as many local ingredients as possible. Including freshly cured vanilla from Taha'a.

That night I sat alone at my table surrounded by honeymooners dining by candlelight, which flickered dramatically under the attentions of the *mara'amu*. As if my solitary romantic status wasn't enough, the evening was enlivened by the arrival of a troupe of young girls from Taha'a to demonstrate their mesmerizing high-speed-hip-twitching-breast-bouncing-eyelid-fluttering Polynesian dances. My sensual appetites would need to be satisfied by the food.

Didier had introduced me to the chef, Veronique Melloul, and I told her that I was particularly interested in Tahitian vanilla. 'It is very different from the Bourbon flavour,' she explained. 'Much more suited for savoury dishes in my opinion, but wait until dinner, and you will see how I use it.'

Veronique did not disappoint. As the Polynesians performed their highly physical *oteas* and *upa upas* I was presented with duck *foie gras* flavoured with Taha'a vanilla served with sweet papaya chutney and a peppery rocket salad with thyme dressing. In the after-taste of the vanilla there was a hint of . . . what was it? I couldn't detect the customary creamy brown flavour of Bourbon vanilla. This was more like liquorice, or perhaps warm cherry. Didier appeared at my elbow with a chilled bottle of Pouligny Montrachet Bouchard. 'You will be having the grilled fish – this will be a good choice, *non*?' *Oui*.

The *Mahi Mahi* – dorado – had been grilled to perfection, its firm white flesh still moist and slightly sweet to the tongue. Veronique had pricked the surface of the flesh with vanilla, the delicate aniseed taste softened further as it mingled with a light emulsion of coconut milk. Accompanying the fish was a golden brown toasted plantain, its singed sweetness offset by a daub of finely puréed pumpkin dusted with cinnamon and almond. After a suitable pause, and time to watch a little more hip-swaying from the extremely fit maidens, I was sipping iced Irish coffee topped with vanilla cappuccino cream.

Tahitian vanilla shares many of the same qualities as Bourbon vanilla, but it has a unique aroma and flavour. The parfumiers and gourmets call it a floral note – the faintly aniseed scent they describe as 'heliotropin' or 'piperonal', and which is technically known to chemists as a phenolic aldehyde. Chefs take advantage of this rich floral flavour by combining Tahitian vanilla with fruit filled desserts. No matter how they are cured, or how long they are stored, Tahitian beans never produce a frosting of white vanillin crystals on their surface. Aside from its idiosyncratic chemistry, Tahitian vanilla is part of another botanical mystery.

As in the Indian Ocean, it was French ships that brought the plant to the South Sea islands, this time from the Philippines: islands which had themselves received various species of the plant from Spanish merchant ships travelling to and from Mexico. In the sixteenth and seventeenth centuries, under the Spanish Crown, Manila had been governed as a dependency of New Spain. Precious cargoes of mother of pearl, damask, chinaware and silks obtained from trade with China were then taken from Manila to Acapulco on Mexico's Pacific coast, and then hauled overland to Veracruz to take ship for Europe. In turn, silver, plants, cattle and spices from the Spanish possessions in Central America were sent in the other direction.

In 1848 the French commander in the Pacific, Admiral Ferdinand-Alphonse Hamelin, delivered several dozen specimens described as '*Vanilla aromatica*' to the Tahitian governor's garden at Papeete from Manila. Soon afterwards, Admiral Louis Bonard is credited with introducing more plants, also from the Philippines, but this time described as *Vanilla planifolia*. Confusion stems from the fact that *Vanilla aromatica* is no longer recognized as a valid botanical name, having often been mistakenly used to describe *V. planifolia* and other close relatives. However, the plants found in Tahiti are now classified as an entirely separate sub-species, *Vanilla tahitensis*.

In Mexico the botanist Miguel Soto had told me that he believed it highly likely that the Tahitian species is a hybrid formed from two closely related Central American species (probably *V. planifolia* and *V. odorata*) but until now their precise identity remains unknown. Even under laboratory conditions, he said, the identifiable genetic differences between these 'parents' and their 'offspring' are likely to be tiny.

Some of the differences between the Tahitian and the Bourbon beans can be seen with the naked eye, but they are even more obvious to the nose. The fruits of *tahitensis* are shorter that their Mexican cousins, and they are less redolent of vanillin when cured. The outer skin of the pods is thicker, and there are fewer seeds inside. They have another peculiarity – they do not split apart when fully mature on the vine, and therefore do not need to be picked as early as the other species.

Most chefs are unaware of the variations in the aroma and taste of the different varieties of vanilla. They tend to classify vanilla quality according to the price they pay for the beans – and rely on the honesty of the brokers who supply them. It is common for chefs to believe they are buying Bourbon beans, when they may in fact be getting an inferior Indonesian variety with very similar characteristics. Due to their scarcity, Tahitian beans have always been more valuable than other varieties, but the islands produce only seven or eight tonnes of their own vanilla each year, and the majority of that crop goes into local products. Like Mexico, the vanilla growers of Tahiti have been through a boom and bust cycle of production, which at times offered the islands excellent revenues. In 1939, Tahiti was able to export more than two hundred tonnes of vanilla, three times as much as Réunion, and more than half the amount produced by Madagascar. During the Second World War, production fell off dramatically but gradually recovered in the 1950s when as much as three hundred tonnes of cured beans reached the international market.

On the outskirts of Papeete, Tahiti's sprawling capital, I visited Marc Jones, a man obsessed with experimenting with the taste of vanilla. Patricia, the Vanilla Queen, had given me his telephone number and within minutes of calling him he was arranging to take me on a tour of his vanilla products business. I tried to tell him that I might not be in the most alert frame of mind having just endured the twenty-three-hour flight from London. 'Hey, don't even think about being tired, buddy! You need a beer, that's the cure for jetlag. I'll pick you up in ten minutes.'

In person, Marc was as full of energy as his telephone manner implied. Without getting out of the car he proffered a firm handshake through the window. 'Climb in, we'll go get you that beer.'

He drove along the coast away from Papeete turning off the main road towards the industrial zone known as Punaruu. Marc stopped outside a modern building decorated with the words Ariki Boutique and a picture of a Tahitian chief adorned with full-body tattoos on the board outside. There were metal tables and chairs outside and a doorway leading into a small takeaway shop selling hamburgers, chips and ice cream. Surrounded by warehouses that were all closed up for the weekend, it seemed like an odd place for a food shop, but while we sat outside a steady stream of customers drove up and ordered snacks. Marc gave me a whirlwind tour of his merchandise: 'Here, look we're doing these T-shirts with vanilla bean designs – whaddya think? Good – or not good? . . . Here's something else – vanilla-flavoured tea, coffee, liqueurs – you name it we're doing it! . . . Now, how about that beer?'

I asked if I could take tea instead. 'Are you sure? Beer will do you good. You really want tea? That's OK – we can do tea.

No problem. But what you really need to try is this – come with me.'

Marc moved outside again shouting instructions to the staff at the food counter to make me some tea. From the cold chest outside he filled a cornet with a mound of what looked like ice cream, but was in fact frozen yoghurt flavoured with local vanilla. 'Isn't that great?' It was.

While I consumed vanilla tea, Marc drank iced beer and explained his love for Tahiti and the vanilla business, although he has also diversified into fast food, macadamia nuts, T-shirts and flavoured liqueurs. 'I'll try anything,' he laughed. 'I've made mistakes, sure, but I'm learning all the time.'

I told Marc that I had come to Tahiti not just in search of vanilla, but also to scuba dive. We shared a love for the sea, and he talked about the best places to see sharks around the outer islands. Going to Taha'a was definitely a good idea, but he recommended a visit to Raiatea too, where he had a business associate called Madame Chane. 'You want to meet her,' he said with a serious look. 'She's the reason I'm here today. She's –' he hesitated a moment – 'she's a human being.'

I told him that I had a list of other names, dealers in vanilla who had promised to meet me during my visit.

'Like who?'

I mentioned a name. 'He's an asshole!'

Another name. 'He's a prick.'

'Are they your competitors?'

'Nah, that's not it. They think they know things. They all want to talk. But then look at me, I'm talking!' Marc shook his head and laughed. 'I talk too much. Me too, I'm just an asshole. Just a businessman. They're all pricks. You're a clever guy, you'll see.'

The throaty roar of an engine drowned out our conversation and Marc sprang up from the table as a Ford Mustang drew up outside the Ariki store, with its engine revving. The car was painted canary yellow, and a huge Tahitian man with an enormous pot belly levered himself out of the driving seat. He shook hands with Marc, and sauntered into the shop to order a burger.

'Man, you gotta' see this, come here Tim.'

Marc walked around the car several times admiring its paintwork. The owner returned, munching on his food so that grease trickled down his chin as he talked. He told Marc he had just fitted the yellow beast with a brand new engine too, imported specially from Australia. 'Cost money, eh?' said Marc.

'Yeah. Money,' the fat man answered, rubbing his greasy fingers together.

The man drove off in a cloud of sound and Marc shook his head sagely as he watched him go. 'Money's bad, man. You'll find out. Oh, yeah. Money's a shitty thing. It's a *bad* thing. Money doesn't matter. People matter, that's what Tahiti taught me.'

Marc forced me to eat another frozen yoghurt as he told me about his life on the island. Originally from the USA, he had been here twenty years, and had married a Tahitian woman, a relative of Madame Chane.

'I tried to go back to the States once,' he confessed. 'I cried, man. I just cried when I sat on that aeroplane and tried to leave. Madame Chane, she's a real human being – she bankrolled me when I started out. She didn't have to help me, but she did. That's why you gotta' meet her.'

I asked him about his dealings with Patricia, the Vanilla Queen, from California. 'Hey, you've met the queen. But now you're gonna meet the empress. You see. Madame Chane is the real thing. Nobody knows vanilla like she does. You gotta' take her a gift. Then she'll talk to you.'

'What kind of thing?'

'Don't worry, I'll give you some stuff.' Marc went back into the Ariki Boutique and emerged with an armful of merchandise. He handed over four T-shirts, a bottle of vanilla liqueur, several packets of his own brand of vanilla-flavoured coffee, some tea and several sachets of vanilla beans.

'I can't take all this stuff,' I protested at his generosity. 'Surely Madame Chane doesn't need vanilla?'

'No, just give her a shirt from me. That'll be cool. Tell her I told you she was the Empress. Give her whatever you like, and give the rest of the stuff to whoever you like. Take it home, I don't care – it's a gift. You're a human being.'

Today, Uturoa boasts that it is the largest town in French Polynesia outside Papeete. Once I reached Raiatea, Madame Chane had given me explicit directions, and said that if I got lost – as she put it – *en ville*, I could always ask someone how to reach the *Maison Vanira* – the Vanilla House. What she hadn't explained was that Uturoa only possesses about six streets, so getting lost wasn't really a possibility.

There were just two thoroughfares, one facing the yacht marina and behind it, separated from the seafront by a short row of shops, a longer and wider main street. This busier route led me past the modern post office, a pharmacy and a supermarket. The buildings were mainly quite unattractive cement blocks with overhanging awnings shading the pavements from sun and rain. One or two older wooden buildings survived, like old teeth surrounded by plastic dentures. They were bleached and weathered by the sun with tall slim doorways leading into cool interiors. The main attractions in Uturoa seemed to be the Aurora furniture store — '*tout pour votre confort*' — and the Galeries Fuchon advertising marine engines, waterproof paint and fishing supplies. Just past the Jade Garden Chinese restaurant stood the oldest and shabbiest building on the street decorated with a red and white signboard advertising Coca-Cola, and above it in smaller lettering the words Maison Vanira. The first floor windows were grimy, obscured by thick dust and with many of the panes cracked and broken. There were no windows at street level, just plain undecorated wooden panels covering the façade, with a pair of doors leading into a dimly lit room with a bare concrete floor. I began to question whether Marc Jones had been too fulsome in describing the owner as an empress.

Inside the gloomy edifice there was very little evidence that this was any kind of shop. Tucked into one ill-lit corner there was just one small glass-fronted display case containing half a dozen rather dusty bottles of vanilla extract, a single bottle of *Monoi Tahiti* perfume and several bars of dark brown vanilla-scented soap. Beside the stand stood a rickety wooden table where a Tahitian woman with the dimensions of a Sumo wrestler was sorting through a bundle of cured vanilla beans. Behind her there was an archway leading into a back office area, where I could see a desk completely submerged in papers. As I approached the table a short fierce-looking Chinese woman appeared from behind the archway and stared at me. She had wiry grey hair which stood up all around her head as if it had been furiously back-combed, and she wore a purple cotton smock dress decorated with bright yellow flowers. With both hands she clutched a voluminous straw handbag and as I introduced myself she rocked back and forth on her heels, swinging the bag against her knees.

'Madame Chane?'

The woman nodded, her chin bobbing up and down with short powerful movements, but she didn't speak. I handed her one of the shirts Marc had donated, and she placed it on her table without opening it. Then I tried asking if she could show me any of her stock, which I said I knew to be of the very best quality. Seemingly unimpressed by the compliment, she simply nodded again, and threw a disparaging glance at the table where the Tahitian woman was sorting the beans. 'There, vanilla.'

I examined a few of the beans, saying how well they had been cured. But it was clear Madame Chane wasn't ready to talk. Whatever I said she simply flicked her head back and sniffed. I began to wonder if she understood anything I was saying.

'We go now,' she said decisively after a few more moments of rocking. Then she gave some instructions to the woman, and fluttered the fingers of one hand at me with a palm downwards motion to follow her outside. There was a dusty estate car parked on the street nearby and she climbed in, pulling out into the traffic without a backward glance. The car smelt strongly of vanilla. We took a slow tour of Uturoa. I was glad of the sedate pace, as Madame Chane was barely tall enough to see over the steering wheel of her car. Whatever I said, I couldn't turn her attention to vanilla. 'Post office,' she declaimed in her staccato style as we passed it. 'Ferry.' 'Town Hall.'

The entire circuit of Uturoa, complete with one-word commentaries on all of the main buildings, took no more than five or six minutes, and then we headed out of town where Madame Chane parked outside the island's only smart hotel, the Hawaiki Nui. 'We eat lunch.' It was more of a statement than an invitation.

The restaurant was empty, but Madame Chane chose a table in one corner of the room. 'More private,' she said quietly. Each time our waiter approached the table she would stop talking and begin the nodding motion with her chin. She had another mannerism which involved a problem with her upper front teeth. At least two of them appeared to be false, and when she did speak in sentences of more than a couple of words they tended to slip. She would then throw her head back and click the teeth back into place with a voluble sucking sound. Once we were alone she admitted that she hadn't wanted to discuss anything to do with her business in front of her staff.

'I can't talk about vanilla in front of those people,' she whispered, indicating the Tahitian restaurant staff.

'Why not?'

'The Tahitians are . . . *fiu*.' She used a local expression, difficult to translate, which combines a sense of fecklessness, laziness and ennui. But, Madame Chane added, 'Talking about vanilla can also be dangerous. It got my brother killed.'

'How?' I asked, startled at this sudden and completely unexpected revelation.

'*Ass-ass-iné*,' she hissed, stretching the word out to double its natural length. The effect was dramatic, combined with a wild rolling of the eyes and a triple dose of clicking and sucking as the denture failed to cope with the extra sibilance she had injected into the word.

She explained that a few years earlier, her youngest brother, Robert, had been robbed and beaten to death at the Maison Vanira after it became known that he had a large consignment of vanilla beans on the premises. The murderer had been a Tahitian. Like most ethnic Chinese in the islands she didn't classify herself as Tahitian.

Jeanne Chane said she was in her seventies, although she

didn't want to name the precise year of her birth. She wanted me to know that she could trace her Chinese roots back to 1918 when her grandfather had sailed to the Society Islands from Canton. After succeeding as a local trader he had then sent for his son, Chan Fook Wan, who had made the long journey to the islands with his own family. As a child she had been brought up in a household filled with the smell of vanilla, a business she learned by a process of simple absorption. She remembered, at the age of five, sitting on the porch of the house with her grandmother and other women, massaging the oily beans to make them straight as they dried. The family's fortunes became centred upon the collecting and curing of the beans. As a successful shopkeeper, her grandfather built up the necessary capital to buy and sell large quantities of vanilla. Like many of the businessmen in Tahiti, her father succeeded, she believed, because the Tahitians themselves were not interested in working hard at any form of regular commerce. 'They fish, they make babies,' she chortled girlishly. '*Fiu!*'

After lunch we climbed back into the creaking station wagon and drove south towards a modern vanilla plantation that she said was being partly financed by European Union money. 'They want to encourage young people into growing vanilla,' she said dismissively. 'But they forget the price can fall from one year to the next.' Like most of the large traders, Madame Chane doesn't farm the vanilla herself; she buys the beans when they are cured and exports them. Other dealers told me she had cornered the market on Raiatea and Taha'a for years, buying more than half the vanilla available.

The plantation had been laid out under shade netting and the plants were being trained up concrete posts. There seemed to be no one in attendance, but Jeanne Chane walked between the rows of plants inspecting the leaves, stopping occasionally to nod vigorously in the direction of a plant she thought I should take a closer look at. There was a spot of mould at the base of one of the vines and this provoked an outburst of chin waggling and teeth sucking that left me in no doubt that she disapproved. We drove back to Maison Vanira, and she told the Tahitian woman at the trestle table that she could finish work for the day. Once we were alone she made me a cup of very strong tea and allowed me to sit in the back office. Among the mountain of papers on her ancient desk she quarried some dog-eared awards for vanilla production she had accumulated over the years.

There was a stained and tattered certificate of merit from the 1990 *Concours Vanille*, and a framed award stating that Madame Chane had been a six-time winner of the Ordre du Mérite Agricole in Papeete. Another from the Ministry of Agriculture and Fisheries attested to her contribution to maintaining the highest standards of vanilla curing. Among all the detritus I spotted a small souvenir packet of vanilla beans from the Maison de la Vanille, at Saint André in Réunion. It was brittle with age.

'I know this place very well,' I volunteered proudly, expecting her to be interested in the island on the other side of the world. I wondered if she knew the story of Edmond Albius.

'Ah!' Madame's chin stabbed the air and she screwed up her face in disgust. 'Not like Tahitian vanilla.'

As I was leaving, Madame Chane asked me if I had a wife. When I said I had, she rummaged in a drawer and found a small bright square of gift wrapping into which she folded a bar of vanilla soap. 'You take, you take,' she said, pressing it into my hand. It struck me that Madame Chane hadn't said whether she herself actually liked the smell of vanilla.

My question brought forth another bout of rapid nodding. '*Hah*,' she said, in a quiet matter of fact way, then stared at me impassively for several seconds. 'I am forced to.'

It was an avowal of duty, rather than something she felt. A very Chinese reply.

On the eastern shore of Taha'a I met Carlos Lo Sam Keow, one of the vanilla curers who supply dried beans to Jeanne Chane. She had told me that Carlos produced good quality beans, and it was clear that he had set up his system in a methodical way. At the back of his house he had a collection of old freezer chests, which he had adapted to use as storage boxes for his bundles of dried vanilla. Disconnected from their power supply they provided a perfect airtight means of keeping the beans in good condition until they were ready for shipping. To inspect the beans, Carlos led me outside and up a narrow wooden ladder onto the roof. On several dozen wooden trays there were hundreds of thousands of plump brown vanilla pods arranged in orderly rows on the corrugated tin. Carlos drove his fingers into the trays, turning and sifting the beans and offering me a handful to examine. They were slightly shorter than the beans I had seen so often in the Indian Ocean, but they were also thicker of girth. Even within Tahiti it seemed there were variations in the type of vanilla plants being harvested.

'We call these beans *tiarei*,' Carlos explained. 'They are the ones we have the most of here on Taha'a. But on Huahine island they have the *ha'apape* with narrower leaves and a longer bean, but not so much flavour.'

'Is it another species?'

'No one is sure!' Carlos grinned. 'There are a lot of theories about this plant, you know. They first noticed the difference in the *ha'apape* about a hundred years ago, so maybe it's just a local variation. There is another sort too, we call it *potiti* which has even shorter pods, but is definitely not as good for flavour or scent.'

Madame Chane had been understandably coy about the amount of vanilla she might buy in a year, but Carlos was happy to tell me what his own contribution to the island's turnover might be. 'Naturally, the price changes every season,' he said. 'But if you take last year as an example, I took about five tonnes of green beans. That gave me one and a half tonnes when they were cured and they cost me about $225,000. They sold for just about $300,000.'

Carlos's $75,000 profit seemed like a good return for what amounted to less than five months' work. Especially if world prices continued to rise.

'Yes,' he smiled. 'But I have a big family, and I need to have a lot of capital to stay in this business every year. The way prices are rising it's getting harder and harder to find the cash to buy the green beans.'

Carlos Lo Sam Keow was just one of Madame Chane's suppliers, but on Taha'a alone there are about three hundred and fifty small scale vanilla farmers. In Uturoa it was clear that the simplicity of the dilapidated Maison Vanira was in stark contrast to the amounts of money she needed to maintain her place as Tahiti's pre-eminent dealer in beans. Like so many Chinese traders in far-flung corners of the world she guards her secrets well, and has little in the way of visible material wealth to show for her labours. After her brother's murder it would seem like a wise course. Jeanne Chane reminded me very much of a Chinese family friend who always refuses gifts on birthdays and at Christmas. Her belongings are kept to a minimum and she has no time for extraneous possessions. Unlike Madame Chane, my friend is not a wealthy woman but she always insists on distributing small amounts of cash to her nearest and dearest. It is the only thing worth hoarding. And, like Madame Chane, my friend is never separated from her large handbag which always contains cash and her passport. Whatever else these Chinese matrons hide in their portmanteaux remains a secret.

In a small plantation on the edge of Hurepiti Bay, I pollinated my first vanilla orchid. The little flower was just one of a hundred blooming that morning and it would scarcely matter if I failed. Even so, it was an effort to keep my hand steady as I reached out to take the slender central petal. The finely serrated lip quivered between my thumb and forefinger. I pulled back the tissue, tearing the thin material to reveal the tip of the column inside, the whole structure slightly narrower than the rubber on the end of a pencil. Holding the remains of the lip under my left thumb I could finally see the organs that had rested within its shelter. There, at the tip of the column was the tiny bright yellow ball of pollen hanging from the bulging hood of the anther. Now, very gently, for the operation.

I had a toothpick-sized splinter in my right hand and I held it under the little flap that drooped over the stigma. With a minute upwards motion I raised the flap just a couple of millimetres, and pressed the anther with its yellow load down onto the upper surface of the exposed stigma. It was a soundless act, a physical union in which I held my breath. Then, it was done. I had succeeded, but I felt slightly uncomfortable, like some gauche medical student asked to perform a gynaecological procedure on an older woman. The whole process felt like a mixture of minor surgery and sex.

'Good, try again.'

The voice belonged to the plantation owner, the serendipitously named Alain Plantier, who hovered at my shoulder watching my every move. We walked between the rows of vines, looking for a flower at a convenient height, and one which was hanging at a readily accessible angle for my novice skills. This time I felt more confident, pulling the lip aside in one smooth movement. But I was too brutal, and in lifting the rostellum I pressed too hard. The anther and pollen ball snapped off. I realized what a skill it would be to fertilize two thousand vanilla orchids in a day, a tally the planters expected of their best workers in Madagascar.

Alain Plantier is a French yachtsman who arrived on Taha'a twenty years ago by boat and fell in love with it. He looks more like a painter than a farmer, with faded baggy cotton trousers rolled at the knee, a droopy pale blue cotton singlet and a soft straw hat with a decidedly feminine domed crown. Very un-macho pink-thonged flip-flops on his deeply tanned feet completed his outfit. Softly spoken, and difficult to gauge, he said he had a military background, and that he and his Italian wife, Cristina, had spent several years sailing the world until they found the perfect spot to stay. Now, he grows a little vanilla, and lives in a simple house just a few yards from the small jetty where he moors his yacht in Hurepiti Bay. On the shaded terrace of their house, Cristina served us from a large glass jug of water flavoured with lemon juice squeezed from the fruit in their own garden. On the wooden slats of the jetty a slim teenage boy with golden skin lay with his feet dangling in the water. 'My nephew,' Cristina explained. 'He is visiting for a few weeks. Some European company for our son.'

Bright light shone from the blue water as we talked. 'Do you like carambole?' Cristina asked. 'What do you call it in England?'

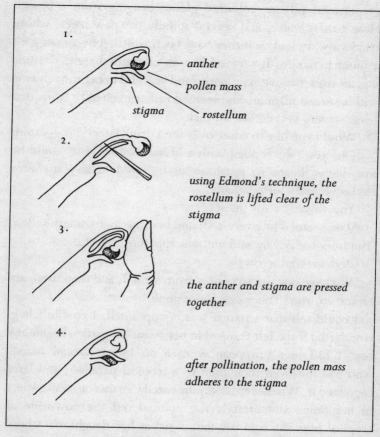

The manual pollination of the vanilla orchid is a delicate process

'Star fruit.'

I had to admit I had always found the soggy yellow-skinned things rather dull. 'Yes,' Cristina nodded indulgently. 'By the time they reach London they will be – but here, tell me if they taste like this.' She proffered some sweet slices and I realized I had misjudged the fleshy angular fruit. Nearby I could see grapefruits, fulvous coloured globes hanging from a branch close to the house, and several spindly pawpaw trees, whose trunks always look as if they have been whittled by a man with a blunt penknife. It seemed like an enchanted spot. Cristina was an attractive woman, petite and graceful in her movements with a serene manner. She seemed rather excited to learn that I was staying at the Taha'a Pearl.

'Would you like to come over for a drink later?' I suggested.

'Oh, yes,' she replied with a broad smile. 'That would be fun, we've heard so much about it, but I believe it's very exclusive, only for residents.'

'You would be my guests.'

Alain seemed uninterested, and became increasingly sullen. 'I'm busy today,' he said without apparent regret.

'Perhaps tomorrow?'

'We have our son to collect from school, and then there are errands to run. This week is not good.'

I could tell that Cristina was disappointed. I couldn't help wondering if she felt trapped in her beautiful garden beside the bay. I had met European women on Indian Ocean islands who had followed their men to a tropical paradise, and later regretted it. Whenever I complimented Cristina on some aspect of her home and lifestyle she pointed out the downside of tropical life. She told me that a girl at her daughter's school had died of Dengue fever, and that living in paradise was not as easy as it might seem. I compared some of my own experiences of living in Seychelles, and Cristina nodded. 'So, you understand.'

'Do call me at the hotel if you change your mind,' I offered.

Alain drove me back to the jetty at Tapuamu to catch the boat back to the hotel. We passed fields of taro, their giant leaves on rhubarb-pink stalks creating a carpet three feet off the ground. There were plantations of *nono* trees (*Morinda citrifolia*) too, their ugly green fruit shaped like potatoes but soft as rotting flesh to the touch when ripe. I knew the fruit from Seychelles, but couldn't resist stopping to pick up one to take a sniff. The scent is indescribably foul, a combination of truly bad soft cheese and unwashed socks with a hint of dead rodent. It reminded me of a cat my mother once owned when I was small. My sister and I used to dare each other to smell the cat's breath, which we decided after extensive experimentation could only be described as 'yellow'. In Tahiti, growing the *nono* has become a lucrative business, since it is believed to have almost miraculous medical value, especially in the USA where some people believe it is anti-carcinogenic. To make the juice more palatable it is mixed with other flavours. The Tahitians have long used the fruit as a poultice for victims of stone-fish poisoning, and they will sometimes eat the noisome flesh as a general tonic.

We drove over the high ridge overlooking the deepwater bay at Ha'amene. Alain stopped his jeep and fetched a machete from the boot, expertly slicing the top from a fresh coconut so that I could drink while we took in the view. The bay was a sliver of bright blue water cutting into the rumpled green flanks of the land. Alain sat down and pushed his straw hat back to mop his brow. He seemed to relax a little as we talked, and there was no trace of his earlier bad mood. 'I could never go back to Europe,' he said suddenly. 'Everything adapts to Tahiti, even the vanilla has changed its chemistry here.'

We sat quietly for a time and he would occasionally get up to collect a piece of leaf or plant from the thick vegetation nearby. He had become an expert on the local vegetation, and knew the Tahitian names for all of the plants, as well as the Latin. He showed me the stately Hotu tree (*Barringtonia asiatica*), with bright pink flowers and fruits shaped like miniature ox hearts. Inside there are bitter seeds that the islanders used to grate and crush into a piece of coconut fibre sacking. Thrown into the lagoon they will temporarily stun fish without poisoning them. Alain fetched a plantain from another tree and showed me the violet dye from its skin that early missionaries had relied on as ink when they first arrived in Tahiti. A rosewood (*Thespesia populnea*) was valued as a treatment for bites from giant centipedes, and it too yielded a bright yellow pigment. It is as vivid and tenacious as oil paint and I have kept a smear of it on the pages of one of my notebooks to remind me of Ha'amene Bay.

11. Murder in Madagascar

There were six people squashed inside the battered little Renault 4 as it trundled along the bumpy dirt road to Ankadirano. In the front sat the driver and two bodyguards, while the rear seat was occupied by two young men and a middle-aged woman. The bodyguards were necessary because the woman, Seraphine Bakidy, and her younger colleagues were carrying cash — six hundred million Malagasy francs, almost one hundred thousand US dollars. In Madagascar, where most families live on less than three hundred dollars a year, it was a king's ransom, easily enough to get them all killed. But Seraphine and her companions had no choice. They were on a vanilla-buying expedition, visiting the small-subsistence farmers dotted around the bush communities north of the main town of Antalaha.

Antalaha is the southernmost point of the triangular patch of coastline that produces more than 90 per cent of Madagascar's vanilla. Seventy miles inland to the west is Andapa, and eighty miles due north is Sambava. Another one hundred and twenty miles further north is Vohémar, the furthest point of the great island where vanilla is grown. The first letters of these towns have been put together to spell S-A-V-A, a useful shorthand for describing the fertile vanilla region. Today, about 80,000 people here rely on vanilla for a crucial part of their earnings, and the local people have a saying: 'Everything here works because of vanilla. If the vanilla goes, the people will go.'

Renault 4s are still probably the commonest cars in Madagascar, and the Malagasy manage to keep them going under difficult conditions for what appears to be an infinite lifespan. A large number of the eight million Renault 4s that were ever built and are still running, are on the road in Madagascar. For a long time they were the only type of car available as taxis. For the last forty years these basic little cars have been the standard mode of transport. Seraphine Bakidy's car was distinguished only by the fact that it was blue, whereas the vast majority of the Renaults you see are white or brown or dark green.

Seraphine and her companions had already bought almost two hundred kilograms of cured vanilla during the day. The work of negotiating with the farmers is slow and often difficult, with hours of preamble to be sat through before a price is even mentioned. The vanilla they had secured was packed into the small boot of the car, with more on the roof under a tarpaulin. At the tiny village named Masovariaka, the Renault was unexpectedly stopped by a group of villagers who had mounted a simple roadblock with tree branches laid across the dirt track. The men of the village wielded a selection of clubs, sticks, heavy stones and machetes. At least four of the villagers carried hunting rifles. As the blue Renault came to a halt, an excited mob began rocking the small car back and forth, smashing at the windows and kicking in the panels on the doors. They shouted at the occupants to get out.

Seraphine opened her door and was dragged from the vehicle, screaming at the villagers for an explanation. A strong blow to the head knocked her to the ground, where she lay unconscious with serious injuries. Left for dead by the angry crowd, she saw nothing of what happened next, as the five men she had been travelling with were all pulled from the car. The driver and the two bodyguards put up a fight and managed to flee down the road, escaping with cuts and bruises and hiding out in the thick forest until darkness fell. Seraphine's companions on the back seat were not so lucky.

Jean de Dieu Tsarafidy and Jean Louis Sanasy were both in their early twenties, just getting started in the vanilla business and like Seraphine Bakidy they were carrying cash. The villagers beat them unconscious and tied them with thin rope around their arms and legs. Then they lynched them, and as they hung suspended like chickens from a tree, they were each shot in the chest.

The occupants of the little Renault could not have known that two days earlier another blue car had visited Masovariaka. The car pulled into the small settlement at dusk, and an armed gang terrorized the villagers, forcing them to hand over several dozen kilograms of cured vanilla. The theft was a devastating financial blow to the small community, and they were out for revenge.

When it was discovered that she was still alive, Seraphine Bakidy was given first aid by some of the women in the village, and her unconscious body despatched by bush taxi to the regional clinic at Sambava. She would spend four months in hospital recovering from her injuries. Meanwhile, the driver and the two bodyguards reached Sambava alerting Seraphine's husband, Gilbert Gilbert, to the tragedy. Gilbert reacted fast, assembling a gang of his own and driving fast to Masovariaka. By the time he got there it was a ghost town: the inhabitants had fled into the bush. Needless to say, there was no trace of the six hundred million francs. Frustrated by the incident and enraged at finding the bodies of the two dead vanilla collectors, Gilbert Gilbert's men set fire to the village, razing it to the ground.

On my last visit to the SAVA region, the kids were riding bicycles on the dusty streets of Antalaha. Dozens of bright, shiny mountain bikes newly imported from China that cost fifty dollars apiece, cheap by European standards but extremely expensive for Madagascar. On several small houses there were even new satellite dishes, and I had spotted numerous people using mobile telephones. 'Oh yes, because of the vanilla prices there are a lot of rich people here now,' Georges Randriamiharisoa explained as he wrestled the steering wheel of his Land Cruiser to negotiate another massive pothole in the road. Georges is president of the Groupement National des Exportateurs de Vanille de Madagascar (GNEV), an organization set up to represent vanilla dealers and to coordinate production policy in the region. He also runs one of the biggest vanilla curing operations in Antalaha, the sleepy port at the southern end of the SAVA region. Much of Madagascar's crop takes ship here for the main exporting centre at Toamasina two days' sailing down the coast. The port at Antalaha is no more than a broken-down concrete jetty, but it is the only way, apart from exorbitantly priced air freight, of getting the vanilla out of the region in large quantities.

'The boom in vanilla has brought in a lot of cash,' said Georges. 'A lot of the older people have bought bicycles but they just wheel them along the road – they don't know how to work the gears. They just want people to know they have the money to buy them.'

Every jolt of the vehicle made me feel sick, and I had serious doubts that I could make the short distance from Georges' house to the vanilla depot without vomiting. I didn't want to be sick in front of Georges, because I suspected that it was the dinner he and his wife Clarice had provided the night before that was making me feel ill. It had started innocently enough with a delicious fruit salad made with fresh pawpaws, kiwi fruit and lychees. Then came the coconut sorbet to refresh the palate before the main course. It was duck. The bird appeared on the table whole, its head and beak still attached and glazed with a rich vanilla sauce. There were blackened vanilla pods emerging from the charred beak and several more scattered throughout the slivers of meat and juice that were heaped upon my plate. Bright green uncooked vanilla leaves were strewn across the dish as garnish. There was also an enormous joint of pork studded with cloves, and Clarice had insisted that I should have a serving of each. Finally, came dessert: deep-fried bananas with a syrup made from honey, sugar, rum and again, a dozen large sticks of vanilla. Clarice is a tiny birdlike woman, with enormous dark eyes and a rather imperial manner, accentuated by a penchant for richly embroidered cheong-sams. Between courses she summoned servants from the kitchen by tinkling a little brass bell which she kept at her elbow throughout the meal. Within seconds, a man in a starched white cotton jacket would appear to receive instructions from his mistress.

After a restless night disturbed by violent dreams I could barely face the idea of breakfast. Some cold cuts from the pork joint arrived at the table, and I had to confess to Clarice and Georges that I wasn't very hungry. 'It's the heat,' said Clarice, shaking her head pityingly. 'But you must eat to keep up your strength.' She rang her little bell, and issued some instructions to the cook who appeared silently at her side. A few minutes later I was given a plate of sliced pawpaw, its moist orange flesh dotted with small green seeds. 'You must eat a few of the seeds,' Clarice commanded. 'They are good for the stomach, just a few mind – they can be poisonous if you eat too many.'

'Come,' said Georges, as I mopped up the last of the pawpaw. The seeds were hard and bitter, but I convinced myself they would be an antidote to the sweet bulk of last night's enormous feast. 'We will go to the warehouse, and you will see what we have to do to keep our vanilla safe.'

Georges manages the curing plant at Antalaha for one of Madagascar's most successful vanilla houses, the Ramanandraibe company based in the capital, Antananarivo. Working in partnership with a large American firm, they supply much of the island's best vanilla to America and Europe. As we drove, Georges told me that with the price of vanilla at its highest ever, he had started keeping a gun in his bedroom. One of his sons who lives nearby had been shot at one night by men trying to break into his house. The men wanted to force him to open up the warehouse, so that they could steal vanilla. Fortunately, he too had a gun and was able to return fire, scaring the gang away.

The sign on the wall said *Ramanandraibe Exportation, Produits et épices de Madagascar*. Georges swung the Land Cruiser through the gates and into the vanilla compound, waving at the group of security guards standing nonchalantly by the entrance. During daylight, their main job was to keep an eye on the staff. An open-sided warehouse stretched for a hundred yards down one side of the yard, and opposite was another long building where Georges had his office. Under the porch at one end of the building there were dozens of colourful rattan baskets lined up tidily in rows. Beside each bag there was a pair of rubber flip-flops. 'They belong to the workers,' Georges explained.

'We make them leave their lunch and personal possessions here so that they can't hide vanilla in the bags.'

In the open-sided shed opposite the office there were dozens of women sitting at wooden tables sorting and packing vanilla beans. They sat under the shade of a sloping corrugated tin roof talking quietly as they picked through the beans in front of them. Supervisors in blue overalls moved up and down the row of tables, occasionally telling the women to stop talking and concentrate on their task. Some sections of the line had been given shade from the sun with heavy grey woollen blankets suspended from the tin roof. They flapped gently in the morning breeze.

Georges led me along the line of tables to show me the different sections of the line. 'Let's start at the beginning,' he said, leaving the shelter of the verandah and heading for the far end of the compound. Behind the long warehouse was a small concrete building with a raised area to one side. There were large cylindrical cane baskets arranged in neat rows, the containers for the beans when they were dipped. A trench had been cut into the floor at one end, like the pit in a car mechanic's workshop for inspecting the underside of vehicles. Georges explained that this was where the fire was laid to heat the large tubs of water into which green beans would be dipped for the killing phase of the curing. It was the same process I had seen in Mexico and Réunion, the only difference being that at Ramanandraibe Exports everything seemed very streamlined and efficient. Instead of an open wood fire there were tall gas cylinders arranged in the pit to feed the fire. Georges' operation was clearly set up to handle very large quantities of vanilla beans.

Behind the dipping shed there was a fenced-off garden area, where I spotted vanilla vines being trained along bamboo supports. 'Do you grow vanilla here, too?'

'Oh no, these are just experimental varieties,' said Georges, leading me into the garden. It was just a few square yards of earth, but there were more than a dozen separate vines, several of them with leaves of a different size and shape from the ones I had seen elsewhere. Georges gently stroked a leaf from one of the vines between his thumb and forefinger. 'This one, see it has a label —"A55" — it gives a very high percentage of vanillin in the beans, but there is a snag. It is prone to disease, and it can't take much sun. It's a shame, because the vanillin content is as high as four per cent, compared to the normal yields of around two per cent.'

After the nursery it was time to see what Georges called the analysis centre, where a woman in a white lab coat presided over a set of digital scales, a number of test tubes and petri dishes, and a machine with a label on it that said Jenway 6400 Spectrophotometer. The lady in the white coat told me it could measure the vanillin content of the beans by shooting a concentrated beam of light through them. She had some paperwork to discuss with Georges, and I stepped outside to wait in the yard.

I found myself at the edge of the compound, next to a lavatory block where two elderly men wearing the regulation issue Ramanandraibe blue overalls stood guard. Women from the vanilla shed who needed to visit the lavatory had to stand still and be frisked, airport security style, by the old men. While I was waiting two women approached, and as I watched the men caught my eye and winked lasciviously as they gave the women's buttocks a firm squeeze that clearly had nothing to do with finding vanilla. The women didn't seem to mind.

Georges reappeared and led me back towards the warehouse. At one end there was a high-ceilinged room filled with shiny metal boxes, the size of large biscuit tins. These were the boxes that would be piled into containers for the long sea voyage to the USA and Europe. The room was dark and cool, but the boxes reflected the available light, capturing my image and twisting and distorting my features like funfair mirrors. I wondered how much vanilla Georges could have on site at any one time.

'Well –' he paused, as if afraid that someone could be listening – 'we can have five hundred tonnes here at the peak of the season. But,' he added hurriedly as though he had said something he shouldn't, 'we try not to let so much stock stay in one spot for more than a few days.'

Even at an average price of just $200 a kilogram that would mean the vanilla here would have a retail value of $100 million on the American market. Georges could tell I was making the calculations in my head. 'But see, we take precautions,' he said, leading me to the back of the shed. The walls had been built of double-thickness breezeblocks, and inside the brickwork a steel frame extended from floor to ceiling. 'You would need explosives to get through that wall,' he said gravely. 'And we would hear the bang. My men would be able to get here before any significant amount was stolen.' I told him I wasn't planning a raid, and he gave a thin-lipped smile.

Back at Georges' office there was a muscular man with very dark skin sitting on a plastic chair clutching a leather briefcase to his chest. His name was Justin Jao and he had bright flickering eyes and an open, intelligent face. He was one of Ramanandraibe's vanilla collectors, just returned from a trip in the 'bush' as Georges termed it, and he was here to report on what he had seen. He told us that he had been gone for three weeks, travelling with four armed guards and walking into the most inaccessible areas for two or three days at a time to find the farmers who had beans to sell. I asked him how much vanilla he might collect on a typical trip.

'Before the prices went so high, maybe a tonne in ten days, but now four or five hundred kilos is all I can carry enough money for.'

Justin explained that, although he worked principally for the Ramanandraibe company, he was in effect a freelance businessman. It was up to him to make the best deal possible with the farmers in the bush.

'Ramanandraibe give me a cash advance to buy vanilla beans for them, OK? But they tell me I have to use that money to buy only the best quality vanilla available. They are very strict. They want 60 per cent of the beans to be longer than 14 centimetres, 35 per cent of them to be no less than 12 centimetres, and only 5 per cent can be shorter than that. But, if someone else will pay the same amount, or more for beans that don't make the grade, I can sell to them – then I pay back the cash advance Ramanandraibe gave me.'

Georges nodded sagely as Justin explained the system. 'It's true,' he said. 'I have sixty collectors, and I have to trust them to bring me back the money I advance them. Sometimes, they come back empty-handed and tell me they have been robbed, but how can I be sure?'

Justin laughed, showing a mouthful of strong yellow teeth against mottled gums. 'We collectors sometimes take a chance! If Ramanandraibe rejects what we bring back we have no choice but to try to sell it to another exporter. But we still owe Ramanandraibe their advance, or the equivalent in beans. If the other exporter knows we are desperate to sell he won't give us a fair price and then we might not have enough to pay back the original advance.'

Curers, like Georges, also protect themselves by reserving the right to give the collectors a lower price if the beans they bring in are too moist, or not of the right quality. Georges wanted me to know that he acted strictly according to the rules, and he produced a chart listing the different grades of beans and what he expected to pay for them. The varying qualities were set down according to rules drawn up by the government, he explained, showing me a piece of paper entitled *Arrêt Interministeriel No. 4911/99 MCC 12/5/99*. There is a certain obsession with bureaucracy in Madagascar which almost thirty years of independence from French rule has done nothing to alleviate. 'This means all the exporters are treating the collectors in the same way,' Georges said defensively. 'The exporters all meet once a year and agree to these rules, otherwise there would be chaos!'

The highest quality was called 'NFN', meaning '*non-fendu noir*' – black not split. Beans more than fourteen centimetres long were known as 'extra', and there were subdivisions of grades by colour, quality and length all the way down to 'split cuts', short remnants of vanilla beans which had also split open. Each category had a price, and Georges was forever adjusting the figures on his chart to suit the market. 'If you think the collector has a tough time,' he said, 'remember I have to deal with the foreign buyers, and they drive a hard bargain too. You see, they have different uses for the beans,' he continued. 'If they are just making vanilla extract then it doesn't matter if the beans are shorter, or split, because they will pulverize them and heat them anyway, to extract the flavour. But the gourmet-grade beans for chefs, and for the high quality ingredients market, they have to look as good as possible. And they must taste as good as they expect of a real Bourbon bean.'

I asked Justin if the farmers were happy with the very high

price they had been getting recently. His coal dark eyes flickered from side to side.

'They are happy of course, but they always ask me why the price is so high now. Until a few years ago the government set the price for vanilla and it stayed the same for more than twenty years. They don't understand the free market, only that they can ask for more money. Now they wait until later and later in the season to sell the beans so that they can get a better price, and some of them are starting to hoard. But many are too scared to keep the vanilla in their house.'

'Yes,' Georges interrupted. 'But another problem we have is that some farmers are picking too early. They don't want the risk of someone stealing the beans, but it means the quality of the flavour is not so good.'

'Don't the beans need to stay on the vine for a long time to ripen?' I asked.

'Oh yes', Georges nodded vigorously. 'But after two months they have already reached their maximum weight and length. And we buy by weight in the first instance. Of course the farmer gets a good price per kilo, but the quality of the flavour is very poor unless it is allowed to stay on the vine for at least six, preferably eight months. That's where the special Bourbon taste comes from and that's what the foreign buyers want. They don't care what price I've had to pay to the farmers.'

Meanwhile, the problems of security and a volatile price for vanilla were causing the same problems for the farmers and curers that I had seen in Mexico. I told Georges a little of what I had seen there. 'We also try to make rules,' he said, shaking his head as if it was a hopeless task. 'We have imposed curfews; no one is allowed to drive a car with vanilla on board after six p.m. And you can go to prison for selling someone else's beans.' He rummaged in his desk drawer and produced a little wooden stamp studded with fine pins. 'This is my personal mark; the vanilla council has registered these four letters "AOXA" in my name. I prick the beans I grow with this as soon as they are big enough, and this is supposed to mean no one else can sell them.'

'Does it work?'

Georges turned his palms upwards and shrugged. 'With this crazy money around, nothing is guaranteed. If a curer is offered beans at a very good price it can be hard to say no.'

As president of the vanilla exporters' association, Georges was desperately concerned to help the farmers maintain Madagascar's reputation for producing the highest quality vanilla in the world. He told me that two years previously, representatives from the European Union had visited his factory and asked if he could find forty farmers to whom some basic financial aid could be given. Within a year he had established one hundred groups representing 14,000 farmers, all of whom were committed to protecting the quality standards for which Bourbon vanilla is known. In small ways the association was achieving success.

'We found that the farmers were trying to increase their profits by semi-curing the beans they had for sale,' Georges explained. 'They were storing them in plastic bags as a way of heating them rapidly – but plastic makes the beans go mouldy. We have used the EU money to distribute 60,000 blankets for the farmers to use for the sweating process instead of plastic.' The GNEV also distributed thermometers and timers so that the farmers could monitor the sweating process more accurately. It all sounded encouraging, but Georges remained downbeat.

'Maybe we can achieve something in the long term, but I'm afraid that people are too interested in making quick money.

And you know, in the last few years we in Madagascar have had cyclones and a sort of civil war to cope with as well. It's not easy.'

In the afternoon Georges had work to do, and I was left to explore the compound on my own. The open yard between the offices and the warehouse was made of concrete and unbearably hot. I retreated to the covered verandah of the warehouse where the women were sorting and packing the dried vanilla. They had upturned packing cases for chairs and I asked if I could occupy a spare place at one of the long tables. The five women working there were mostly young, shy and nervous, giggling and casting their eyes downwards if I spoke to them. Most of them wore their hair in tight plaits which they curled up on top of their heads so that it was out of their way as they worked. Their braids were dressed with coconut oil so that they shone like woven vanilla beans. Their fingers were as nimble as weavers', flickering over the pile of dark brown pods on a grey woollen blanket laid across the table. The cured beans were stacked in neat circular bunches and bound with pale strips of raffia which they tied with neat little bows around the middle. The rolls, each containing a hundred pods, looked like miniature bundles of kindling. The oil on the surface of the beans caught the light and made them glisten, and some of the vanilla had a reddish tinge, like stray ginger hairs in a dark beard. The women's fingernails and the skin around their cuticles had been dyed black by the pods. One of the women told me that they were paid about three dollars a day for working with the vanilla.

'Is that a good wage?'

'Oh yes.' There was general assent. 'We would get half that if we worked with cloves or rice.'

There was a hypnotic appeal in watching the sorters going

about their task. They spoke in hushed tones, casting occasional glances towards the supervisors who walked up and down the line of tables. I began to talk very quietly too, and it felt like being back at school, afraid of being caught by a teacher. One woman, Angelina, was slightly more forthcoming than the rest, and after a time she asked shyly if I could answer a question. She said that she and her colleagues had been told that vanilla was worth a lot of money outside Madagascar.

'If this is true, we don't understand what the *vazaha* do with the vanilla,' she said, using the Malagasy word for stranger, and which they apply to any foreigner. 'Why do they pay so much for it?'

I tried to explain that it was the taste and smell of vanilla that made it valuable. Angelina's eyes widened. 'Is that all?'

The women clearly doubted what I had said, staring at each other with suddenly serious expressions. It was clear they thought I was lying, and I felt as if I had let them down with my explanation. None of them would look at me. They talked animatedly for a while in their own language, evidently debating whether what I had told them could make any sense, but nervous about pressing their enquiry. Finally, it was Angelina who spoke to me again. 'We believe there must be another reason,' she said, staring at the ground. 'Is it because you can make dynamite with it?'

'No, it is really for food. When we *vazaha* cook, we like to add vanilla just because it is a special taste. And we cannot grow it in our country. That is why vanilla from Madagascar is so important. It is the best in the world.'

The compliment to Madagascar brought forth a round of smiles, and the atmosphere improved again. In this region, where rain is plentiful and the soil is fertile, people have not endured poverty and hardship like those further south. With fish and rice, fruit and vegetables in good supply there is no malnutrition here and the local ethnic group, the Betsimisaraka tribe, are better off than most. They are also the most skilful at growing and curing the vanilla, which has recently become such a big earner. Vanilla is not, however, something the Betsimisaraka ever use in their own cooking, and the women still doubted that foreigners would pay a lot of money for the beans.

'What about tyres, do they use vanilla to make tyres for their cars?'

A klaxon sounded to signal the end of the working day, and Angelina and her colleagues began to tidy away their work. The supervisors moved down the line of tables collecting the last bundles of tied beans to return them to the safety of the warehouse. The women began to troop out of the warehouse, gathering near to the main gates to be frisked again before they left for home. Then they picked up their little rattan bags and ambled through the gates like factory workers anywhere at the end of a tiring shift. As I waited for Georges, the compound seemed very quiet and still, but the smell of the vanilla hung over everything like a sweet cloud.

12. Ice Cream and Perfume

Following Edmond's discovery, the manual technique for fertilizing vanilla orchids spread slowly but steadily from Réunion to the neighbouring Indian Ocean islands. By 1866 it was being grown in Seychelles and Mauritius, and by 1870 it had reached several areas of the Great Red Island, Madagascar. Like Réunion, these Indian Ocean islands (even those controlled by the British) had a stock of French-speaking planters whose livelihoods were threatened by the diversion of shipping through the Suez Canal. Fortunately, many of them would have vanilla beans to sustain them. By the late nineteenth century 80 per cent of the 30 tonnes of vanilla reaching Europe each year came from the French colonies. Planters in the Congo tried growing it, as did the British in India and Ceylon, with even the US Department of Agriculture showing an interest in developing plantations in their newly annexed territories of Hawaii and Puerto Rico. In most cases these countries would eventually abandon vanilla cultivation as too labour intensive when compared to other crops. However, thanks to the techniques perfected on Réunion, growing and pollinating vanilla orchids under suitable tropical conditions was no longer a great mystery. As far as the commercial supply of the luscious beans was concerned, the work of the Mexican orchid bees in allowing the vines to bear fruit had been entirely displaced by human activity.

In the south-west Indian Ocean getting the vanilla vines to grow from cuttings was not a problem. The easiest means of establishing a vanilla plantation was simply to obtain some slips of about two feet long from an established vine, and transplant them. The plants were, after all, robust enough to survive long sea voyages. As they grow, the vines need to be supported on a tutor, and any of several dozen species of trees and shrubs will do, including varieties of pine like Casuarina and shrubs like the Barbados nut which will not grow too tall. The vine will then send out aerial roots of its own which help it cling fast to its support. Once established, a mature vine sends down stems which hang downwards, eventually reaching the ground and producing roots for a new stage of growth. Early planters knew that cuttings needed to be transplanted at the end of the dry season and the base of the plants had to be given plenty of mulch. Vanilla likes moist heat, a hilly well-drained site and just the right amount of sunshine and shade. The vines cannot tolerate temperatures lower than about 6°C, and prefer the temperature range between 21° and 32°C. They also need as much as 3,000 mm of rain, fairly evenly distributed throughout the seasons. In the SAVA region of Madagascar the vines get exactly what they need.

In a good year Madagascar produces more than half of the world's natural vanilla, approximately 1,200 of the 2,000 tonnes of beans available to importing countries. By the beginning of the twentieth century the pattern for modern-day vanilla production was well established. The amount grown and cured by Madagascar outstripped Mexico, Réunion, Comoros and Tahiti several fold. No plant was as widely used in confectionery and perfume as vanilla. The demand for natural vanilla in Europe and the USA was driven in part by the industrialization of the food industry, the burgeoning market for processed foods and an increasing appetite for small luxuries, especially ice cream.

From its early beginnings in the middle of the nineteenth century, commercial ice cream production increased rapidly alongside improvements in technology, such as steam power, mechanical refrigeration, electrical motors and new freezing processes. In America in particular, it is fair to say that ice cream acquired a position of cultural prominence. Not only did Thomas Jefferson expend great effort to obtain his supply of vanilla 'batons' from Paris, but according to household records his presidential predecessor, George Washington, spent more than two hundred dollars on ice cream for official entertaining during the summer of 1790. The nation credits Nancy Johnson, from Philadelphia, with the first patent for a successful hand-cranked ice cream freezer in 1846. Until her invention, making ice cream was extremely physically laborious, a task best left to servants. A mixture of cream, sugar, eggs, salt and vanilla had to be agitated by hand with a wooden spoon in a tin bowl, surrounded by ice. Johnson's machine made the process faster, and the mixture smoother. Inside a large tin with a removable lid, she adapted an S-shaped 'dasher' that scraped the sides of the container as it churned, preventing large ice crystals from forming and ruining the result. Johnson's ice cream churn cost three dollars, cheap enough for most middle-class households to afford. By 1877 more than seventy improvements had been made to the design of the original churn, speeding up the process. By 1878 ice cream was being shipped all over the country and it could be stored in ice cellars for several months.

In 1851, a Baltimore milk dealer named Jacob Fussell converted his milk unit into the first ice cream plant in the United States. By the end of the century, the ice cream parlour was a feature of even the smallest town. Americans also claim as their own the invention of the ice cream cone, in 1896. Other ice cream achievements included ice cream sodas (1874), ice cream sundaes (1881), Eskimo Pies (1920) and Popsicles (1923).

When America opened its arms to a renewed flood of immigrants from Europe in the 1920s, and processed them on Ellis Island in New York, the new citizens were rewarded with their first 'American meal'. The Commissioner for the island decreed that it should contain ice cream, a substance unknown to many of the new arrivals. Some of them mistook it for frozen butter, and tried to spread it on their bread.

The American obsession with the frozen dessert continues. This is a country, after all, where July has been designated official 'Ice Cream Month', and where the third Sunday of July is officially 'National Ice Cream Day'. This celebration of ice cream owes its inception to a Senate Resolution proclaimed by President Ronald Reagan on 9 July 1984. Reagan's proclamation was apparently issued as a result of lobbying from the International Ice Cream Association, part of the International Dairy Foods Association whose members represent more than 85 per cent of the total volume of milk, cultured products, cheese, ice cream and frozen desserts produced in the United States. The industry is now worth $70 billion a year. According to the official wording of the presidential decree, the country recognizes that 'ice cream is a nutritious and wholesome food, enjoyed by over ninety percent of the people in the United States. It enjoys a reputation as the perfect dessert and snack food.' And the amounts consumed 'provide jobs for thousands of citizens and contribute substantially to the economic well-being of the Nation's dairy industry'.

The majority of the vanilla beans imported into the USA are used for making vanilla flavour extracts and essence. Naturally, much of that flavouring eventually goes into ice cream. I discovered that ice cream makers, large and small, were surprisingly reluctant to let me see their factories in action. Time and again, well-known companies on both sides of the Atlantic made plans to allow me to watch them making their famous ice cream and then cancelled the arrangement. Eventually, an ice cream executive told me why. 'Look, we don't need publicity of that sort,' he said, asking not to be identified. 'It's the same with any food product – no one will take the risk that you might reveal how simple the manufacturing processes are, and then people might start questioning the value of what they buy in a tub of ice cream. Most of our added value,' he continued, 'is in marketing the product as something people *want* to eat – let's face it, they don't *need* to eat ice cream. None of the big boys want to stick their neck out and risk you writing something that doesn't fit with the brand image.'

One household name brand of ice cream prides itself on its 'home-made' image, and even offers public tours of its factory. Explaining that I was simply interested in seeing the final incarnation of vanilla beans as they end up in a tub of ice cream, I asked if I could watch the process at close quarters. After months of negotiation, they said I could take the public tour, but visiting the factory floor would be out of the question. It was the same story in America, the UK and France.

Finally, I did visit an ice cream plant. A vanilla importer with family connections in the ice cream trade arranged it, but said, 'they don't really want publicity'. Tucked into the gently rolling landscape of northern Pennsylvania there is an old farm which once operated as a dairy. The farm is still there, but the dairy business has taken over much of the land for factory space. It now makes 26 million gallons of ice cream each year.

I watched 6,000-gallon milk tankers unloading their swishing white cargo into the loading bay and saw them test each batch for unwanted antibiotics, freshness, butter-fat content and protein. Buckets of frozen pasteurized egg yolk were mixed with sugar, bulked up with skimmed milk powder, whey powder and stabilizers before being poured into giant steel vats and liquefied with milk. Inside an enormous labyrinthine network of steel tubes and wire grilles I heard the liquid being homogenized by being sheared under pressures of 2,000 pounds per square inch. Throbbing, churning, warming mixtures were batched and blended in 3,000-gallon steel tanks that looked like fat space rockets. Every stage of the process was monitored and measured by computerized control panels. There were people involved, but surprisingly few, mainly to pour the raw ingredients into the mixing tanks, and keep an eye on the gauges. Finally, the white liquid came down a spout into rectangular steel vats holding 500 gallons of mixture. Enormous paddles stirred the opaque pools, while nearby gauges were programmed with selected recipes. The amount of cream, the viscosity and the amount of air (crucial to ice cream consistency and flavour) were all punched into the great machines while flavourings were added. Forked metal arms upended tubs of unctuous bright yellow peanut butter and swarthy variegated brownie butter, too sweet to taste on their own. And there, in a great creamy swirling lake was the vanilla ice cream.

In the middle of the assembly line it passed through a pair of freezers as big as lorries, chilling it to semi-liquid hardness at a staggering 1,600 gallons an hour. It glooped down a hose into cardboard tubs whose lids dropped from a conveyor with a satisfying *pock-pock-pock* sound and then flew along a track to be wrapped in cellophane and placed on trays for loading. In a refrigerated warehouse there were men in winter coats, woollen hats and gloves so thick their fingers wouldn't bend. The temperature was −40° Fahrenheit and in one section great fans produced a wind chill that took it down to −70°. The freezing conditions were needed to make sure each carton reached a core temperature of −20° before it was shipped. A battered ghetto-blaster pumped out a barely tuned radio station as they piled the cartons onto palettes and loaded them into refrigerated lorries. In the dim light of the warehouse they laboured, only their eyes showing through swaddling scarves. My nose started to crackle inside as the mucous froze, and dressed in lightweight clothes I was desperate to leave. The tubs were frosted with ice. Quickly smearing the rime away I peered at the side of a carton so that I could read what it said. *Ingredients: Cream, Nonfat Milk, Sugar, Vanilla, Vanilla Bean.*

As the population increases, the consumption of ice cream grows steadily in the USA, somewhere between 2 and 3 per cent each year. Food manufacturers fight vigorously for a share of that market, because the annual domestic sales of ice cream alone in the USA are worth more than $20 billion. Vanilla remains the most popular flavour, accounting for more than a third of the 1.25 billion individual ice cream products sold annually. In quantity, that figure translates into just over 22 litres of ice cream for every individual in the country each year. In the UK we consume a mere 8 litres each per year, while the Scandinavians manage almost 13 litres. British ice cream buyers choose vanilla 90 per cent of the time.

Worldwide, annual global sales of ice cream now top 13 billion litres, a figure which is likely to rise as previously untapped markets, such as the Far East, expand. In countries like China, a burgeoning middle class is being tempted to spend its money on what the flavouring industry calls 'non-essential foods'. Western dietary habits are spreading fast, along with the developed world's waistlines.

In principle, the demand for natural vanilla should continue to rise. Apart from ice creams, many of the best known colas contain real vanilla, as of course do the specific 'vanilla' versions of these drinks. Flavouring essence made from cured vanilla beans is an essential part of these products' carefully constructed flavour identity. The art and science of creating food and fragrance compounds is itself an enormous industry, with an annual value estimated at over US$16 billion. Market leaders in the field, such as the Swiss-based Givaudan corporation and its American rival International Flavors and Fragrances, have combined sales of more than $4 billion annually. To manufacture the individual (and carefully concocted) tastes which give their products its identity, food makers need vanilla. Flavour suppliers, essence manufacturers and food companies all have to find sources for good quality vanilla beans, either through their own direct efforts or through a broker who knows the market well. It is a process shrouded in secrecy.

Food manufacturers are always reluctant to divulge the details of their ingredients, in spite of labelling regulations which purport to tell consumers what they are buying. Both in Europe and the USA, there are regulatory standards governing the way in which vanilla 'extract' is made, and specifying that it must be made with *Vanilla planifolia* or *Vanilla tahitensis*. The basic industrial strength of extract also requires that 100 grams of beans are used per litre of 35% alcohol (13.35 oz per gallon), to produce what is known as 'single-fold' extract. Chefs and cooks will use this type of extract, but commercial ice cream makers will need three- or four-fold extract – made with three or four times the amount of beans per litre of extractive alcohol. To economize, food manufacturers using real vanilla are often tempted to switch to an artificial substitute – usually made with vanillin, a chemical which occurs in vanilla beans but can also be synthesized from other materials, including coal tar.

Part of the mystery and sensuous appeal of the vanilla bean comes from its complex chemistry. During curing, when the beans are dipped in hot water, the structure of their cell walls is disrupted, provoking an enzymatic reaction which allows ferulic acid to degrade and eventually transform itself into vanillin and vanillic acid. Commercial vanilla beans are judged, in part, on the amount of vanillin they contain – usually around 2 per cent, but occasionally as high as 3 or 4 per cent. Beans which are cured too rapidly will not develop high quantities of vanillin.

Vanillin, just one of several hundred chemicals in vanilla, is known to chemists as $C_8H_8O_3$ (4-Hydroxy-3-methoxy-benzaldehyde). For more than a century it has been possible to synthesize vanillin, and today it is the most commonly produced flavour compound in the world with an annual market of 12,000 tonnes. It is cheaper and stronger than natural vanilla flavour and widely used in food manufacturing, household scents and as an anti-microbial agent in fruit purées. Safe for human consumption, it is also more chemically stable at high cooking temperatures, but more importantly it saves manufacturers money. For American ice cream manufacturers, vanilla extract typically costs around 73 cents per gallon as opposed to about 12 cents per gallon for artificial vanilla flavour made with vanillin from other sources. In premium grade ice cream

In the late nineteenth century vanilla extract became a staple ingredient in home baking and ice cream

this means natural vanilla extract would account for as much as 3 per cent of the cost of ingredients, a significant figure in such a competitive market. Ice cream made with natural vanilla would, however, probably taste better. I say probably because many consumers have never tasted the difference. Tests conducted by flavour manufacturers have revealed that many people prefer artificial vanilla, simply because it is the taste they know.

This is depressing news for vanilla growers. Less depressing is the rapid growth in recent years of products whose brand image relies on their perceived excellence based on all natural ingredients – ice cream brands like Ben and Jerry's and Häagen-Dazs are obvious examples. These rely heavily on consumers identifying them as above average products, and the manufacturers hope people will buy them because they associate their product with excellent ingredients. In effect, it is safe to assume that the more expensive a product is, the more likely it is to contain natural vanilla.

Vanilla extract (in tandem with vanillin) is a staple building block for flavour around the world. It is widely used in the production of chocolates, bakery products, ice creams, chewing gums, dairy products, cocoa drinks, pharmaceuticals, fragrances and deodorants. There has never been a more versatile food ingredient.

Vanilla is also an important ingredient in perfumery, where it provides a warm, sensual base 'note', the term parfumiers use to divide and describe the different elements in their fragrances. The top note is the scent you get when you open the perfume bottle, the so-called signature of the aroma which makes the first impact. This is the most volatile element in the fragrance and it is the one which is often lost after a short time. Next comes the middle note, especially when the perfume is applied to the skin, where it is warmed and absorbed. The middle note remains active over several hours. Later, perhaps in the evening, the nose picks up the base notes of the scent, the less volatile but more sensual parts of the aroma. Here, vanilla can be used at the very heart of a perfume. The parfumier's art rests in combining the volatile and the heavy notes to generate what they call an evaporation profile. The less volatile notes are the ones which impart high sensuality to the fragrance, the vanilla, amber or musky elements of the mixture. And, just as in the food industry, some of the most expensive ingredients come from nature. Vanilla imparts a deep rich, balsamic note to perfume. Vanilla has contributed to some of the most memorable perfumes of the past century, including *Shalimar* by Guerlain, and Chanel $N^o 5$. More recently it has been an element in Thierry Mugler's *Angel*, Yves Saint Laurent's *Opium*, *Dune* by Dior and *Tresor* by Lancôme. Jean-Paul Guerlain once remarked that 'vanilla has a secret charm, a power to evoke tastes and aromas in equal measure. It can be suave, sublime, or sensual and it has conquered the palette of the parfumier.'

Perfumery requires different chemical skills from baking or ice cream making. Instead of vanilla extracts, the parfumiers must use very high concentrations of the vanilla aroma. The most highly refined of these products is 'vanilla absolute', extracted using liquid CO^2 or hydrocarbon solvents, creating a liquid which is completely soluble in ethanol and perfume oils. 'Vanilla absolute' costs approximately $5,000 a kilogram, and is therefore used for only the highest quality fragrances, whereas the same amount of vanillin for perfumery costs less than $20. Once again, higher priced products will be more likely to contain the real thing.

Away from the rarefied atmosphere of the great perfume houses, the scent of vanilla has been the subject of other experiments. Malaysian chemists have reported that vanilla may be an antidote for certain virulent jellyfish stings. It also repels many insects, and one American lady told me that she remembers her mother smearing vanilla extract on her arms and legs to guard against mosquitoes during hot autumn nights.

Olfactory researchers have calculated that 90 per cent of what we call 'taste' is actually 'smell'. If we cannot smell whatever it is we put into our mouths, then we are unlikely to be able to identify its taste. Dietitians have used the relationship between taste and smell to help persistent over-eaters to lose weight. In a scientific study at a London hospital, severely obese patients were given scented patches (similar to the nicotine patches used by smokers) to affix to their skin. According to Catherine Collins, the hospital's chief dietitian, those exposed to a vanilla scent lost the most weight – several pounds more than other patients.

Other studies have shown that vanilla-like odours seem to have a calming effect, and some hospitals add it to their air-conditioning systems in the belief it will promote a more tranquil atmosphere in the medical environment. Meanwhile, Dr Alan Hirsch at Chicago's Smell and Taste Foundation has carried out extensive tests on the erotic potential of certain odours. Vanilla, he found, had the ability to increase involuntary blood flow to the penis in men while they were sleeping. However, he points out that numerous smells had a similar effect, and the smell of pumpkin pie gave a particularly impressive result. Vanilla performed creditably, however, and seemed most effective with older men, perhaps suggesting that they associated the smell with pleasant childhood memories.

In the 1950s the soda-jerks of America's drugstores would announce the arrival of attractive female customers to the kitchen staff by shouting, 'Vanilla!' On one level it was an innocent double entendre, but on another it conveyed the hidden, sensuous overtones of the flavour itself. They implied something delectable and tasty, but disguised it with a commonplace term. The trend continues, although the innocence of the soda fountain has been lost. As a racial epithet, chocolate and vanilla are sometimes used as synonyms for black and white. In recent years the term 'vanilla' has been applied extensively by bankers to describe investments that are relatively risk free, the suggestion being that the financial returns will not vary from what is expected of them. Implying that they might bring higher than average returns, one respected financial newspaper recently carried the headline: 'Government Investment Certificates are no longer just plain vanilla!'

There is a song entitled 'Vanilla Sex' by the underground punk band Nofx:

> *So stay in your missionary position*
> *I hope that you got bored to death*
> *There's no way I'm going through life*
> *Having vanilla sex . . .*

The lyrics alerted me to a hitherto undiscovered sexual terminology, in which 'vanilla sex' is used to describe conventional heterosexual relations rather than anything involving bondage or other arcane sexual practices. The phrase 'plain old vanilla' has become synonymous with standardization and blandness. It hardly seems fit for the luscious substance.

Given its commercial ubiquity, it is no surprise that the USA is the world's largest importer of vanilla beans. The men who procure the beans are a small band of individuals with extremely specialized knowledge of their commodity. Once upon a time they were gentlemanly types from the East Coast who based themselves in the Philadelphia and New Jersey area where they could easily handle and inspect incoming cargoes of beans arriving by ship. As prices have peaked in recent years, the prospects of high profits have drawn inexperienced, but extremely wealthy, speculators into the market. Some of these speculators have been attracted by the prospect of doing business on a purely cash basis. It is also the kind of trade with the potential to attract dirty money. In the face of increasing competition for the raw material they need, the vanilla brokers – old and new – have acquired a reputation for ruthlessness. Vanilla beans from Madagascar are at the heart of their trade.

13. The Admiral's Legacy

The east coast of Madagascar is spectacularly straight when seen from the air. It makes the island look like a great ear that has been surgically sliced off some giant's head. The ear in question would have a surface area twice the size of Great Britain, since Madagascar is the world's fourth largest island. The west coast is more bulbous, and irregular, and off the north-western tip the four Comoros islands sit like little flecks of discarded flesh. When the sea is calm there are eddying swathes of red in the shining blue ocean adding to the notion that this land is bleeding. The billowing red flux might as well be blood, since it is made by the rich earth being swept away into the sea after the tropical rains. Much of the ancient forests that held the soil in place have been cut down to make way for cattle, or simply to provide firewood for the fast-growing population. Flying inland towards the capital, Antananarivo, perched on its high plateau, you can't miss the bare patches of earth. The red clay scars reveal where the Great Mother, as the Malagasy call their home, is being rubbed raw. Every time I see it, I feel a stab of pain.

Up close, the bare earth is the colour of dried apricots; a dramatic backcloth for the display of mudbrick houses topped with thatch. I can see water buffaloes pulling ploughs through terraced paddy fields and farmers bent double tending to their staple crop. The Malagasy love their rice, and proudly proclaim that they consume more of it, per capita, than the Chinese.

There were soldiers on the tarmac at Ivato airport as the plane taxied towards the terminal building. Close to where my plane parked there was another Boeing 737, rather shinier than the one I had taken from Africa. The polished tail plane was decorated with the elegant fan shape of the traveller's palm, and in man-sized lettering the fuselage bore the words REPOBLIKAN'I MADAGASIKARA. The president, Marc Ravalomanana, had recently acquired the plane for his official use, a controversial move in a country with so many financial problems. The plane had reportedly cost $12 million, something of a bargain, but it seemed like an ill-advised display of hubris, especially when the state airline Air Madagascar was in dire financial straits and had virtually abandoned much of its internal network due to a shortage of aircraft and aviation fuel. The plane also seemed an awkward asset for the man who had finally ousted the island's corrupt former dictator, Didier Ratsiraka.

Ratsiraka, otherwise known as the 'Admiral', came to power in 1975, leading the *Avant Garde de la Révolution Malgache* (AREMA). The Admiral developed a peculiarly idiosyncratic brand of politics known as Christian-Marxism. With help from North Korea and the Soviet Union he effectively destroyed Madagascar's economy, turning the island from a net exporter of rice into a country dependent on handouts from the eastern bloc. Meanwhile, he fomented racial discontent between the Merina tribe of the central highlands and the more 'African' peoples of the coastal regions. It was an astute strategy, assuring him of votes from the impoverished, illiterate masses and at the same time allowing him to intimidate the intellectual and aristocratic highlanders. The Merina (pronounced *mairn*), the clan which ruled Madagascar from the beginning of the nineteenth century, are distinctly un-African in appearance, tracing their origins back to the time when settlers from Indonesia first reached the islands two thousand years ago. They provided Madagascar with a feudal, aristocratic hierarchy and a monarchy which was abolished by the colonial French. Ethnically and economically, the Merina dominate the central plateau and the capital, Antananarivo, but Ratsiraka came from the coast, playing up his humble peasant origins in keeping with the spirit of socialism.

In good Marxist tradition Ratsiraka established a Supreme Revolutionary Council, and even produced his own little book of aphorisms, but unlike Chairman Mao's it was green instead of red. Under his rule, the country fell quietly, but steadily, into a mire of poverty, corruption and infrastructural decay. Far from bringing power to the masses of the lowlands, the revolutionary era allowed centralized state power to strengthen. Antananarivo and its predominantly Merina elite became the epicentre of power, wealth and corruption. As the roads fell apart, the provinces became even more remote, and in many cases virtually inaccessible except for those fortunate enough to be able to travel by air. Antananarivo, with its picturesque clay bricks, pitched medieval roofs and rolling hills, might be one of the world's most beautiful capitals. Instead, it became a twilit city beset by potholes, power cuts, bubonic plague and cholera. Arriving to report for the BBC in 1988, I still remember my first sight of hovels built from sticks on the pavement, with small groups of semi-naked children gathered outside. Nearby, their parents were tending fires for making charcoal, the whole family covered in soot like a miserable vision of Victorian urban squalor. The wealthier families barricaded themselves into their houses at night and employed watchmen and guards to protect them while they slept.

Vagabonds and cut-throats stalked the streets while Ratsiraka was holed up in his massive palace well away from the city. One day I took a taxi out of the city to catch a glimpse of the building. We stopped on a hill half a mile away to survey the presidential enclave from on high. Within minutes a military lorry thundered along the dirt road to where my driver had stopped. It blocked us in, and twenty soldiers leapt out brandishing AK47s. They demanded to know what I was doing, and why I might be taking photographs of the presidential palace. I managed to convince them that I was simply a tourist interested in the view, and that I didn't know that the monstrous, Korean-designed palace was of any significance. They let us go after pushing my driver around a bit, warning him not to bring any more *vazaha* up this road.

In 1991, as the eastern bloc began to disintegrate, the Admiral was quick to proclaim that it was time for a change of philosophy, and he took steps to liberalize certain parts of the economy. The island was in dire straits, with the World Bank estimating that by 1990, some 70 per cent of the population was living in poverty, twice as many as at independence three decades earlier. It was now officially among the ten poorest countries in the world. Pressure from the World Bank and other key donors was being put upon Ratsiraka to bring in economic reform. Without aid from the Soviet Union, the Admiral had no choice, and he agreed to liberalize key industries like petroleum, telecommunications and transport, as well as some aspects of food production. But crucially, vanilla would remain under state control. For years, foreign exporters had been forced to abide by a set price of around US$70 a kilogram, most of which went into 'government' coffers. Ratsiraka wasn't about to let anyone else take a share.

Vanilla and politics have never been far apart in Madagascar. Although the amount of vanilla produced worldwide is relatively small as an agricultural commodity, in Madagascar it is a vital part of the economy. Since 1900 vanilla has consistently represented a large share of the country's export earnings, and it is the only economic area in which Madagascar has an opportunity to influence a world market. The island consistently accounts for half of the world's vanilla production. Under Ratsiraka, the government imposed an 80 per cent tax on every kilogram of vanilla beans that left the island, making vanilla responsible for a staggering 10 per cent of national income. The combination of monopolistic Marxist export control and the fact that Madagascar dominated the market by virtue of sheer size, led to interesting benefits for those controlling the industry. Ratsiraka inherited a system set up at the behest of French economic advisers at the time of independence. A stabilization fund in the form of a parastatal company, the *Caisse de Stabilisation*, had been created to restrict exports, and so capitalize on Madagascar's dominance in world production. Meanwhile, the price paid to farmers was kept low, to discourage excess production and any resultant fall in price. For a century Madagascar had been the key player in the world market for natural vanilla, and as the largest exporter could easily influence world prices. The high quality of Bourbon vanilla also gave Malagasy exporters a lead. In addition, although there were at least 60,000 vanilla farmers, the internal vanilla trade in Madagascar was dominated by a select elite; those with the financial muscle to deal in such a valuable cash crop. To cement their position, an international 'Vanilla Alliance' was created with its neighbours Réunion and Comoros. Each country then agreed to an annual quota of exports so as further to control the world price.

There were negative consequences to all this rigid control. First, Madagascar started stockpiling vanilla, beans that it didn't want to export for fear of allowing supply to exceed demand. Malagasy exporters were in effect paid a subsidy for those vanilla stocks that were not exported. Allegedly, these would also serve as a buffer to be sold if the country ever experienced a poor crop year. The Caisse paid them a fee for storing this stock. Inevitably this led to corruption, with exporters and curers claiming the fee for stocks that never existed. As Ratsiraka's regime became increasingly corrupt the Caisse started paying fees only to those vanilla exporters in favour with the regime. Some exporters were given a better deal than others if they paid off the right people in the Ministry of Finance. It was not unknown for vanilla to be exported as 'cloves' so as to avoid paying the full complement of government taxes.

A further consequence of state intervention in the Malagasy vanilla industry was that Indonesian vanilla growers saw an opportunity. In competing with Madagascar, the Indonesians were faced with Bourbon beans of superior quality and what economists call oligopsony: a situation where a small number of buyers influence the price paid for an agricultural product. Indonesia started to increase its own production, and sell them at a lower price. The Indonesians couldn't compete on quality, but they could certainly increase the amount they grew. This was important, because buyers from the USA realized that when it came to making vanilla extract, there was no need to buy gourmet-grade beans from Madagascar. As Georges Randriamiharisoa had explained to me in Antalaha: if the beans were simply going to be mashed up and have their flavour extracted, it didn't really matter what they looked like. For many food applications, there was no reason to pay top dollar for immaculately sorted and graded Bourbon beans. However, food manufacturers might still choose Bourbon beans for their consistently higher vanillin content. Indonesian beans would be cheaper, but manufacturers might need to use twice as many to achieve the same strength of flavour.

In the last decade of the twentieth century, Madagascar's internal political upheavals were to have a devastating impact on the vanilla trade. Ratsiraka was voted out of office in 1993, and replaced by President Albert Zafy, who promised true democracy and the birth of a genuinely free-market economy. The new president increased economic reforms, and abolished the *Caisse de Stabilisation*, replacing it with the Madagascar Vanilla Institute (IVAMA). The Institute did not have a monopoly over the amount of vanilla that could be exported, but it was staffed by essentially the same people who had run the Caisse.

In 1996, disillusioned with continuing corruption and the lack of economic progress promised by Zafy, the Malagasy electorate voted Ratsiraka back into power. It was a classic case of 'better the devil you know'. The consequence for vanilla trade was that Ratsiraka promptly abolished IVAMA, hoping to get his hands on the vanilla industry once again. However, pressure from the World Bank and the International Monetary Fund meant he could no longer insist on total state control over the crop. With official price fixing no longer in force, the government had to content itself with imposing a tax of around US$21 per kilogram on vanilla exports. Those who had pressurized the government to adopt free-market principles in the vanilla trade also made a mistake. They assumed that the market was inelastic, that world demand would remain at similar levels no matter the price. In fact, the vanilla business showed great elasticity of demand, and prices fell in the face of excess supply. By 1996 the price of vanilla had more than halved, to roughly $25 a kilogram. In the following year it dipped below $20 a kilo and remained at that level until 2000. The peasant farmers of the SAVA were being paid 50 cents a kilo for green beans.

No one knows how much corruption there has been in Madagascar's vanilla market, but it seems highly unlikely that such a key industry would have escaped the kind of financial skulduggery that characterized many government operations during Ratsiraka's reign. It seems probable that businessmen with vested interests in the export trade would have had to make a deal with the *ancien régime*. The Admiral's era coincided with the period when Madagascar supplied just over 70 per cent of the world's vanilla. Fortunes had been made with vanilla, and the men in charge of selling the crop to foreign buyers were unlikely to give up their role in its trade. Thanks to Ratsiraka, they had no local competition.

Although the 1996 elections had returned the Admiral to power, his new role as a democratically elected president left him considerably weaker than he had been in the seventies and eighties. Having had a taste of freedom, ordinary Malagasy people were no longer afraid of showing their displeasure at government inefficiency and crumbling living standards. In Antananarivo the collapse of communism had spawned a remarkable cult of civil disobedience and a culture of truly massive public demonstrations. It was not unusual to see half a million people blocking the streets of the capital whenever the government made an unpopular decision. In the nineties general strikes also became something of a popular pastime.

At the very end of 2000 a parliamentary election was held, and although Ratsiraka's AREMA party did well in the provinces, a boycott by opposition voters rendered the poll almost meaningless. However, Ratsiraka remained in power as Madagascar adheres to the French system of one round of legislative or parliamentary elections, with a separate contest for the presidency. When it was time for presidential elections in December 2001, the opposition candidate, Marc Ravalomanana, claimed victory. His party represented something new, the promise of a fresh start for the island. Ravalomanana was a self-made millionaire, a man who had built his fortune on dairy products, especially yoghurt. A devout Christian, he called his party *Tiako i Madagasikara* – I Love Madagascar. If nothing else it had a more appealing ring to it than most of the other 133 parties contesting the election which included names like the 'Party Uniting Common Efforts' and 'Work, Justice and Development in Harmony'.

Victory at the polls was not enough to displace the Admiral. Didier Ratsiraka simply refused to acknowledge defeat, brazenly claiming that Ravalomanana was corrupt. For the first few months of 2001, violent protests and riots between rival factions caused chaos in Antananarivo. The Supreme Court ruled that the votes should be recounted, and the two rival presidents agreed. The court found in Ravalomanana's favour, but then the Admiral simply refused to go. He declared a state of martial law, and for seven months Madagascar effectively ceased to function as an economy. There were two presidents, with Ravalomanana installing himself in the government offices in the capital, and Ratsiraka setting up a rival regime on the coast at Toamasina. Apart from being his home town, Toamasina is also the main port of entry for ships arriving in Madagascar, and the only port from which supplies can easily reach the capital by road. Troops and supporters of Ratsiraka mounted a blockade, and bridges and power lines were blown up to cut off access to Antananarivo. The capital ground to a halt. The two rival presidents each created his own administration, including naming their own governors for the Central Bank. But neither man could gain access to Madagascar's finances, since almost all of the national cash was kept in the American Federal Reserve. Unsure of whose administration was the legitimate government, the US simply blocked access to the funds until the political dispute could be resolved. Air Madagascar ran out of fuel.

While the political situation in Madagascar was chaotic and the road to true democracy decidedly rocky, the vanilla growers, curers and exporters were also contending with the forces of nature. On the night of 2 April 2000, an intense tropical cyclone hit the vanilla-growing region on the north-east coast. Cyclone Hudah was 250 miles wide, and travelling at almost 200 miles an hour. Centring in on Antalaha, it destroyed an estimated 1,000 acres of vanilla plantations, perhaps a fifth of the total, prompting fears that the 2001 season would see a shortage of beans available for export. Since the demise of the government cartel several years earlier, Madagascar had been gradually, and covertly, getting rid of its surplus stock of vanilla. There was little, if any, left with which to make up the shortfall. In 2000 the vanilla price doubled, hovering close to $50 a kilogram. Vanilla dealers watched in alarm as an historic economic bubble began to grow.

At one stage during the impasse between Ravalomanana and Ratsiraka in their rival capitals, it was mooted that Madagascar might split into a collection of provincial federations, each running its own economy. Rumours spread that Ratsiraka would keep the SAVA region, and its all-important vanilla industry for himself. The political chaos of 2002 and the uncertainty over the amount of vanilla likely to come onto the market following the previous year's hurricane, combined to create understandable nervousness in the market. Without state control of the export price, the stage was set for this mixture of nerves, civil unrest and canny exporters to send the price of good quality vanilla sky high. Speculators, eager to push up the price, were happy to exaggerate the potential negative impact of both the weather and the civil war when talking to foreign buyers. They created a frenzied atmosphere in which foreign buyers were desperate to secure supplies of cured beans, and committed themselves to contracts at prices that were more than double what they had paid the year before.

Far from stabilizing the price, as some analysts had predicted, the free market had caused the price to go into uncharted territory. In 1999 foreign buyers had been accustomed to retail values of between $25 and $40 a kilogram for their cured vanilla, but by 2001 the figure had shot up to $150. By 2002 Malagasy exporters were expecting $250 a kilo, and by 2003 the price had reached almost $400. Similarly, heavy rains during the 2002 season led to a shortage of beans reaching the market in 2004. The rains had a doubly negative effect; they caused flowers to drop from the vines preventing them being pollinated, and they lowered the air temperature, causing the vines to produce fewer flowers. Due to the delay between picking the beans and when they appear on the supermarket shelves the vanilla traders knew that the weather in 2002 would have a serious impact on supermarket prices in 2004, another factor to include in their negotiations. Some buyers feared that premium grade vanilla would reach a retail price of $500 a kilogram. They were correct.

Meanwhile, the political crisis between Ratsiraka and Ravalomanana was finally resolved in July 2002, when the Admiral agreed to go into exile in France. Ravalomanana's victory in the previous year's elections was recognized by the international community and he set about establishing his new 'corruption free' government for the island. Government officials were given large pay rises in an effort to obviate the need for them to accept bribes.

Ratsiraka might have fled the country, but the sight of the soldiers on the tarmac at the airport reminded me of the first time I had come to Madagascar. Back then, dozens of rather scruffy soldiers had been in attendance at the airport, and they also manned the immigration booth inside the terminal.

I had been in Seychelles, and my flight connections meant spending a night in Mauritius. Early that morning, just three hours before I was due to catch the Air Mauritius flight to Antananarivo, I had fallen and injured my ankle, tearing the ligaments on both sides and, as I learned later, causing a slight break in the bone. I couldn't put any weight on my foot at all, but I was so determined to get to Madagascar that I refused to go to a hospital for treatment, as missing my flight to Antananarivo would have meant a three-day wait for the next one. I assumed that within a few hours I would be able to see a doctor in Antananarivo. At least I would be on the magical island I had always wanted to visit. My ankle had swollen to three times its normal size, and the Mauritian hotel had summoned a pharmacist from a nearby village to give me first aid. He inspected my grotesquely swollen joint and grandly pronounced that a fracture was almost certain. On learning that I was insisting on going to the airport, he disappeared, returning a little while later with some gel, which he said would help the pain. It turned out to be haemorrhoid ointment, but it did have the effect of numbing the skin. I remember clearly the long walk from the aeroplane to the terminal building, shuffling and hopping along on my good leg as best I could. The night before

I broke my ankle I had also developed an extremely volatile stomach upset, necessitating frequent and violent visits to the lavatory. Now I would have to allow extra time to get there.

My only contact in Antananarivo was Voahangy Rakotoarivelo, a journalist who worked for the BBC on a freelance basis, and she had come to the airport to meet me. Her eyes widened in dismay when she saw my swollen leg. I assumed I could go to a clinic and receive treatment, but she shook her head. 'No, Tim,' she said sadly. 'There is no clinic I can recommend. If it needs an operation, you would have to go back to Mauritius or England.'

I wondered if Voahangy was being overly cautious, but while I was in Antananarivo I met the British Ambassador. He confirmed that seeking medical assistance in Antananarivo was not advised. His deputy, whom I knew slightly, had just been flown to Mauritius for medical treatment. The man had been accidentally stabbed while rehearsing an amateur dramatic presentation of an Agatha Christie play. During our meeting, the ambassador said something that I have never forgotten. 'This country has minerals, oil, and an amazing natural environment. It also has a sophisticated population. It is a land of enormous potential. And,' he smiled benignly, 'it always will be.'

My memories of that first visit consist, in part, of an endless succession of extended visits to extremely primitive lavatories, and of taxi rides in the ubiquitous Renault 4s, along the worst roads I had ever encountered within a city. I had seen bad rural roads in Africa, but I had never seen a capital with countless potholes along the main streets that were big enough to swallow a car. There were no streetlights that worked, and no foreigner dared journey out at night without a torch. Driving seemed only marginally safer. At night, the drivers had the disconcerting habit of flicking their headlights on only if they were approaching a major junction. Otherwise, they drove without them, telling me that headlamp bulbs were impossible to obtain. The taxis would also switch off their engines whenever there was the prospect of a decent glide downhill, economizing on petrol. Because of my broken ankle I often took relatively short taxi journeys, rather than present myself as a slow moving target to the muggers and potholes that riddled the streets. Once, a taxi driver took me from an office on a hill all the way into town at night without ever switching on his engine, coasting all the way and laughing wildly at the effort of controlling the car without letting it lose momentum. He laughed even more wildly when I suggested that the fare should be reduced in accordance with what he had saved on petrol.

Air Madagascar also made an impression on me. Attempting to fly to Antsiranana at the northern tip of the island, I had spent an entire day shuttling between the capital and Mahajanga on the west coast. Twice we took off for Antsiranana only to return to Mahajanga because the pilot had been warned of an approaching storm. Unfortunately, radio contact with Antsiranana was unreliable and he didn't want to risk flying into the airport in case the weather was truly bad. On our second landing at Mahajanga I hobbled over to the airport control tower. There was no impediment to visiting the tower, and I shuffled up the steps to the control room. It was one of those towers with a mushroom shaped blob at the top where, ordinarily, the controllers would have large picture windows on all sides giving a clear view of the tarmac. The windows were there but they were all broken and the lone controller was exposed to the elements. He seemed happy to have a visitor, and he explained to me that he was attempting to make contact with his colleagues at my destination, Antsiranana. He was using a telephone, one of those old cumbersome models with a large wobbly cradle for the heavy Bakelite handset. On the side there was a little handle which he whirled energetically to obtain a line. It wasn't working, and we chatted for a few minutes about the difficulties of flying in Madagascar. He explained to me that my flight would have to return to Antananarivo. Then he gave me a wink, and looked at my heavily bandaged ankle. 'Monsieur should go to the front of the queue,' he said amiably. 'There may be some trouble.'

Unfortunately, we were now so late that there were people jostling for space on the plane, passengers from Mahajanga expecting to join our aircraft on its return flight from Antsiranana to the capital. I took the controller's advice and eased myself close to the metal barrier which prevented passengers wandering onto the apron. Pointing at my bandaged ankle I asked the soldier at the barrier if I could be allowed through ahead of the crowd. A small cash advance paved the way. I was halfway across the tarmac when I heard the stampede behind me. It had been announced that seating for the return flight to Antananarivo would operate on the *place libre* basis. In other words, whoever found an empty seat and claimed it, could have it. In spite of my ankle, I managed to make it to one of the last free places on board and watched as those left standing in the aisle were ordered off the aircraft by soldiers with guns. It wasn't pleasant, and I then felt guilty for getting a seat. Women with babies cried. Men in suits produced papers claiming they needed to reach the capital on urgent business. It was all to no avail, and eventually, the hapless stragglers were removed and we returned to Tana, ten hours after we had left on what was scheduled to be a two-hour journey.

Madagascar had a deep effect upon me, and I returned several times to witness some of the political transformations that followed the collapse of Christian-Marxism. Some things improved, others did not. In 2003 I noticed that apart from the President's spanking new aeroplane, the collection of rusting Soviet-built military aircraft that had always decorated the periphery of Ivato airport had been removed. The soldiers mounting guard and casting a wary eye over the arriving passengers were still heavily armed, but they were now smartly dressed.

Driving into Antananarivo also brought a pleasant surprise – the giant potholes which had blighted the capital had all been repaired. Traffic hazards still included men pulling rickshaws laden with bricks and firewood but all along the route there were new buildings in various stages of construction, and many of the ancient Renault 4s seemed to have been replaced with new Japanese models. People told me that the political crisis of the last few months had kept tourists away from the island but there were plenty of *vazaha* to be seen around town. In Antananarivo I met oil prospectors, airline industry executives and agricultural exporters all trying to make contact with the president's office in the hope of securing an entrée into the newly liberated markets abandoned by cronies of the old corrupt regime. There was definitely an air of hope and renewal in the air.

At the Antananarivo Hilton little had changed. The building itself is not attractive, a rather straight up and down block with a large open foyer and a couple of restaurants. On previous visits I had sought refuge in the foyer as a place to conduct interviews for the BBC, relatively sure I would find a reliable supply of electricity and comfortable sofas on which to sit. BBC travel budgets did not however allow me to stay there.

Even in the dark days of AREMA-led corruption, the hotel had always been one of the places where the city managed to retain a little glamour. In a small arcade next to the lobby there were boutiques selling crocodile leather shoes and handbags, finely embroidered linen and silk shawls all made in Madagascar. It was the place where foreign businessmen stayed, and where those with a little spare cash could use the casino on the top floor. I had once done rather well at roulette there, parlaying my small travel allowance into a satisfyingly large pile of Malagasy francs.

This time I wasn't counting my pennies quite so avidly. From my room there was a view over Lake Anosy, where the French built their memorial to Madagascar's First World War dead. Surmounted by Winged Victory the tall column of the memorial sticks up like a candle from its little island in the centre of the lake. It is a noble thing, in direct contrast to the hovels and shacks where the poor of Antananarivo live out their lives. There was a thunderstorm approaching, making the sky a dark mass of fulminating rain clouds. The lake is surrounded by jacaranda trees and their purple blossoms made a garland fit for any hero. That night the rain cleared the streets of all traffic, and as there was no point in trying to leave the hotel I decided to revisit the casino.

The croupiers were petite young Malagasy women, with shining black hair and smooth brown skin. The air was thick with the smell of strong cheap tobacco, and the clientele were predominantly oriental men, chain-smoking and sipping at tumblers of whiskey brought to their tables by elegant waitresses in short skirts and waistcoats. The men, many of them visiting Taiwanese sailors and traders, played blackjack or jostled for a space at the roulette tables, slapping down their chips in a frenzy, stretching their stocky torsos across the baize to slip in an extra bet even as the croupiers cried *rien ne va plus*. The men made croaky *har har* sounds when the wheel stopped

The Malagasy have turned vanilla production into a lucrative art

spinning, and the noise didn't seem to vary much whether they won or lost. The croupiers, with their large brown lemurian eyes, were impassive, scooping up the losing chips with blank expressions and never smiling at the gamblers. I played roulette for an hour, staying at the table only until I started to lose. On this visit it was my own money at stake, and I wanted to keep it. I also wanted to get a good night's rest. There was more travelling to do, and I was waiting for the arrival of Henry Todd, the world's most important vanilla buyer.

14. Vanilla Prince

Henry Todd is tall, dark and quite handsome. His hair is thick, and cut short to reveal a widow's peak. Fit and slim, his tropical lightweight suit hangs immaculately from his broad shoulders. On his feet there are suede Gucci brogues and under his jacket there is a crisp Jermyn Street shirt. The porter at the door of the Madagascar Hilton knows him well, and immediately arranges to pay for the taxi that has brought him from the airport. The porter understands that Todd rarely carries any cash, mainly because he travels too frequently to bother exchanging his coins and notes for local currency. Todd has only one small piece of luggage: he visits the hotel so regularly that they allow him to leave a set of clothes here. The women behind the reception desk at the Madagascar Hilton all smile broadly at *M'sieur Todd*, handing him the key to his room with the minimum of formalities. Henry is the scion of the family-run company that buys almost half the vanilla beans in the world.

It is February, and after much negotiation, Todd has agreed to let me travel with him to the SAVA region while he investigates the state of the vanilla crop. It has taken a long time to arrange this trip, since Henry is constantly travelling.

In an average year he will make between fifty and seventy long-haul flights, and as many short hops to visit clients within the USA and Europe. His working life is a constant, punishing round of regular visits to Paris, London, Philadelphia, Chicago and other regional cities on both sides of the Atlantic. Perhaps eight times a year he will be in Madagascar, a journey that will always involve time in Antananarivo as well as flights to Antalaha, Sambava and perhaps Vohémar. He will make the same number of visits to India and Indonesia, and occasional trips to Uganda and the Comoros. Few of these places can be reached with a single flight. To reach Madagascar he often flies overnight from Europe to Johannesburg, picking up a three-hour connecting flight to Antananarivo. Sometimes he arrives via Mauritius or Nairobi. Each year, Henry Todd spends around $200,000 on his airline tickets alone, and he told me once that he had accumulated about one million air miles on his account with British Airways alone.

The firm that he works for is called Zink & Triest, an old-established firm of vanilla dealers acquired by the Todd family in the 1960s. For several years now, Henry has been responsible for acquiring the vanilla that Zink & Triest imports into the USA. In the trade he is known as Henry 'Junior', since his father, Henry 'Senior', did the same job for many years and now manages operations from the company headquarters in Pennsylvania. Zink & Triest imports vanilla beans and then sells them to extract producers, to flavourists and in some cases directly to food and beverage manufacturers. They will never reveal the identities of their individual clients, but it is safe to say that there are few people using natural vanilla who have not done business with Zink & Triest.

Henry greets me with a warm handshake. We have met before, but on a rather formal basis, and I know he is wary of revealing too much about the vanilla trade. 'Hi Tim, glad you could get here,' he says cheerfully. 'We'll catch up later. Right now I have a meeting in town with some important people. I just had a phone call about it when I was coming in from the airport.' As we are talking, two Malagasy men in suits come through the swing doors and greet Henry in French. He is bilingual, and generally talks as rapidly in French as he does in English. He tells them he will drop his bag in his room and five minutes later I see him depart with the men in a four-wheel-drive vehicle with smoked glass windows. Later that day I learn that his important meeting was with President Ravalomanana. Interestingly, the president's office had turned down my repeated requests for an interview for the BBC, saying that he was preparing to go abroad the very next day and wasn't able to see anyone. However, it seemed he could clear his diary for the world's biggest vanilla dealer. That night I received a phone call from Henry Todd telling me to be ready to leave Antananarivo early the next morning. We would be going north to visit some vanilla growers.

The coterie of vanilla dealers who dominate the international market are all well known to one another. Their club is a small one, where contact is unavoidable, and face-to-face business relationships are kept cordial. As I learnt more about the business, and the men who run it, something became clear. Rumours and counter rumours are a significant part of vanilla brokerage. It is partly why the brokers keep their movements as secretive as possible.

In Madagascar, Mexico, India and Indonesia the farmers spread rumours about the amount of vanilla they think will be available during the next season. They hope to frighten the curers into offering them a better price for green beans. In turn, the curers spread rumours among the farmers about how much the foreign buyers are willing to pay for the dried product. They want to make the farmers believe that it is the foreign buyers who set the price, rather than themselves. Meanwhile, the international brokers spread what they call 'market intelligence' to their customers about how much vanilla may or may not be available during the forthcoming year. It often suits the smaller buyers to exaggerate the effect that their larger rivals are having upon the price. They can blame other dealers for paying too much or too little for vanilla, claiming that it is the largest dealers who make the market. And among the small band of international vanilla buyers, the men who import the cured vanilla into the developed world, there is always time for a little gossip.

As I got to know many more of these major dealers, the cracks in the brotherhood began to show. On many occasions I was told that there was only one reason for the recent and ongoing crisis in the vanilla market. 'It's Zink & Triest,' other brokers would whisper discreetly, and always with the admonition that they must never be quoted. 'Let's face it, Z&T have more cash than anyone else – it's in their interest for the market to go sky high. No one else has the money to compete with them. They've been encouraging the price rises, so that they can force everyone else to the wall – then they'll corner the market.'

If I pressed them further, some dealers would get personal. 'It's Henry "Junior",' said one. 'He's behind all this.' The thesis seemed to be that Todd was a young man, eager to make his mark in the industry by fair means or foul. Apart from a vague supposition that it might be in Zink & Triest's interest to drive their competitors out of business, there didn't seem to be anything more specific behind the claims. However, the

awe with which these rivals spoke of Henry 'Junior' made m
curious. I wanted to learn more about the background to th
Todd family's dominance of the vanilla world.

On a cold winter's day I took a plane from Chicago over
frozen Lake Michigan to reach the Midwest town of Kalamazoo
The southern end of the vast lake was a milk white gatherin
of mammoth ice shards and the streets of Kalamazoo wer
slithery with slush. It is an average-sized town, with a universit
and a strong sense of community spirit, somewhat burdene
by its faintly comical sounding name. At the small airport a
Battle Creek the newsagent was selling souvenir mugs, T-shirt
and pencils with the slogan: 'Yes! There really is a Kalamazoo.
The town might have remained more obscure had it not bee
for the popular Glenn Miller song 'I've Got a Gal in Kala
mazoo', which was featured in the 1942 film *Orchestra Wive*
and nominated for an Oscar. It didn't win, although the lyri
cist Mack Gordon may have taken some solace from the fac
that he lost to Irving Berlin's 'White Christmas' at the 194
ceremony.

Henry Todd's great-great-grandfather was one of Kalama
zoo's most prominent citizens. The company he set up in 186
still has its headquarters in Kalamazoo, and I was keen to learn
something about the dynasty that has come to dominate the
vanilla trade. Albert May Todd had nothing to do with the
tropical vine, but he built a considerable fortune on anothe
plant: mint.

Albert Todd was one of ten children born to a New Englanc
family who could trace their stock back to a Yorkshiremar
called Christopher Todd, who arrived in the colony in 1638
He married into a family of successful bakers and the family
have stayed with food ever since. When Albert May Todd wa

born in 1850 his family was living in Michigan, where the cultivation of mint was a well-established industry. As a teenager, Todd began experimenting with growing his own crops, learning how to distil the oil, which in the nineteenth century was still regarded as a virtual panacea. Peppermint-flavoured lozenges were a standby in any medicine chest and Spirit of Mint was regarded as a cure for flatulence, colic and even depression. The process of mint oil extraction was comparatively simple, requiring little more than a large copper boiler in which fresh mint would be steamed and the oil collected by condensation. Mint production spread in tandem with the expanding population of the north-eastern United States as settlers travelled west and up into Michigan in search of farmland. By the middle of the nineteenth century the Midwest's production of mint oil was a big enough business for excess production to be shipped back to Europe.

In 1869, at the age of nineteen, Albert Todd formed the 'Nottawa Steam Refined Essential Oil Works' in collaboration with his elder brother, Oliver. One of the factors affecting the price that could be fetched for mint oil was its purity. Albert concocted a steam jet system for further refining the oil, and the Todds' 'Crystal White Oil of Peppermint' acquired a reputation for excellence and reliably good quality. The brothers made enough money to allow Albert to attend Illinois University in 1873, where he studied chemistry. However, the strain of studying while keeping an eye on the business was apparently too much for him and Albert became ill, undertaking a voyage to Europe in 1874 to recuperate. The voyage evidently provided a cure, since young Albert was able to undertake an extensive walking tour, during which he visited eight countries.

The trip greatly influenced his subsequent career, both financially and culturally. On a visit to England he discovered a variety of mint that was not being cultivated in the USA, a strain known as Black Mitcham, from Surrey. He brought some cuttings of the new mint back to Michigan and quickly found that it was hardier than the plants already in cultivation. With his background in chemistry, Albert Todd continued to perfect his method of distilling mint oil that yielded a purer product than any of his rivals'. In 1876, Albert Todd exhibited his wares at the Centennial Exposition of the United States, held in Philadelphia to celebrate a hundred years of independence from Britain. Todd was awarded a medal for his 'Crystal White Double Distilled Oil of Peppermint', and a cash prize which he invested in some rare books. It was the beginning of a library and an art collection that would eventually become something of an obsession with the mint grower.

On a snow-filled morning in Kalamazoo I found myself in front of a classic red-brick Art Deco industrial building on Douglas Avenue. A fine collegiate-style entrance led into a small foyer. There on the wall was an oil painting of the man himself, Albert May Todd, the man they called the 'Peppermint King'. Painted in 1918, it shows him sitting in a finely carved armchair and wearing a sombre three-piece suit, with wing collar and a dark bow-tie. This is no soulless portrait of a captain of industry: his features are thoughtful and in his right hand there is a book, his forefinger marking the page as if he has just been interrupted while reading poetry. The portrait and the panelled walls combined to make the lobby feel more like the entrance to a gentlemen's club in New York than part of a provincial factory. There was something else unexpected about this place: it actually smelled of mint.

The Todd building is not normally open to the public, but my visit had been arranged in advance. A fresh blast of mint-scented air filled the lobby as a panelled door swung open and Ian Blair, a former vice-president of the Todd company, emerged to give me a tour. Ian had married into the Todd family, eventually rising to the post of financial controller for the company. 'I'm officially retired now,' Ian explained. 'But I guess I've become something of a company historian over the years. Let me show you around.'

Behind the reception area there was a network of corridors leading to a more modern extension to the building where the mint business was located. I had to wear a white lab coat and protective goggles before being allowed into the production areas. There wasn't a great deal to see: a succession of large metal cylinders, an automated labelling system for plastic drums containing mint oil and a laboratory where a small team of chemists were testing samples of mint oil. Ian explained that the mint oil business hadn't changed a great deal since the time of Albert May Todd. As he talked, the similarity with the vanilla business became clear. Like vanilla, mint is a natural plant product valued for its specific flavour properties. It is processed in a relatively simple manner and sold on in processed form to large-scale food manufacturers as an ingredient in other products. It is also an industry that requires high standards of purity, because as with vanilla, industrial mint users require an ingredient which is chemically stable and consistent in flavour.

Ian was cautious about discussing what happened to the mint oil after it left the A. M. Todd factory. 'You know, the food industry is very sensitive,' he said sheepishly. 'We have to sign confidentiality agreements with the people we supply, and agree not to discuss what we do for them.'

As we returned to the wood-panelled surroundings of the main building I began to understand something of the scale of success Albert Todd had enjoyed. In a small display cabinet there was a bottle of the original 'Crystal White' peppermint oil produced by A. M. Todd at the 1876 exposition. A. M. Todd oils garnered medals at other trade fairs, including the Paris Exposition of 1900. More telling and remarkable than the ephemera of the mint oil bottles and labels from early product lines was the art upon the walls. Large oil paintings were dotted around the executive offices. Here was a copy of Velázquez's Venus on one wall, copied from the National Gallery in London. 'In those days it was common for American collectors to commission copies,' Ian explained almost apologetically. 'If you couldn't obtain the real thing, you could at least get a very good artist to reproduce the ones you liked.' Apart from copies of European masters, there were numerous originals by American artists, with pride of place going to a work by William Robertson Leigh from 1914. Entitled 'The Great Spirit', it depicts a Native American brave sitting on an escarpment and staring over a great expanse of mountain scenery. Ian seemed keen that I properly appreciated this particular work. 'Out of all his collection, that was Todd's absolute favourite,' he said. 'He was very keen to promote artists who painted Americana.'

Aside from becoming a patron of the emerging school of 'Western' artists, Albert Todd made a further eight visits to Europe between 1907 and 1923, acquiring oil paintings, porcelain and sculptures. There were first editions of Tennyson, William Morris and Edgar Allan Poe. He also bought a fifteenth-century edition of Dante's *Divine Comedy*, rare illustrated works of natural history by Audubon and original editions of 'Captain Cook's voyages'. When he died in 1931, aged eighty-one, much of his collection of twelve thousand books and hundreds of paintings passed to the University of Michigan and other public institutions. He once wrote, 'I am having a good time buying what I don't need and never can use.

But the people can use them, get joy and inspiration from them . . .'

Todd was a capitalist and an entrepreneur with a social conscience. A supporter of prohibition, he also founded an organization called the Public Ownership League of America, whose aims were to foster public control over railroads and utility companies. 'He was definitely a reformer,' Ian explained. 'And we always joke that he was the last Todd who was a Democrat!'

Albert Todd was elected to the United States Congress in 1896, the first Democrat elected in Michigan for almost fifty years. In one of the display cabinets I spotted a campaign lapel button with the slogan: 'Pay your taxes, Worship God / Vote for the Honorable A. M. Todd.'

In business, Albert Todd was not content to simply buy mint from other farmers; he realized that having his own plantations would enable him to make larger profits, and also to control more closely the quality of the plants he was harvesting. In the 1890s he acquired large tracts of land not far from Kalamazoo, property that had been considered unsuitable for farming due to being waterlogged. In Michigan these areas were known as the Mucklands. Todd invested in digging extensive drainage ditches in these wetlands and set up his own mint plantations, one of them named Mentha. Mentha developed into a settlement in its own right, acquiring its own shop, school, post office and railway station, and Ian showed me pictures of the impressive wooden buildings and immense steam tractors from the era.

Apart from being an astute businessman, Albert Todd's fortune was significantly increased by developments in American consumerism that flourish to this day, namely chewing gum and toothpaste. Kalamazoo is relatively close to Chicago, where a man named William Wrigley was in the soap-making business. To encourage shops and salesmen to take his product he would offer them extra incentives, such as free packets of baking powder to give away to their customers. The baking powder proved more successful than his soap, so Wrigley switched products. To promote the baking powder he offered free packets of chewing gum. Again, the samples proved more popular than the product they were meant to promote. In 1894, after experimenting with various flavours, Wrigley produced Spearmint – the world's most popular chewing gum. Wrigley's was not the only company that needed mint oil, and by the turn of the century Albert Todd was supplying firms such as American Chicle, Beechnut, Colgate and Procter & Gamble. Within a few years, peppermint-flavoured gum and spearmint-flavoured toothpaste were to become worldwide phenomena.

The dynasty that Albert Todd created from mint plants is still flourishing. In time Albert May's son Albert John ('A. J.') took over the business, followed by his son A. J. 'Junior'. A. J. 'Junior' was succeeded by Albert John Todd the Third, and then Henry W. Todd became the fifth generation to take up the reins as president of the company. It is his son Henry 'Junior' who is now responsible for acquiring the vanilla stocks.

The world of international vanilla dealers has always been tight-knit, or at least limited in its membership. In the 1960s the A. M. Todd company was still principally dealing in mint. At the time, a Philadelphia vanilla broker named Bernard Champon was working for the Zink & Triest company, a partnership formed by a former professional tennis player 'Bill' Triest and his business associate, Jack Zink. They relied on Bernard Champon to buy their own vanilla stocks, since he spoke French and they did not. When Zink and Triest began to think about retiring the Todd company received a tip-off that the business might be for sale, and they made an offer. The mint industry was stable, but no longer expanding significantly and it was time to diversify. To trade successfully in vanilla would require the same sort of skills they had used to dominate the mint industry – and a healthy amount of investment, something the Todds could also provide.

Today the A. M. Todd group supplies ingredients for the food, beverage, flavour, fragrance, cosmetic, and dietary supplement industries. Their clients produce toothpaste and sports drinks, chewing gum and pharmaceuticals – all products that rely on achieving highly specific flavour characteristics as part of their distinctive identity. Henry Todd 'Junior', great-great-grandson of the 'Peppermint King', may be relatively young, but with antecedents like this, he can hardly be called an upstart.

Henry Todd took me back to Antalaha in a chartered plane. 'I usually don't have time to wait for the Air Mad schedule,' he explained as we climbed on board. 'They don't have daily flights to a lot of the places I need to visit, and I'd end up getting stuck somewhere.'

Away from Antananarivo, Henry was visibly more relaxed, and he had exchanged his tropical suit for a pair of jeans, sandals and a crisp white polo shirt. During the flight, which involved landings at Toamasina and at Sambava to top up with fuel, we took turns to sit beside the pilot. I discovered that Henry and I shared an interest in aeroplanes, a common affliction among people who fly alone frequently. I told him about a friend of mine with whom I played a game involving points according to which aircraft, which airlines and which airports one had visited. Behind his slightly cool professional exterior there was a man with a good sense of humour and a wide-ranging awareness of current affairs. The fact that I had travelled to many of the places he knew well provided another bond.

At Antalaha Henry's mood changed again. There was a delegation of people waiting to meet him at the airport when we landed. As our small Beechcraft taxied towards the terminal building, Henry warned me that for the next two days we would not be alone. 'Apart from you,' he confided, 'there are a lot of other people who've been asking to see our operation down here. I figured that it was better to let them all come at once. That way the farmers will only get to see one bunch of *vazaha* tramping *en brousse* through the vanilla plantations.'

'Why does that matter?' I asked.

'You know, the farmers see foreigners around, they get excited and the price starts going up straightaway. They don't get a lot of white folks around here, so they always figure anyone they see is here to buy vanilla.'

Georges Randriamiharisoa, president of the vanilla exporters' association and the Ramanandraibe curing house, was one of the delegation at the airport. There was also a collection of other people to whom I was introduced in bewilderingly quick succession. They included a young American man from Zink & Triest who was visiting Madagascar to obtain some auditing information on the vanilla trade, and two men from large flavour and fragrance manufacturing companies, one in France and one in the USA. A commercial attaché from the US embassy in Antananarivo had also made the journey, saying that he was newly arrived in Madagascar and he wanted to find out more about vanilla as a key export crop. There was another American, an elegant older woman who told me she had come to Madagascar to make a feasibility study of vanilla farming. She said she was working as a consultant for an aid agency that wanted to persuade coca growers in Colombia that vanilla might be a viable alternative to the drug trade. She, and all of the other people present, wanted to pick Henry Todd's brains.

That night Henry and I stayed at a large colonial-style house overlooking the waterfront at Antalaha. It had been acquired by Zink & Triest as a base for when Henry needed to stay in town. There were thick wooden shutters on the doors and windows and the furniture inside was made of heavy hardwood. It was neither comfortable nor particularly appealing to look at.

'There was an old French guy and his wife who lived here for thirty years,' Henry explained. 'He decided to go back to France and he left all this furniture in the house when he went – I think he made some of it himself.'

The house was grand, but rather run down. Henry smoked a cigar and drank a glass of whiskey as we sat on the porticoed verandah overlooking the overgrown garden with its small empty fountain and a collection of untidy flower beds. He had a habit of peppering his conversation with French words, a language he had first studied at Dartmouth College in New Hampshire. Semi-permanent residency in Paris and his constant involvement with Madagascar meant that Henry was perfectly bilingual.

'Did you learn French because you knew you would end up in the family business?'

'No, not at all,' Henry said, fiddling with his cigar, which seemed in danger of going out. 'I had no intention of working with my dad. I wanted to be a banker and after college that's what I did. Then I had a car accident and broke my leg very badly and ended up spending a lot of time in hospital. I guess after that I decided I wanted to do something other than sit in an office all day getting stressed about stuff that doesn't really matter.'

'But isn't vanilla trading stressful?'

'You know, Tim, it is. *Goddamit!*' Henry's cigar had finally fizzled out. He went in search of some matches and returned a minute later, and I wondered if it was an excuse to change the subject. But he returned to my question. 'Vanilla is so stressful I can't even light a cigar these days,' he joked. 'No, seriously, it can be stressful but no two days are ever the same. And I love places like this. Can I carry on doing it for another ten years? Maybe not. But when the travelling gets too much, I remind myself that if I end up back in the States in an office one day, I'll miss all this.'

I felt I was getting to know Henry better, and I broached the subject of some of the rumours I had heard about Zink & Triest. 'Are you ruthless?' I asked.

Henry drew on his cigar for what seemed a long time. 'I don't accept that characterization,' he finally replied, without showing any emotion. 'We're the biggest exporters and that gives us a certain amount of leverage in the market. People don't like that. Would I do something that I considered unethical to beat my competitors? No. I think you have to maintain a reputation for straight dealing if you want to survive in this business. And we've survived through some very tough times. If we were ruthless we would have dropped some of our smaller customers when the price of vanilla went through the ceiling. We didn't, and we've lost money on occasion honouring our contracts. Is that ruthless?'

'Where do you see the vanilla farmers in all this?' I asked, curious to know Henry's perspective on their situation.

'Right now,' he said earnestly, 'they're doing great. But this market can't sustain these prices indefinitely. When it crashes, it's gonna crash big-time. Say what you like about state control, but Malagasy farmers got something good out of it. They knew what price they were getting and they didn't care how long it took to cure their beans. They turned curing into a genuine art form.'

'Are they getting too much money for their beans now?'

'In the sense that the market is unbalanced, yes. I think an export price of around $60 a kilo would make everyone happy, and still give them a fair wage.'

I knew I had heard that figure before. In Mexico, Victor Vallejo had proposed a similar price as giving the farmers a fair deal. Surprisingly, Henry 'Junior', the world's biggest vanilla buyer, and Victor, the farmer's champion, were talking the same language.

A few hundred yards along the seafront there was a rusty freighter tied up at the dilapidated jetty in front of a deserted customs house. 'That's the boat that takes our vanilla to Toamasina,' said Henry. 'One of the reasons we bought this house here is that we can keep an eye on what's going on at the dock. One of our rivals had an incident recently where he loaded three containers onto a boat and flew up to Toamasina to make sure it got onto the boat to Europe. When it arrived the containers were empty – the thieves had hijacked the boat and used acetylene torches to cut the hinges off the container doors!'

I tried to find out a little more about some of the people who had been at the airport that afternoon. Henry was frustratingly discreet whenever the conversation veered towards anyone with whom he did business. 'Like you, they all want to know about vanilla,' Henry said guardedly. 'The guys from the flavour houses want to see how the vines are doing – then they think they'll have an idea about the size of next year's crop. They'll use that knowledge to try and second-guess me on price.'

*

The next day we all left in a convoy of four-by-four vehicles to drive to a plantation halfway between Antalaha and Sambava, a distance of about twenty-five miles. The road was dry and in poor condition, but it passed through some of the island's prime vanilla land. Tiny villages, comprised entirely of simple huts covered in sun-bleached palm thatch, flashed by and we left them behind in clouds of orange dust. Women and children sat beside the road sorting through carpets of red and brown chilli peppers and cloves. Young boys tended solitary cows on the grass verge outside the villages and there were naked ebony-skinned men with hard-muscled torsos bathing in muddy streams. A traffic jam formed at a narrow wooden bridge across a lagoon within sight of the sea. I decided to walk across it and met three little boys who wanted to show me a fish they had caught. It was no more than four inches long but they were proud of it and beamed at me in triumph as I took a photograph. On the lagoon there were men fishing from dugout canoes and the boys told me with wide eyes that upstream there were crocodiles.

This was fertile land. Jackfruits like grotesque scrotums hung from trees beside the road. Banana trees and cashews grew plentifully, and we passed women with baskets of fruit balanced upon their heads. They carried everything that way: one with a pile of freshly washed laundry, another some gnarled manioc roots and another, miles from any visible shop, had just a single can of Coca-Cola perched on her tightly braided top-knot.

Occasionally we stopped. Henry would lead us into the trees to inspect vanilla vines growing close to the road. The vines were in flower, and whenever we stopped, farmers emerged from their huts near by to discuss how many pods might be produced in the next season. At one plantation a young boy came out to join the group wearing a T-shirt decorated with a portrait of Osama Bin Laden. The man from the American embassy stared at it as though it might spring to life. 'Why do you think he's wearing that?' he asked me in a whisper.

'Who knows?' I tried to reassure him that he hadn't stumbled on an Al Qaeda connection to vanilla. 'I suspect he was given it – he may not even know who Bin Laden is. These people aren't even Muslims.'

The talk turned to vanilla. The American from the flavouring company was particularly enthusiastic about what he saw. 'Look, these vines are plump and healthy,' he said, fingering a green strand. 'With all this biomass, I'm sure they will produce plenty of flowers.'

Henry, as well as the farmer and Georges Randriamiharisoa, who had come with us, thought otherwise. Yes, they said, the vines were healthy, but that had no bearing on how many flowers they might produce. That would depend on previous years' production too. 'We have had good crops for the last three years,' one farmer explained. 'Even in the year of the bad cyclone the vines that survived grew many pods. But now they need a rest. We see this every few years, when the plants have given many pods they have to slow down for a season to get their strength back.'

As everyone made their way through the trees, stopping now and then to inspect vanilla vines, I asked the flavour manufacturer why he thought he knew more than the Malagasy farmers, and Henry. 'Look, this is all a mind game,' he sneered. 'The exporters want me to think next year's crop will be small so that I'll get scared of not getting the beans I need. But I'm not swallowing it.'

'Why would it suit Zink & Triest to tell you there were fewer beans available?'

'They want to scare me into thinking I might not get the

beans I need for my own customers. I might get pushed into signing a contract early in the season, so they can guarantee a good price,' he virtually snarled. 'But I'll always buy from several sources anyway, so no one can get me over a barrel.'

For three hours we passed through village after tiny village, the jeeps sliding across the ruts and potholes, rearing up and sliding down like beetles negotiating cracks in a pavement. Small children waved and ran alongside as we passed by Ambodimangamaro, Andrapengy, Manambato, Maromokotra, Antapolo and Ampahana. 'I did this journey a few months ago when it was raining,' said Henry. 'It took nine hours.'

When we reached the new Z&T plantation it was an idyllic spot, some miles from the nearest village. Neat rows of vanilla vines grew on natural tree supports on a gently sloping hill surrounded by thick forest. 'We've got about seventy hectares here, but we've only planted half of it,' Henry explained. 'We put in almost sixty thousand vines in 1999 and they're just starting to fruit well.'

Out of earshot of the rest of the group I asked Henry what the advantage would be of owning a plantation. 'Hopefully,' he said, checking if any of the hangers-on were about to appear, 'we can control the quality of the crop – and we can apply what we know about how to get the best from the vines on a more consistent basis.'

'Won't people think you're just trying to maximize profits by cutting out the small farmers?'

'You know what, Tim?' Henry had slipped into corporate mode again. 'Whatever we do we'll be the bad guys. When the price is high it's our fault – and the food industry blames us. When the price is low, it's the farmers who say we're ripping them off. Right now Madagascar is at a really dangerous period in its vanilla history. Plenty of other countries are starting to sell good vanilla. But with prices so high we are really struggling to persuade our customers not to switch to artificial flavours. What Madagascar has is quantity *and* quality. But now that the government isn't guaranteeing the farmers a price they have no security. When the price of vanilla crashes – and believe me it will crash – we want to make sure we can still obtain a reliable supply.'

The issue of creating modern plantations worries some environmentalists. Traditional vanilla plantations use existing forest species as tutors on which to train the vines. If you create a more efficient plantation it may mean clearing areas of natural forest, and planting rows of tutor-trees which may not be indigenous. Plantations which have been cleared will support almost twice as many tutor-trees. Critics of Zink & Triest told me that they feared that the company wanted to turn vanilla production into some kind of global agri-business, and that they planned to set up their own plantations to create a monopoly on vanilla production. I repeated the theory to Henry, but he just smiled.

'Yeah, I've heard those stories. But what the people who repeat them don't seem to understand is that monopolies are a fairy tale. They only exist under dictatorships where they can be enforced. Anyone who's ever tried to farm vanilla on a large scale knows what a headache it is. The security you need to protect thousands of acres of plantation is a nightmare, and actually makes it uneconomic. And anyway, even if we dominated the market, we're still going to have to obey the laws of supply and demand. Maybe we could slow a price crash down a little bit because of the volumes we trade in – but when the market falls, it falls.'

Every time Henry said anything, someone wrote it down. The woman from the aid agency also carried a video camera with which she filmed much of what Henry said and did. I asked if I might have a copy of the tape for my own use. 'I couldn't possibly do that,' she snapped aggressively. 'My clients have paid for this information and everything I do for them is highly confidential.'

She was forever asking about the conditions under which the farmers lived and how much they would expect to earn from vanilla. The men from the flavour manufacturers were concerned about the same issues, but seemed particularly keen to hear how Henry planned to stop the farmers demanding more money for their crop. Meanwhile, the man from the US embassy was interested in all aspects of vanilla production, and clearly had no background in it at all. He had a very small notebook and he stuck close to Henry's side, occasionally asking me to confirm something someone said in French. His command of the language was weak, and the flavour manufacturer didn't speak French at all, forcing Henry to spend his day translating everything that any of the farmers said. He also had to translate questions from English into French, and by the end of the morning he was losing his voice.

After a tour of the vanilla plants we were taken to the newly finished plantation manager's house. It sat on a rise with a clear view over the surrounding land and its serried rows of vines. A team of women scurried to and from the kitchen block to serve us lunch on the shady verandah. An enormous platter of lobsters appeared, enough of the scaly beasts for us all to have three or four apiece. There was chilled wine and fresh Malagasy coffee to accompany the cheeseboard served as dessert. Everything on the table, except the rice which accompanied the lobsters, had been transported up the bumpy road to the plantation from Antalaha ahead of our arrival.

At the foot of the hill I could just make out a row of thatched huts nestling in a hollow on the edge of the cleared land. Henry had told me that the plantation had its own workers' village, somewhere for the women who fertilized the flowers to stay during the pollinating season.

I left the table to explore. Up close the houses were small and square with pitched thatched roofs. Net curtains twitched in the breeze at the open windows. Two little girls, perhaps four and five years old, sat on the wooden steps leading up to the porch of one of the houses. They held hands and shrieked in fear as I approached and a woman appeared at the doorway to see what had happened. Her name was Marta, and she beckoned me up the step with a smile. The porch led into a single living and sleeping area, with just a single wooden chair to sit upon and a narrow bed in one corner of the room. I wondered if the family all had to sleep in it together, and Marta laughed, saying that as her husband wasn't employed here on the plantation it didn't matter.

'Do you earn good money with vanilla?' I asked.

'Very good,' she nodded vigorously. 'I will stay here three months and the plantation will give me rice. They will pay 10,000 Malagasy francs [£1] a day, twice as much as any other crop.'

Marta showed me her small kitchen area, with a back doorway leading out to an outside sink and a clothes line at the rear of the house. There was no electricity this far from Antalaha, and the back yard had a stone hearth with a large black cooking pot sitting on a wire frame above it. Some children's clothing, presumably belonging to the little girls, was hanging out to dry. Two tiny pairs of shorts, two T-shirts and a towel swung on the line. All of them were extremely threadbare, scraps of cloth barely held together by their seams. I had wanted to see how the plantation workers lived, but the tiny clothes reminded me of my own young children and made me extremely ill at ease. I felt ashamed to be inspecting the workers' poverty.

I climbed back up the hill and found that the rest of the group were waiting to leave. The lady from the aid project seemed to be swaying slightly, perhaps as a result of the wine. She asked where I had been.

'I went to see the workers' village.'

'Oh, what a good idea. I should have thought of that,' she said. 'How was it?'

'Fine.'

We made the return trip to Antalaha at speed, our drivers anxious to reach the town before nightfall. I asked my driver if it was unsafe to travel in the dark. 'Only because of the holes in the road,' he said. 'But in the curing season it is very dangerous. Sometimes robbers will throw sticks of dynamite at a truck if they think it has vanilla on board.'

The pace of life by the road had slowed. In the twilight at Manambato a girl sat swinging a cloth to fan the flames in a metal brazier for the evening meal. A cow arched its back to piss copiously outside its owner's hut. The women with their mats of cloves and peppers had gone, as had the smiling, waving children. On the bridge where I had seen the three boys with their tiddler of a fish the sky was a scarlet cloth above the leaden lagoon.

Two days later Henry Todd and I took a plane north to the town of Vohémar. The strain of the group tour had taken its toll and Henry was exhausted. Now, the accountant, the embassy man, the flavourists and the woman from the aid project had gone their separate ways and Georges too was back at work at Ramanandraibe's warehouse in Antalaha. On the way we stopped for fuel, this time at Sambava, halfway to our destination. Once again there were no commercial flights due that day and we had the airport to ourselves. As we waited to climb back into the Beechcraft another small aeroplane landed and taxied to a spot on the tarmac a few yards from where we stood. It was a jet, a more expensive model than our own, and instead of one pilot it had two, attired in neat uniforms. They unfolded the steps and stood smartly on the tarmac as an Indian-looking man in a blazer and tie emerged from the cabin. Two other men followed him down the steps, and I recognized the same representatives from the two flavour companies who had been with us in Antalaha.

'Who are they with?' I asked Henry.

'He's one of our competitors,' he replied. 'Someone we used to work with, but we fell out when we found out that he was involved in some stuff we didn't like.'

A chauffeured car pulled up close to the executive jet, and the three men climbed in without acknowledging our presence.

'Did you know the guys from the flavour companies were going to see him?'

Henry shook his head. 'It's not something we would discuss. But I could have guessed – none of our customers want to rely on a single source for their vanilla. He's a major player, and a lot of people suspect him of speculating in the vanilla market: driving up the price when it suits him for a short-term profit.'

It was difficult to get Henry to say any more, but when I returned to Antananarivo I made my own enquiries. It emerged that the businessman had previously been very close to the Ratsiraka regime, but had only recently started dealing in vanilla on a large scale. The rumour mill said Z&T had cut their ties with him because they found his buying techniques indisciplined, and he was costing the company money.

In the succeeding days I began to understand something of the complexity of dealing in vanilla. Henry Todd's job was to gather as much information as possible about the vanilla market. On each visit to Madagascar he needed to physically inspect the vanilla vines on as many plantations as possible, and speak to as many farmers, collectors and curers as he could. He would then compare this information with what he was told by his suppliers, not just the large exporting companies like Ramanandraibe in Antalaha, but also the much smaller firms in the provincial towns. Henry also had to cast a careful eye over the business practices of the firms he was buying from. At the same time he must try to find out what his rivals were offering to pay for cured vanilla, and balance his own offers of a contract against what he estimated his customers in the United States and Europe would be prepared to pay.

Henry took me to a succession of meetings in small musty offices behind little wooden shops. Cheaply produced calendars sponsored by builder's merchants or shipping companies were pinned to cracked plaster walls, and ancient wooden desks were piled high with hundreds of pieces of paper. In Vohémar there was Gerard Dubosc, a Merina with close-cropped hair and dancing brown eyes. He fiddled with a calculator while he talked, continually punching in figures while he answered Henry's questions. Whenever Henry queried anything about the sums being discussed, Gerard rolled his eyes heavenwards and spread his hands. 'Ah!' he would say. '*Les spéculateurs!*'

Another day, we took tea with Roger Athoy on the balcony of his house. He was an elderly Chinese man wearing a singlet stretched over a rotund belly and baggy cotton shorts that seemed in danger of falling down about his ankles. His hair was slicked straight back from his brow and he dabbed at his eyes and forehead with a handkerchief while we talked, complaining that he was suffering a bout of malaria. There was a stuffed hawksbill turtle nailed to the wall above his chair.

As in Tahiti, the vanilla curers and exporters seemed often to be of Indian or Chinese origin, men with cash to spend on acquiring stocks from the native growers. 'It's often the case,' Henry agreed. 'Even in Uganda. These people have a long history in trade.'

On a rolling green plain outside Vohémar we met a Frenchman named Christophe. He was tall and lean with tightly curled hair, a trim moustache and a selection of heavy gold chains around his neck. Christophe wanted Henry to see his new vanilla plantation, a venture he said represented an investment of several million dollars. It wasn't yet producing vanilla in commercial quantities but he felt sure that next year he would have something special to sell. So far, they had planted almost ninety acres of vanilla, and Christophe said he hoped he would eventually produce eighty tonnes of crop per annum.

Everyone in Vohémar seemed to know Christophe. He sped around the tiny town on an off-road motorbike, and people told me I should be careful because they believed he had once been a mercenary. They whispered that his nickname was 'Capitaine Paff!' – a French term for 'Pow!', the noise made by a gun.

One of Christophe's pieces of jewellery was an eighteen-carat gold pendant in the shape of a scuba diver, and he told me that he had once made a lot of money diving for red coral in the Mediterranean. He said he had been given a 'special permit' to dive off North Africa. Apart from the vanilla plantation, Christophe also had a business growing marine algae for cattle feed. 'It has plenty of iodine; very good for cows,' he said. He also owns a crocodile farm.

On our last day in Vohémar Henry arranged for us to meet

a friend of his called Serge Rajaobelina. Serge runs a charity named Fanamby, working to preserve a small evergreen forest in an area known as Loky-Manambato. Serge told me that Henry had been making donations to the project but until now, he had never had a chance to take him there.

'How far is it?' I asked as we climbed into yet another jeep.

'Just a couple of hours,' Serge replied cheerfully. However, it was already two o'clock in the afternoon, and although he said we would be back well before dark, I had a sense of foreboding about how long the journey might take. According to the road signs, Daraina, the town closest to our destination, was only twenty miles away. 'We are working there with a local community,' Serge explained as we jiggled and lurched against each other while the driver negotiated the uneven road. 'We want to encourage them to preserve a patch of forest that is home to an extremely rare group of lemurs. It's a population that has only recently proven to be a separate species, and one of the most endangered primates in the world.'

At one bad patch in the road we met an enormous lorry with a broken axle blocking the traffic in both directions as a group of men, passengers and drivers, tried to repair it with rope and pieces of metal. The lorry had slewed across the road leaving room only for pedestrians to pass. I asked one of the men how long it would take to fix. 'Two days,' he said with a shrug. 'Maybe three.' The women and children travelling in the truck were already setting up a makeshift camp in the long grass nearby, unable to do anything except wait for the vehicle to be repaired. The children were sent to find firewood for cooking while their mothers began assembling pots to boil water. Meanwhile, behind the accident, a queue of eight or nine other lorries all filled with people and baggage sat patiently in the mud. Serge's driver enlisted the men from one of the lorries to cut a path through the bush nearby for our jeep to pass. They piled up brushwood and sticks under the wheels of our vehicle to get it over the most uneven ground and after half an hour we were able to drive on.

The landscape was a monumental swathe of plains and hills, lush vegetation and ochre earth. Five hours later, with the light fading rapidly, we jolted down a rutted track to a tiny settlement, perched on the banks of a narrow river bed. About forty people live in the collection of huts, which can hardly be called a village, and many of them gathered shyly around Serge as he explained that we, the *vazaha*, were here to see how the Fanamby project worked. He told me that his main efforts were concentrated on making sure the villagers didn't cut any trees down and reduce the available habitat for the lemurs.

The dry season had reduced the river to a trickle, and the river bed was full of logs and dead tree trunks. The villagers had taken advantage of the low volume of water to divert its flow into a succession of crude channels and sink holes. Half-naked men, women and children sprawled in the mud. Their faces, hair, clothes and skin were all dyed the same milk-shake brown, slick with water and gloop as they pushed handfuls of slimey mud through crude round sieves. They were panning for gold, tiny flecks of unrefined ore which they would sell to businessmen, many of them from the Far East, who make the long road journey here to the Daraina Forest. In the tall gum trees overhanging the river there were lemurs with bright round eyes watching the activity below.

Serge explained that the Daraina lemurs are a small population of golden-crowned sifakas – one of five families that make up the genus. Like most of Madagascar's fauna, the lemurs and their kin are endemic species, remnants of ancient times when the great island was attached to the giant continent of Gondwanaland. Ancient or not, the villagers protect the sifakas, believing them to be sacred spirits whose existence must be guaranteed if the gold is to be found in the river. The people who share the forest have pronounced the lemurs *fady*, or taboo.

'God gave us this river,' one of the men explained to me. 'And the lemurs have always lived here with us. We are so lucky to have this place, and we must keep others away so that they do not cut down the forest.'

'Do you have any gold?' I asked the man.

He nodded and reached under his shirt for a small leather pouch tied around his neck. Gently, he untied the knot and tipped the contents of the pouch into his hand. Several nuggets, the largest no bigger than a dental filling tumbled into his palm. It was dull, dirty ore, but it represented a serious amount of money to the village.

Not far from where we stood, Henry had scrambled across the river bed to the far bank. He was standing staring up into the branches of a slender tree with two boys from the village. One of them showed Henry a banana and then made a clucking noise with his tongue, as if he were calling a horse. Within seconds, a rustle and a swaying branch announced the arrival of a mother lemur with a tiny baby clinging to her back. No more than eighteen inches in height, she had thick white fur, with a delicate pale russet patch between her ears as if she had dipped her head into a tub of cinnamon.

The lemur sat stock still at the juncture of branch and trunk, assessing the two creatures standing below her with a fixed stare. Then, cautiously, she turned away so that she could shimmy backwards down the tree trunk until she was just within arm's length of Henry. The boy passed him the banana and Henry held it out. The lemur grasped the fruit with delicate black fingers, holding it in her teeth and chattering as she scampered upwards to a high branch to feast in peace. Henry stood and grinned up at the lemur, his face flushed with pleasure.

At Daraina, Serge had arranged for his staff to provide some food for us before we hit the road. There was grilled chicken, barbecued zebu meat and a selection of cheese and bread. By the time we returned to Vohémar it was past eleven. Christophe and some other vanilla dealers were waiting at the guesthouse, expecting Henry to join them for dinner. We were all exhausted but the owner of the guesthouse had fresh lobster and tuna ready to place on the grill.

'Do we really have to eat dinner again?' I asked.

'You don't,' Henry muttered. 'But I do. It's business.'

He was right, his job really wasn't like being a banker at all.

Epilogue

In Mexico I once journeyed through the mountains of Oaxaca which lead down to the humid plains of Veracruz. Here, long before such things were written down, men first transported the wild vanilla plants they had plucked from the dense forests of south-eastern Mexico. To the north and west lie Cordoba and Jalapa on the ancient trade routes to Tenochtitlan. Beyond those cities is Papantla, in the land of the Totonac. East and south, the band of moist forest feeds directly into the jungles of Chiapas, and down through Guatemala and along the isthmus of Central America towards Costa Rica. From their home in southern Mexico the plants were distributed all along this route, wild vanilla tended and tamed by the people who valued its precious scent.

For days I travelled through the countryside, passing forgotten villages in lonely valleys, and lumber camps shaded by tall trees. Crossing the high Sierra Juarez, the barrier between Oaxaca City and the Gulf Coast, I camped in forests of pine and oak and in the bright clean mornings there were tufted eagles above the steep slopes. Eleven thousand feet up I stood at La Cumbre, the highest point in the mountain range and saw the track of the *Camino Real*, the ancient route from Oaxaca City to the port of Veracruz. Thousands of years before the Spanish came to Mexico, men from the Pacific Coast travelled this way to trade with the people of the Gulf Coast. Withered spindle pines stood up like totems against an endless sky and there was neither sight nor sound of man.

Leaving the cool high ground for the coastal plain I warmed myself with *frijoles de olla* and *tlayuda* – steaming black beans and lightly toasted tortillas. They were made on an open fire by Tia Aquino, an eighty-year-old woman who provided meals for anyone passing through. She told me she had twelve children, but she and Fidel, her husband of fifty-eight years, had lost count of exactly how many grandchildren they now had. Afterwards, in a tiny tin-roofed hut at the foot of the mountains I came to a village with women roasting cocoa beans carried from Chiapas. The hut had no electricity supply and they were making chocolate as part of a cooperative to generate an income for their community. In the hot room a rich scent filled my lungs as I watched them grinding the cocoa beans by hand and mixing the powder with sugar, cinnamon and vanilla. They churned the mixture with long-handled wooden spoons as it warmed over a charcoal griddle. To cool the chocolate they spread it out on a table covered in ceramic tiles, patting it and squeezing it into thin rectangular blocks, or sometimes into thick cylinders which they cut into slices that ended up as rich brown discs like oversized chocolate coins.

Years later, in an English country kitchen the bean lies on the cutting board, a sliver of rippled darkness against the pale wood. Chef picks it up and slips the point of a sharp knife into the flesh near one end. It is moist but firm, and the knife moves smoothly from right to left splitting the pod in two. The two halves of the fruit's outer flesh are still attached to each other at the tip, like an ultra-slim banana peeled back to its base. He turns the knife, angling it away from his fingers and pressing down against the lower flap of the bean, pushing the edge of the steel along its length to scour out the moist seeds. He takes another bean from the box and begins again.

There is milk and cream warming in the pan. Twelve fresh golden egg yolks glisten in a bowl. He adds sugar to the eggs and whisks them rapidly until the mix lightens, not quite white. The pan comes off the flame and he scrapes the gleaming black treasure into the mixture, along with the eviscerated pods. They are limp. Now the eggs and sugar join the liquid. Back to the heat it goes and he begins to stir, stopping the sugar from catching on the base of the pan. Now and then the beans appear, like logs in a flood, dark flecks of seed and flesh speckling the swirling yellow flow. After a short time it thickens and he pours the mixture through a sieve into a white bowl. Two dark whole coffee beans are dropped into the liquid, along with the spent pods. Now, he covers it close so that a skin will not form, and places the bowl in the fridge to steep and cool. Tomorrow, when the flavour is full, it will be turned into ice cream.

Chef hands me the spoon to taste. He cannot know what he offers. It is the story of a Mexican orchid, and the scent of an Indian Ocean island.

Acknowledgements

It would have been impossible to write this book without the resources of the Royal Botanic Gardens at Kew. Dr Phillip Cribb, Deputy Keeper of the Herbarium, has been an invaluable and supportive source of reference on all matters relating to orchids, and greatly eased my research in the Herbarium and Library. Inside the library I am indebted to Craig Brough, Barbara Lowry and Anne Marshall for their patience in helping me track down early botanical works relating to the history of vanilla cultivation. Special thanks must go to Marilyn Ward, the Illustrations Curator, for her help in obtaining reproductions of so many relevant early botanical drawings and paintings.

Thanks also go to the library staff at the Archives départementales in La Réunion where I obtained so much valuable information about the early days of Bourbon, and the life of Edmond Albius. Madame Emmanuelle Vidal, who knows the collection better than anyone, was particularly kind. Réunion's foremost historian Daniel Vaxellaire shared his deep knowledge of the colonial history of the island. Susan Mordan and the Reference Staff of the US Library of Congress in Washington were also unfailingly efficient and helpful.

In spite of frenetic business schedules dictated by the vanilla crisis of the last three years, many people in the vanilla trade made themselves freely available to help. In the USA, I must thank Jeff Lehman of Shank's Extracts in Lancaster, Pennsylvania for his expert knowledge and hospitality, as well as for allowing me access to his remarkable collection of vanilla memorabilia. In New Jersey, Bernard Champon of the Haiti Essential Oil Company was generous with his recollections of twentieth-century vanilla broking history. Hank Kaestner, vanilla consultant extraordinaire, gave me the benefit of his many years in the trade, and much insight into hidden aspects of the industry. Thanks too, must go to Craig Nielsen at Nielsen-Massey Vanilla in Illinois for allowing me to visit their factory, and to Ernie Pinckney at Turkey Hill Dairy in Pennsylvania who knows as much as anyone about making ice cream. In California, Patricia Rain (the Vanilla Queen) has been generous in her support for my book while engaged in writing her own. She shared her passion for the plight of vanilla farmers, as well as so much of her detailed knowledge of Mexico, especially the Totonac culture and legends.

At Zink & Triest, I am indebted to Henry Todd 'Senior' in Montgomeryville, and Ian Blair at the A. M. Todd Company in Kalamazoo for sharing so much of their extensive knowledge of family history, and the mint and vanilla industries. Henry Todd 'Junior' deserves special mention for his encyclopaedic grasp of every aspect of the vanilla trade and for his friendship and hospitality. He also interrupted his merciless travel schedule many times to take telephone calls from a desk-bound author.

In Mexico, where the story of vanilla began, Agustín Arroyo was a remarkable and indefatigable guide and host, sharing his passion for Veracruzano music and all manner of aspects of his country's unique history, cuisine and culture. Manuel Diaz-Cebrian and Lupita Ayala at the Mexico Tourist Office in London also provided invaluable assistance with travel and contacts. Thanks also go to Duncan and Jacqueline Wood in Mexico City for hospitality and assistance with Spanish translations of early documents. Paulette Levy of the Universidad Nacional Autónoma de Mexico also helped with the etymology and translation of Totonac vocabulary. In Papantla, 'the city that perfumed the world', warmest thanks go to Victor Vallejo, Pastor Gutierez Rivera and Javier Carreira Dueñas. In Mexico City, deepest thanks to Miguel Soto, the world's foremost expert on vanilla botany who shared so much of his specialist knowledge and love for this remarkable plant.

In Madagascar my very warm thanks go to my friends and fellow journalists Voahangy Rakotoarivelo and Honoré Razafintsalama for their hospitality and guidance over the years in Antananarivo. In Antalaha, thanks to Ramanandraibe Exports, and to Georges Randriamiharisoa, President of the Groupement National des Exportateurs de Vanille de Madagascar, and his charming wife, Clarice.

In Tahiti I thank Marc Jones in Papeete, Jeanne Chane on Raiatea, Alain and Cristina Plantier on Taha'a, and Didier Rougé-Biscay at the Taha'a Pearl Beach Resort.

Travel-writing commissions have provided a valuable subsidy on many of the journeys I took to research *Vanilla*. I am particularly grateful to Sarah Spankie at Condé Nast Traveller for the opportunity to use material gathered while on assignment for the magazine in Réunion. Graham Boynton, travel editor at the *Daily Telegraph*, deserves similar thanks for allowing me to visit Tahiti. Practical travel assistance was also received from Rebecca Aldridge at American Airlines and Sarah Hopkins at Air New Zealand.

In London, Nigel Phillips was an expert source of wisdom on ancient manuscripts, Stuart Redler was generous with his professional photographic advice and assistance, while Dr

Nicholas Walton at the Institute of Food Research in Norwich gave his expert input on vanillin synthesis. Margaret Dean at gourmetvanilla.co.uk provided useful information on Indian vanilla production. At Givaudan in Zurich, Dr Roman Kaiser gave generously of his many years' experience in scent and fragrance research, and his colleague Thomas Muench gave me a delicious tutorial on ice cream flavour descriptors. Thanks also to Chef de Cuisine, Michel Roux, for allowing me into his famous kitchen at Le Gavroche in London and for sharing his memories of vanilla. For anyone interested in discovering just how versatile an ingredient vanilla can be, I suggest a visit to The Vanilla Pod in Marlow-on-Thames where restaurateur Michael Macdonald is a truly gifted chef. And, on so many journeys away from home I must acknowledge the repeated hospitality of Geoff Weg, Lenore Reese and Josh Isenberg in Los Angeles and New York.

Without my wife Jessica, this book would not exist. As always, her clear-sightedness and meticulous editing skills have been an essential part of the writing process. I must also thank my literary agent Natasha Fairweather, at A. P. Watt, for her wholehearted support and advice during the planning, writing and execution of this book. I am also extremely fortunate to have an enthusiastic and passionate editor in Rowland White at Penguin Books.

Select Bibliography

Andrews, H. C., *Botanists' Repository*, London, 1808.

Arctander, Steffen, *Perfume and Flavor Materials of Natural Origin*, New Jersey, 1960.

Bauer, Francis, *Illustrations of Orchidaceous Plants*, London, 1830–38.

Bechtel, H., Cribb, P. and Launert, E., *Manual of Cultivated Orchid Species*, Dorset, 1981.

le Bellec, Fabrice, *Le Grand Livre des Fruits Tropicaux*, Réunion, 1999.

Berliocchi, Luigi, *The Orchid in Lore and Legend*, Oregon, 2000.

Bouriquet, Gilbert, *Le Vanillier et la Vanille dans le Monde*, Lechevalier, Paris, 1954.

Bouvier, Nicolas, *Une Orchidée qu'on appela Vanille*, Metropolis, Geneva, 1998.

Brookes, R., *The Natural History of Chocolate*, London, 1730.

Brown, Mervyn, *Madagascar Rediscovered. A history from early times to independence*, London, 1978.

Bruman, Henry, 'The Culture History of Mexican Vanilla', *Hispanic American Historical Review* (Michigan), vol. 28, 1948.

Burnett & Co., *About Vanilla*, Boston, 1900.

Calkin, Robert R. and Jellinek, J., *Perfumery, Practice and Principles*, New York, 1994.

Chabin, Michel, *Letters of Ferréol Bellier-Beaumont and Eugène*

Volsy-Focard, Archives départementales de la Réunion, 1981.

Chamberlain, John, *The Manner of Making of Coffee, Tea and Chocolate*, London, 1685.

Clusii, Caroli, *Atrebatis Exoticorum libri decem*, Leyden, 1605.

Coe, Sophie & Michael, *The True History of Chocolate*, London, 2003.

Colmenero, Antonio, *A Curious Treatise of the Nature and Quality of Chocolate*, transl. Don Diego de Vades-forte, London, 1640.

Cooke, Ian K. S., 'Whiteknights and the Marquis of Blandford', *J. Garden History*, vol. 20 no. 1, 1992.

Correll, Donovan S., *Vanilla: Its History, Cultivation and Importance*, Lloydia vol. 7, 1944.

Couplan, François, *Guide des Condiments et épices du monde*, Lausanne, 1999.

Czestochowski, Joseph S., *The Legacy of Albert May Todd*, Kalamazoo, 2000.

Dampier, William, *A New Voyage round the World*, London, 1697.

De Floris, D., 'Notice sur la culture du Vanillier', *Ann. de l'Agriculture des colonies*, 1860.

De la Cruz, *The Badianus Manuscript: An Aztec Herbal of 1552*, transl. Emily Walcott Emmart, Baltimore, 1940.

Delteil, A., *La Vanille, sa culture et sa préparation*, Paris, 1884.

Denis, Ferdinand, *La Légende du Cacahuatl*, Paris, 1860.

Desmond, Ray, *Dictionary of British and Irish Botanists and Horticulturists*, London, 1977.

Diaz, Bernal, *The Conquest of New Spain*, transl. J. M. Cohen, Penguin, 1963.

Dressler, Robert L., *Phylogeny & Classification of the Orchid Family*, Cambridge, 1993.

Dupont, R., *L'Archipel des Seychelles. Ses ressources naturelles, sa faune entomologique et son évolution économique*, Port Louis, 1938.

Edwards, Michael, *Perfume Legends: French Feminine Fragrances*, HM Editions, 1996.

L'Emery, Nicolas, *Dictionnaire universel des drogues simples*, Paris, 1733.

Felter, Harvey, *King's American Dispensatory*, 1898.

Fenaroli's *Handbook of Flavour Ingredients*, vol. 1, George A. Burdock (ed.), London, 1994.

Galbraith, S. J., *Vanilla Culture: as practiced in the Seychelles Islands*, Department of Agriculture, Washington, 1898.

Genders, Roy, *A History of Scent*, Hamish Hamilton, 1972.

Groom, Nigel, *The Perfume Handbook*, Chapman & Hall, 1992.

Hernandez, F., *Rerum Medicarum Novae Hispaniae Thesaurus seu plantarium, animalium mineralium Mexicanorum Historia*, Rome, 1628.

Hirsch, Alan R., *Scentsational Sex*, Element Books, Boston, 1998.

Hofland, Barbara, *A Descriptive Account of the Mansion and gardens of White-Knights*, London, 1820.

Hooker, W. J., *A Century of Orchidaceous Plants*, London, 1851.

Hughes, Ivor, *Vanilla*, Monograph, USA, 1926.

Jensen, H. R., *Chemistry Flavouring of Chocolate Confectionery and Cocoa*, London, 1931.

Kaiser, Roman, *The Scent of Orchids*, Givaudan Fragrance Research, Switzerland, n.d.

Kamen, Henry, *Spain's Road to Empire*, Penguin Books, 2002.

Landin, James E., *American Essence*, A. M. Todd Foundation, 1969.

Lecomte, H. and Chalot, C., *Le Vanillier, sa culture, préparation et commerce de la vanille*, Paris, 1901.

Lépervanche, Jean, *La Vanille et Edmond Albius*, Revue Agricole, 1918.

Loddiges, Conrad & Sons, *The Botanical Cabinet: consisting of Coloured Delineations of Plants from all countries*, vol. VIII, London, 1823.

Lopez, Ruth, *Chocolate: the nature of indulgence*, New York, 2002.

Lucas, Raoul, *La Réunion, île de vanille*, Ocean Editions, Saint-André, 1990.

Ly-Tio-Fane, Madeleine, *Mauritius and the Spice Trade: the odyssey of Pierre Poivre*, Paris, 1970.

Miller, Philip, *The Gardener's Dictionary*, second edition, London, 1740.

Morren, Charles, 'On the Production of Vanilla in Europe', *Ann. Nat. Hist.*, March 1839.

Morton A. G., *History of Botanical Science*, 1981.

Musée Internationale de la Parfumerie Grasse, *Vanilles & Orchidées*, Aix-en-Provence, 1993.

O'Connor, J. E., *Vanilla: Its cultivation in India*, Calcutta, 1881.

Paddington Society, *Newsletter*, no. 57, Feb 1965; no. 75, Mar 1967.

Payet, J. V., *Histoire de l'esclavage à l'île Bourbon*, L'Harmattan (ed.), Paris, 1991.

Pearce, Kenneth, *A Traveller's History of Mexico*, Cassell, 2002.

Perotin, Yves, *Notes Historiques sur des sujets divers*, Archives de la Réunion, 1957.

Piesse, Septimus G. W., *The Art of Perfumery*, Longmans, 1855.

van der Pijl, L. and Dodson, Calaway H., *Orchid Flowers, Their Pollination and Evolution*, Florida, 1969.

Piso, Gulielmus (or Willem), *De Indiæ utriusque Re Naturali et Medica libri quatuordecim*, Amsterdam, 1658.

Pomet, Pierre, *Historie générale des drogues*, Paris, 1694.

Pridgeon, Alec and Cribb, Phillip, et al., *Genera Orchidacearum*, Part 2, Oxford, 2003.

Pulteney, Richard, *Historical and Biographical Sketches of the Progress of Botany in England*, London, 1790.

Purseglove, J. W., *Tropical Crops: Monocotyledons*, Longman, 1981.

Rain, Patricia, *The Vanilla Chef*, Vanilla Queen Press, California, 2002.

Rambosson, J., *Histoire et Légendes des Plantes utiles et curieuses*, Paris, 1868.

Ranadive, S., 'Vanilla', in *Spices, Herbs and Edible Fungi*, Elsevier Science, 1994.

Rasmussen, H. N., *Terrestrial Orchids from Seed to Mycotrophic plant*, Cambridge, 1995.

Redi, Francesco, *Experimenta*, 1675.

Reinikka, Merle A., *A History of the Orchid*, Oregon, 1995.

Richard, Achille, *Monographe des Orchidées des îsles de France et de Bourbon*, Paris, 1828.

Ridley, Henry N., *Spices: A history of their cultivation and use*, London, 1912.

Rolfe, R. A., 'Vanillas of Commerce', *Kew. Bull.*, no. 104, August 1895.

Rolfe, R. A., 'A revision of the genus Vanilla', *J. Linnaean Soc. (Bot)*, vol. 32, London, 1896.

Rosengarten, Frédéric, *The Book of Spices*, Philadelphia, 1969.

Roussin, Antoine, 'Notice sur l'introduction et la fécondation de la vanille', *Bull. des Sciences et Arts*, Réunion, 1862.

Roussin, Antoine, *Album de l'île de la Réunion*, 3 vols, St-Denis, 1860–63.

Salisbury, Richard Anthony, *The Paradisus Londinensis*, 2 vols, London, 1806, 1807.

Shank's Extracts, *Vanilla*, Lancaster, Pennsylvania, 2002.

Soames, Mary, *The Profligate Duke*, Collins, London, 1987.

Société des Amis des Noirs, *Il est encore des Aristocrates*, Archives de la Réunion pamphlet, 1790.

Talon, Monique, *Contribution à l'étude du Vanillier etc.*, Aix-en-Provence, 1960.

Thomas, Hugh, *The Conquest of Mexico*, Pimlico, 1994.

Vaughan, J. G. and Geissler, C. A., *The New Oxford Book of Food Plants*, Oxford, 1998.

Vaxellaire, Daniel, *L'Histoire de la Réunion*, Orphie, 1999.

Volsy-Focard, Eugène, 'Introduction et fécondation du Vanillier à l'île Bourbon', *Bull. des Sciences et Arts*, St-Denis, 1862.

Walton, Nicholas J., et al., 'Vanillin, Molecules of Interest', *Phytochemistry* 63 (2003), Elsevier Science.

de Wildeman, E., *Les Plantes Tropicales de Grande Culture*, Brussels, 1902.

Withner, Carl L., *The Orchids, a scientific study*, New York, 1959.

Zaleta, Leonardo, *The Dance of the Flyers*, Mexico, 1999.

Miscellaneous Official Publications:

Agricultural Census of the Seychelles Colony, Report & tables for 1960. Victoria, 1962.

Exports from Seychelles, Victoria, 1949.

Colbert et Bourbon, Archives départementales de la Réunion, 1983.

Edit du Roy, Donné à Versailles, Portant Règlement pour la vente du Caffé, Thé & Vanille, etc., Grenoble, 1700.